Extras

Extras

The Illustrated Scripts: series 1 & 2
Ricky Gervais & Stephen Merchant

sphere

SPHERE

First published in Great Britain in 2006 by Sphere

A CIP catalogue record for this book
is available from the British Library.

ISBN 13: 978 0 316 03039 7
ISBN 10: 0 316 03039 2

Designed and typeset by Smith & Gilmour, London
Printed and bound in Great Britain by The Bath Press, Bath

Sphere
An imprint of Little, Brown Book Group
Brettenham House
Lancaster Place
London WC2E 7EN

A Member of the Hachette Livre Group of Companies

www.littlebrown.co.uk

CONTENTS

INTRODUCTION

The writing process is the hardest bit about making TV, but also the most enjoyable. At times it can be slow, frustrating work where you feel like you're making no progress and you sit, staring at each other, embarrassed to admit that you've got no idea what Andy or Maggie are going to do next.

At other times, it's just two blokes in a room, trying to make each other laugh, excited because you're on a roll and a silly idea you had in a cafe is still growing and mutating into something you think is hysterical. Those are the best moments, long before you have to start worrying about the schedule or the light fading or wearing itchy wigs: the bit where you're still excited about filling up the blank pages of the script with whatever you want.

Actually, for us, it's a blank wall.

At the beginning of the process we write 'Episodes 1 to 6' on post-it notes and stick them on a wall. The aim is to fill the wall with loads of other post-its, one for each scene. In the first few weeks the post-its go up quickly as we pool all the ideas we've been storing since the last time we did this. Then things slow down and we start to ping-pong ideas back and forth until one of them seems like its juicy enough to make it onto the wall.

Extras was an idea that seemed pretty juicy to us. After the surprising success of *The Office*, we made a very deliberate decision that our next project would not try and repeat the formula that had made that show work. If *The Office* was about an ensemble of four or five main characters, then this would focus on just two; instead of being stuck in the same place each week, we would visit different locations; if David Brent was the central comedy character, Andy Millman would be more of a straight man.

David Brent had been an excuse to get all the observations we had about the petty, pompous people we'd experienced in our working lives off our chests: witless men who recycle other people's jokes and ideas and pass them off as their own.

We wanted Andy to be more like us: more normal, more self-aware, educated and liberal-minded, with a half-decent sense of humour. And, just like us, often paralysed by convention and a conscience, capable of haplessly wandering into agonising social encounters because of a fear of upsetting someone, saying the wrong thing or misjudging a situation. Andy could voice our own frustrations with the world. He'd be an excuse for us to revel in our own neuroses and misanthropy and gripes and grievances. He could relive some of our personal experiences.

We had this character in mind before we knew he would be a movie extra. He was just an ordinary, opinionated bloke: sometimes too honest with people, sometimes too polite. And although that seemed fun to us, it felt as if something was missing.

It was like he didn't deserve to be our main character.

We talked for ages: dreaming up scenarios, dropping him into them, seeing what worked and, although he made us laugh, we couldn't see this Andy character carrying the show. Why?

Even when we put him into a Laurel and Hardy-style double act with Maggie, his best friend, something still seemed missing. We became frustrated, thought about abandoning the idea, talked some more. What was he lacking? What stopped him from being our main character? Then it struck us. *Andy didn't want anything out of life.*

He had no desires or goals. He was just a funny bloke with some strong opinions. He wasn't a leading man unless he was chasing something, unless he had hopes and dreams. He had to care about something so that there would be some jeopardy in his life. We'd learnt with *The Office* that there has to be jeopardy to keep people watching.

The jeopardy in David Brent's life isn't really that his branch might be closed or he might lose his job – the jeopardy is his own ego. He desperately wants to be respected and loved and thought of as a wise, funny, great man. So everything he does is in pursuit of that. And the more he chases it, the more he embarrasses himself. And the more he embarrasses himself, the greater the threat that he's going to realise he is none of the things he wants to be. And, even worse, that he never will be. And if he realises he's never going to be a great man, then his world will come crashing down around him.

So what could Andy want from life? In sitcoms of the past, a character's driving motivation was often social standing. Albert Steptoe, Basil Fawlty, Captain Mainwaring – they were all social climbers with dreams of being respected members of the upper classes. Nowadays, class anxiety seems to have been replaced by a new anxiety. If you ask a kid what they want to be when they grow up, chances are they'll say 'famous'. Celebrity seems to be the world's number one obsession. People's desire for, and fascination with, celebrity is itself fascinating. Being more recognisable than other people is a not a natural human state and the way it changes either the celebs themselves or the people they come into contact with seemed to us to be a rich source of comedy. If Andy had an overwhelming desire to be a successful actor – which, in his mind, would mark him out from the pack – then suddenly we had found his desire in life and the jeopardy in our show.

From there, it was a short step into making him an extra. A film set is a place with a very clear hierarchy: stars, directors, producers at the top; extras (or supporting artists, as they prefer to be known) at the bottom. We loved the idea of taking this character that believes he should be at the top, sticking him right at the bottom and watching him struggle upwards. It gave us an excuse to play around with all our favourite comedy concerns – pomposity, pettiness, rivalry, ambition – and still drop in some observations about familiar everyday stuff, like hiding a golliwog from your boyfriend or lying to a priest to sleep with a girl.

It also gave us an excuse to exploit the talents of some of the people we had met thanks to our own modicum of celebrity. Originally, we intended the real-life movie stars to be the extras in our show. We thought that, as we were focusing on the 'little people', it would be fun to have superstars standing around in the background. But when we found out what people like Ben Stiller and Kate Winslet were willing to say and do, we thought it was a sin not to let them risk their careers and reputations for a few days' work on a new sitcom.

What follows is the stuff that we managed to translate from those post-its on the wall into pictures on the telly. We didn't want to do just another script book – we couldn't understand why anyone would want to read the words instead of just watching the programme – but once we saw Rich Hardcastle's wonderful behind-the-scenes photos we got excited. Rich has a way of making even a rainy day spent standing in a muddy field look glamorous and important.

So here we are: our words, Rich's pictures.

RICKY AND STEVE

EXTRAS
EPISODE 1

CAST LIST
Andy Millman RICKY GERVAIS
Maggie Jacobs ASHLEY JENSEN
Agent STEPHEN MERCHANT
Greg SHAUN PYE
Shaun SHAUN WILLIAMSON

With ROSS KEMP
VINNIE JONES

Mark RAYMOND COULTHARD
Lady Hamilton NATASHA LITTLE
Film Director PETER SULLIVAN
Wardrobe Lady EMMA THORNETT
Chef TONY WAY
Woman in queue
KATHERINE PARKINSON
Female extra EMMA GILMOUR
Woman extra
BARUNKA O'SHAUGNESSY

Written & Directed by
RICKY GERVAIS
& STEPHEN MERCHANT

FILM CLIP: 'HORATIO'

WE ARE WATCHING A TV BIOPIC OF THE LIFE OF LORD NELSON.
IT IS ENGLAND, 1805. LADY HAMILTON IS RUNNING ACROSS A LAWN
TOWARDS A CARRIAGE THAT IS BEING LOADED BY MANSERVANTS.

ROSS KEMP AS HORATIO NELSON IS STANDING NEARBY.

LADY HAMILTON: Horatio.

ROSS TURNS TO FACE LADY HAMILTON.

ROSS: Emma. What are you doing here?

LADY HAMILTON: I couldn't bear to let you go without saying goodbye.

ROSS: You shouldn't have come, Emma. People will talk.

LADY HAMILTON: Let them talk. I'm tired of hiding our love away.
I'm not ashamed of how I feel.

WE CUT BEHIND THE SCENES TO SEE ANDY MILLMAN WAITING OFF-
CAMERA, DRESSED AS A FOOTMAN. HE IS WATCHING THE ACTION,
WAITING FOR HIS CUE.

ROSS: Neither am I. But we both know we shouldn't be together.

LADY HAMILTON: Shouldn't? Who says we shouldn't?

BEHIND THE SCENES, ANDY IS TAPPED ON THE SHOULDER. HE WALKS FORWARD AND LOADS HIS CRATE ONTO THE BACK OF THE CARRIAGE. WE SEE HIM APPEAR IN THE BACKGROUND OF THE FILM CLIP.

ROSS: My conscience. My conscience tells me everything I feel for you is wrong. But my heart, my heart says I can't live without you.

ANDY STANDS BY THE CARRIAGE.

LADY HAMILTON: Promise me you'll return.

ROSS: I promise. Because if Napoleon doesn't kill me, then being away from you surely will.

ROSS AND LADY HAMILTON KISS PASSIONATELY. FROM BEHIND THEIR HEADS WE SEE ANDY EMERGE, EDGING HIMSELF INTO THE FRAME.

DIRECTOR: Cut. Yeah, brilliant, thank you.

SCENE 1. EXT. FILM SET. DAY.

ANDY IS PLEASED WITH HIMSELF.

ANDY: Could you see me?

MAGGIE: Yeah, definitely.

THEY PASS THE DIRECTOR WHO IS EXPLAINING TO THE SCRIPT
SUPERVISOR:

DIRECTOR: Excellent, we'll cut that before that fat little extra gets
his face in? Okay, rest the guys for ten minutes . . .

ANDY REMOVES HIS WIG AND WALKS AWAY.

SCENE 2. INT. STUDIO. DAY.

MAGGIE, A WARDROBE LADY AND ANOTHER EXTRA ARE IN THE
COSTUME ROOM. MAGGIE IS DRESSED AS A MAID. THE DIRECTOR
ENTERS AND ADDRESSES THE WARDROBE LADY.

DIRECTOR: Okay, who are we using for the girl by the carriage?

WARDROBE: We thought this one.

DIRECTOR: (sizing up MAGGIE) Oh, no, no, I said I needed some decent
tits and they're rubbish.

MAGGIE: Well, I could maybe pad them up a bit. Or just sort of like
push them . . .

MAGGIE BEGINS TO ADJUST HER CLEAVAGE.

ANOTHER WOMAN: (gesturing to her own cleavage, desperate to cut in)
You could use these.

DIRECTOR: Bingo.

MAGGIE: We'll bingo these in half an hour after I've had a wee fiddle
with them, I just need to squeeze them.

DIRECTOR: Well, work on them over lunch, yeah?

MAGGIE: Yes.

DIRECTOR: Because at the moment they're just ugh, nothing.

MAGGIE: (wearily) Okay.

DIRECTOR: Good.

THE DIRECTOR LEAVES.

ANOTHER WOMAN: Would it be easier just to use these?

THE WOMAN GESTURES TO HER CLEAVAGE AGAIN.

MAGGIE: Well, no, we made a decision to use mine, so can we just go
with these. If I just squeeze them up . . .

ANOTHER WOMAN: It would be less work.

MAGGIE: You've got padding in the bottom of them.
(TO THE WARDROBE WOMAN)
Can I have some padding?

WARDROBE: We can find some padding.

SCENE 3. EXT.
CATERING BUS. DAY.

MAGGIE AND ANDY STAND IN THE QUEUE FOR LUNCH. MAGGIE IS
MOANING.

MAGGIE: And that cow's sticking her tits in his face. And I said,
'He said he wanted to use my tits, can we just go with my tits please?'

ANDY: I think Meryl Streep went through a similar thing.

MAGGIE: Oh, I know it's not important but—

ANDY: It is important, it is important. I remember Laurence Olivier
having a rant in *Richard III* because they wanted to use stunt testicles
and he said, 'Listen, these gonads are going to be seen because they
went to RADA, you either use the Lord Olivier plums or nothing at all.'

MAGGIE LAUGHS. THEY STEP UP TO THE CATERING TRUCK.

CHEF: Next.

ANDY TURNS TOWARDS THE CHEF.

ANDY: And what do you recommend, my good man?

CHEF: Chicken's the warmest.

ANDY: Is it? I'll have that then.

CHEF CALLS INTO THE VAN.

CHEF: Chicken.

HE SLAPS SOME CHICKEN AND MASHED POTATO ON TO ANDY'S PLATE.
ANDY HESITATES BEFORE PICKING IT UP.

ANDY: Your heart's not in this, is it? Although one of your pubes is I see.

(THE CHEF SCOOPS OUT THE PUBE AND DROPS IT ON TO THE COUNTER)

Oh, straight in there like that, no messing.

CHEF: (examining the hair) It's not a pube, it's a dog hair.

CHEF KNOCKS THE FOOD FROM HIS HAND ON TO THE COUNTER TOP.

ANDY: (to the rest of the queue) It's all right, it's not a pube, it's a dog hair, everyone. I thought it was a pube, it's not, it's just a dog hair. If you do get a hair in there, he just gets it out with his big sausage fingers.

SCENE 4. INT.
CATERING BUS. DAY

MAGGIE AND ANDY ARE EATING AND TALKING.

ANDY: I don't know why I do this.

MAGGIE: What?

ANDY: All this. 'Oh, we'll cut before the fat bloke gets his face in shot.' It's just absolutely demeaning, I don't know why I put myself through it.

MAGGIE: (sympathetic) Because you're an actor.

ANDY: (shaking his head) This isn't acting, getting the back of your head or your arm in a shot. And bloody Ross Kemp in every scene, he gets all the lines. Do you know what I mean? Why is he the star and not me? There but for the grace of God go I.

MAGGIE: (snort of contempt) It's not.

ANDY: It is.

MAGGIE: No, it's not just luck, is it?

ANDY: Why not? We're about the same age—

MAGGIE: (interrupting) No, he's younger than you.

ANDY: No, he's not. We're about the same age.

MAGGIE: (surprised) Is he?

ANDY: Yeah.

MAGGIE: He looks a lot younger than you.

ANDY: (annoyed) You're having a laugh. He hasn't got any hair.

MAGGIE: Well, he's meant to look like that, he's shaved it all off. It's cool, it's like Vin Diesel.

ANDY: (in disbelief) Vin Diesel. Sorry, are we looking at the same bloke? Have another look, right, look at him there, look.
(ANDY POINTS OUTSIDE TO WHERE ROSS IS STANDING WITH A CREW MEMBER)
He looks more like Zippy from *Rainbow*. Look.
(MAGGIE LAUGHS. ANDY IMITATES ZIPPY'S VOICE)
'Hello Bungle, what are you doing in the Queen Vic, Bungle? Phil, why did you sleep with my wife?' Look, look.
(MAGGIE LAUGHS MORE LOUDLY.)
Vin Diesel hasn't got the perfectly round little head that opens and shuts like Pac Man, look at it.

ANDY SMILES AND SIGHS.

MAGGIE: He's got less chins than you as well.

ANDY: One chin! One chin each.

MAGGIE: Yeah, but yours is growing another one.

ANDY: Shut up.

MAGGIE: In five years' time he's still going to look pretty rugged and you're just going to look like a pelican.

ANDY: A pelican? Good, nice one.
(MAGGIE LOOKS OUT THE WINDOW.)
What you looking at?

MAGGIE: Nothing.

ANDY: Well, obviously him.
(ANDY POINTS TO A DASHING ACTOR IN PERIOD COSTUME)
Husband material?

MAGGIE: Could be.

ANDY: And what are you basing it on this time?

MAGGIE: Don't know, but look at him. He looks all dashing and handsome in his green. Why do men not dress like that nowadays?

ANDY: (incredulous) Because they'd get beaten up on the tube.

SCENE 5. EXT.
TEA AND COFFEE AREA. DAY.

ANDY IS GETTING A CUP OF TEA. GREG SIDLES UP, LOOKING SMUG, HOLDING A FILM SCRIPT. ANDY CLEARLY DOESN'T LIKE GREG BUT IS POLITE THROUGH GRITTED TEETH.

GREG: All right?

ANDY: All right, Greg?

GREG: Indeed I am.

ANDY: Good.

GREG: Actually working across the way, Studio H, the big one. Doing a film with Mr Vinnie Jones. So actually just learning a few lines I've got to do with him later.

ANDY: Lines?

GREG: Yes indeed.

ANDY: Well done.

GREG: So what's your part in this epic then? What are you, fourth seaman from the left?

GREG SNIGGERS.

ANDY: Hardly.

GREG: Or something a bit meatier, bit more substantial.
(GREG TAPS ANDY WITH HIS SCRIPT)
You got a speaking part?

ANDY: (shaking his head) No.

GREG: Seriously, how do you survive?

ANDY: (sharply) Don't worry about it, really.

GREG: Digging into the savings?

ANDY: Not really.

GREG: The pile diminishes, does it?
(GREG MIMES BITING HIS NAILS)
'Gotta get some work soon. Gotta get some work soon.'

ANDY: (shrugging) Working all the time, mate. Don't worry about it.
Are your parents still sending you money?

GREG: Yeah, either that or I threaten to sign on.
(GREG SMILES AND RAISES HIS HANDS AS IF TO THE HEAVENS)
And lo the cheque doth cometh in the post. It keeps the wolf from
the door.

GREG SLAPS ANDY ON THE STOMACH WITH HIS SCRIPT.

ANDY: How is the door of the house your parents bought you?
Is that all right?

GREG: Yes, it's fine.

ANDY: Good.

GREG: Look, I've got lines to learn.

ANDY: (drily) Oh, thanks for coming over and sharing that with
me anyway.

GREG: Seriously, mate, something will crop up.

ANDY: Don't worry about it, mate, really. Don't worry about it, mate.
Worry about yourself, mate.

GREG: Stiff upper lip.

ANDY: Yes.

GREG: And other clichés too numerous to mention.

ANDY: Don't mention them then.

GREG: I've got to go.

GREG WALKS OFF. A CREW MEMBER APPROACHES THE TABLE.

ANDY: See you later, mate.
(MUTTERS UNDER HIS BREATH)
Tosser.
(TO CREW MEMBER)
Not you.

SCENE 6. EXT.
BEHIND THE SET. DAY

THE DASHING ACTOR IN GREEN (MARK) IS STOOD IN LINE FOR THE
TOILET. MAGGIE IS PASSING. SHE NOTICES HIM. THINKING ON HER
FEET, SHE JOINS THE QUEUE. THERE IS A WOMAN STOOD BEHIND MARK.

MAGGIE: (to WOMAN) Excuse me, do you mind if I go in front of you
please?

WOMAN: What?

MAGGIE: Can I go before you?

WOMAN: Why?

MAGGIE: (lying, quietly, gesturing to her stomach) I've got a little bit
of a stomach upset.

WOMAN: Oh, okay.

THE WOMAN STANDS BY TO LET MAGGIE IN FRONT OF HER. MAGGIE
SWAPS PLACES AND IS NOW NEXT TO MARK.

MAGGIE: Thank you.
(SMILES TO HERSELF AND TAPS MARK ON THE SHOULDER)
Hello.

MARK: (smiling) Hi there.

WOMAN: (loudly, to MARK and the rest of the queue) I think she wants
to go in front of you, she's got diarrhoea.

(MARK STOPS SMILING)

Don't want it exploding everywhere.

(WOMAN SMILES)

Messy.

MAGGIE: (forcing a smile, crippled with embarrassment) Thank you.

MAGGIE WALKS OFF, HUMILIATED.

SCENE 7. EXT. LOCATION. DAY.

ANDY, HOLDING A CUP OF TEA, WALKS OVER TO SOME EMPTY SEATS AND
SITS DOWN. ROSS KEMP IS SAT NEARBY, WEARING SUNGLASSES. ANDY
LOOKS OVER AT ROSS FOR A BRIEF SECOND AND THEN LOOKS AWAY.

ROSS: (lifting up his sunglasses) Saw you looking.

(HE GETS UP AND SITS IN THE CHAIR NEXT TO ANDY)

Thought I'd better get it out of the way. Yeah, it is me.

ANDY: Hi, I'm Andy.

ROSS: (slapping ANDY hard on the back) How you doing?

ANDY: (nearly spilling his drink) Oh!

ROSS: Sorry, did that hurt?

ANDY: No, it's . . .

ROSS: (showing off) Good, good, because I was worried I might have
hurt you. Don't know my own strength sometimes and, well, if I had
meant to hurt you, you wouldn't have any ribs left, so you got off lightly.

(HE RAISES AN EYEBROW)

Let's leave it there.

ANDY: Okay.

A BRIEF MOMENT OF AWKWARD SILENCE.

ROSS: You know, I love playing military parts.
(CONSPIRATORIALLY)
Well, as you know, I was in the SAS.

ANDY: No, I didn't, I knew you did that TV show about the SAS.

ROSS: Yeah, but how did I know how to do all that shit in it?

ANDY: I assumed you had consultants and stuff.

ROSS: Well, if that's what you believe, then that's what you believe. All right, I wasn't in the SAS for about six months and they didn't say, 'Hey Ross, why don't you give up this acting lark? We could really do with you in Afghanistan.'

ANDY: Did they?

ROSS: Couldn't say. Couldn't say. All I know is, if I ever do get into a fight I'd better have an escape route because I don't want to go to prison for murder, because that's what it would be.

(ANDY LOOKS AROUND, BEMUSED AND DISBELIEVING)

Because my body is a lethal weapon. And me in prison, face like this. Pretty boy.

(ANDY REACTS)

I'd be in the shower just lathering up, a couple of guys would come in wanting a bit of Kemp arse.

(ANDY RAISES HIS EYEBROWS)

I'd see them in the mirror and then

(ROSS MIMES A MARTIAL ARTS MOVE)

... what I'm saying is, you'd best not get into a fight with me.

ROSS PUT HIS SUNGLASSES BACK ON.

ANDY: Sure.

(ROSS STANDS UP AND LEAVES.)

Or a conversation.

SCENE 8. INT. STUDIO. DAY.

A GROUP OF EXTRAS ARE SITTING AROUND, DRINKING TEA AND CHATTING. ANDY AND MAGGIE SIT NEXT TO EACH OTHER IN THE MIDDLE OF THE GROUP. THEY ARE ALL DRESSED IN PERIOD CLOTHES, EXCEPT FOR GREG.

WOMAN EXTRA: (to MAGGIE) What do you do when you're not doing this. What's your day job?

MAGGIE: I work in a pub.

WOMAN EXTRA: (to ANDY) What about you?

ANDY: (smiling) I do this full time, I'm an actor.

WOMAN EXTRA: You do this full time?

ANDY: Yes, yes. Like most actors, I act full time.

WOMAN EXTRA: Yeah, but this isn't really acting, is it? I mean, this is extra work.

ANDY: (now serious) Well, no, 'supporting artist work', isn't it. But this is just pocket money. I am actually an actor.

WOMAN EXTRA: Right. I was going to say because you can't really make a living from being an extra.

ANDY: No.

MAGGIE: (interrupting) No, but he used to have a proper job. He used to, he owns his own house, doesn't have to pay a mortgage (ANDY LOOKS SMUGLY AT GREG WHILE MAGGIE IS TALKING) . . . so he can afford to live on a pittance.

ANDY: (interrupting quickly, annoyed) But I don't live on a pittance though, do I? People pay me to act so—

GREG: (smiling smugly) Yeah, you say you're an actor.

ANDY: Yeah, I do.

GREG: But what have you actually acted in?

ANDY: I've appeared in . . .

GREG: I mean proper acting, not walking in the background. I mean actually speaking?

ANDY: I know.

GREG: Well?

ANDY: (raising his eyebrows) What, you want me to . . . ?

GREG: Yeah.

ANDY: Okay. *My Family*, the Robert Lindsay sitcom.

WOMAN EXTRA: Really?

ANDY: Yeah, it was just a thing, a scene on the bus and the bus conductor come along and said, 'Tickets please' and I just went, 'Yeah sure, no problem.'

GREG: Did you?

ANDY: (rolling his eyes) Yes.

GREG: That was the line?

ANDY: Yeah, he just comes along and he goes 'Tickets please' and I go 'Yeah, no problem, mate, there you go.'

GREG: So if I got that episode and watched it, that's what I'd see you say. 'Sure, no problem.'

ANDY: Well, yeah. Well, I didn't . . .

GREG: What's the line?

ANDY: What's the problem?

GREG: Well, what is the line?

ANDY: The conductor wants the ticket, I'm showing him it.

ANDY MIMES SHOWING THE CONDUCTOR HIS TICKET BUT DOES NOT SAY ANYTHING.

GREG: And what do you say?

ANDY: He asks for my ticket.

GREG: Yeah.

ANDY: And I go . . .

AGAIN, ANDY MIMES SHOWING HIS TICKET BUT SAYS NOTHING MUCH.

GREG: I can't hear what you're saying. No, let's do it, let's do it like it is, actually on the screen. I'll be the bus driver, okay, and you
(POINTS AT ANDY)
just be you, all right, 'Tickets please, can I see your tickets, please?'

(ANDY MIMES SHOWING HIS TICKET AND OPENS HIS MOUTH BUT DOES
NOT SPEAK)
I can't hear anything, no one can hear anything.

ANDY: (shaking his head) Oh, it's years ago.

GREG: But you see that's not proper acting. Okay.

ANDY: Oh, what is it then?

GREG: Well, I can tell you what acting is, I can tell you what I've acted
in to show you what I mean, if you want.

ANDY: Not interested.

GREG: I've acted in, and I'm talking proper speaking parts, in
Emmerdale,
(ANDY GIVES A DISPARAGING SIGH)
Silent Witness.

MAGGIE: (impressed) *Silent Witness.*

GREG: *Silent Witness.* I was a nark in *The Bill,* that was a recurring
character, that was three episodes and really good lines of dialogue.
You haven't even been in the *The Bill,* have you?

ANDY: (laughing) I don't want to be in *The Bill.*

ANOTHER EXTRA: (smirking) You haven't even been in *The Bill*?

ANDY: Listen, I don't want to be in *The Bill.*

WOMAN EXTRA: Have you ever been in *Casualty*?

ANDY: Yes.

GREG: The TV show *Casualty*?

ANDY: Oh, well, no but . . .

TRAILING OFF, ANDY LOOKS AT GREG AND SHAKES HIS HEAD.
GREG SMIRKS. ANDY CLEARS HIS THROAT NOISILY.

SCENE 9. INT.
AGENT'S OFFICE. DAY.

ANDY IS IN A MEETING WITH HIS AGENT. THE AGENT IS SLURPING
LOUDLY FROM A MUG OF TEA. ANDY LOOKS WEARILY AT HIM.

ANDY: Right, this is the deal. You've been my agent now for, what, five years?

AGENT: Yes.

ANDY: And you're not getting me any real acting work.

AGENT: Nothing's coming in.

ANDY: Nothing's coming in. In five years?

AGENT: That's the problem. I know, I'm as annoyed as you are. But you know, I'm not sure there's a demand for little forty-five-year-old blokes.

ANDY: Forty-three!

AGENT: Whatever. You know, I wonder, are you sure you want to be an actor? You've given it five years, nothing's come in. Maybe it's time to just throw in the towel.

ANDY: (as if addressing an audience) My agent, ladies and gentlemen, my agent.

AGENT: No, well, look . . .
(SHAUN WILLIAMSON, WHO PLAYED BARRY IN *EASTENDERS*, ENTERS
IN A TRACKSUIT)
Hello, mate, all right?

SHAUN: Hiya, sorry to interrupt.

AGENT: That's all right, do you know Barry?

SHAUN SMILES AND NODS AT ANDY.

ANDY: All right, Shaun, how's it going? I'm working with a friend of yours at the moment actually, Ross Kemp.

SHAUN: How is he, all right?

ANDY: Yeah, good.

AGENT: (serious) I wouldn't mention Ross's name round here.
(SHAUN LOOKS DOWN AT THE FLOOR, SIGHING)
Ross is sort of mud with Barry because it was Ross that persuaded Barry to leave *EastEnders*. Ross leaves, he goes to ITV, he says,

'It's a million pounds or nothing,' they give him a million-pound contract. So I go to ITV with Barry and say, 'We want a million pounds or nothing.' They chose nothing.

SHAUN: (weakly) They went with the nothing option that time, didn't they?

AGENT: (to SHAUN) And you were, I mean you were upset, weren't you, you were depressed. Couldn't get out of bed for about two weeks. I was livid and, looking back, what I should have done is, I shouldn't have given them the nothing option. I should have gone in there and I should have said, 'We want a million pounds or we want, you know, five hundred pounds' and that way we would have definitely got something.

ANDY: (raising his eyebrows) Five hundred pounds?

AGENT: Exactly, this is it. But live and learn, don't you?

SHAUN: (despondent) This isn't living though, is it?

AGENT: Come on, Barry, don't start that again, mate, I've got loads of stuff for you here.

SHAUN: Like what?

AGENT: Well, there's a light flickering in the gents upstairs, have a look at that. Could you have a tinker with that?

SHAUN: Yeah, I could, I could do that. Could I use your computer later? I've just to get the old new CV knocked up.
(GESTURES TO HIS NEW HAIR IMPLANTS)

AGENT: Yeah, yeah, knock yourself out.

SHAUN: Well, see you.

SHAUN LEAVES THE ROOM.

ANDY: Cheers.

AGENT: All right then, cheers.

ANDY: (angry) Sorry, the reason I'm here is I want to know what your plan of action is. What's your strategy, what is your business plan?

AGENT: (earnest) Well, my plan is when you get some work done I can start making some money, because what I'm not good at is, you know, breaking an act.

ANDY: Oh, so when I'm successful you can deduct twelve and a half per cent, no problem?

AGENT: Fifteen for adverts. That's what I'm hanging on for really.

ANDY: Yes. You're just waiting for someone to call up and give me an advert?

AGENT: That would be amazing, that would be brilliant.

ANDY: (sarcastic) Right, okay. Make sure the phone's on the hook then.

AGENT: (chuckling) You joke about it. It was unplugged for two days, no one noticed.

ANDY STARES AT HIS AGENT IN DISBELIEF. THE AGENT LAUGHS AND TAKES ANOTHER SWIG OF TEA.

SCENE 10. EXT.
OUTSIDE THE STUDIO. DAY.

ANDY AND MAGGIE ARE WALKING ACROSS THE STUDIO LOT TOGETHER.

ANDY: The man does not know where to start, okay.

(ANDY UNFOLDS A PIECE OF PAPER HE'S CARRYING)

This is my CV that he's sending out to people. I mean casting agents, producers. He typed it himself, okay.

(ANDY BEGINS TO READ)

'From 1986 to 1999 Andy Millman worked at the NatWest in Wokingham.

(SHRUGS)

Andy left this comfortable, adequately paid job to try and become an actor despite his age, weight and looks.

(PAUSE. ANDY AND MAGGIE BOTH LAUGH)

Andy claims to be a great actor but has not yet had the chance to prove it because so far he's had no offers except extra work, which as you know is pointless and badly paid. Acting is Andy's dream, if you can make that dream come true, please, please call.'

(STOPS READING AND FOLDS UP CV)

I mean it's like he's writing to *Jim'll Fix It*.

MAGGIE: Oh, you have to fire him.

ANDY: I can't fire him, can I? I can't bear to see his stupid little face. He'd be devastated.

MAGGIE: Yes, but it's your career.

ANDY: I know, I know.

MAGGIE: Well, what are you going to do? I mean, you'll have to find all your own work.

ANDY: Yeah, having a dog and barking yourself springs to mind.

MAGGIE: Well, start today, start now.

(TAPS ANDY ON THE ARM)

Go up to the director and ask him for a line. Ross Kemp. You've spoken to Ross Kemp, haven't you?

ANDY: Yes.

MAGGIE: Go up to Ross Kemp and ask him for a line. Just say to him, 'I thought you were brilliant in *EastEnders*, *Ultimate Force*, I loved you in Spandau Ballet.'

ANDY: (stopped in his tracks) What?

MAGGIE: Spandau Ballet.

ANDY: He wasn't in Spandau Ballet. That was Martin Kemp. Martin Kemp was in *EastEnders* and Spandau Ballet.

MAGGIE: Who's this one?

ANDY: Ross Kemp.

MAGGIE: (confused) Are they not brothers?

ANDY: No. It was Martin Kemp and Gary Kemp were the brothers.

MAGGIE: Well, who is this one?

ANDY: (starting to get annoyed) Ross Kemp.

MAGGIE: Well, who's his brother?

ANDY: I don't know if he's got a brother.

MAGGIE: Yes, he does, he's got that little, the little bald one with the pink face that looks like him.

ANDY: Phil Mitchell?

MAGGIE: Mm.

ANDY: (incredulous) His on-screen brother. Phil and Grant Mitchell, but they're not really brothers.

MAGGIE: (insistent) Yes, they are, they're the Mitchell brothers.

ANDY: What do you mean 'the Mitchell brothers'? You know his name is Ross Kemp.

(STARES AT MAGGIE. SHE LOOKS BLANK)

What bit's confusing you?

MAGGIE: (quietly) The brothers.

ANDY: The brothers?

MAGGIE: What?

AN EXTRA IN A SILVER FUTURISTIC OUTFIT WALKS BY. ANDY POINTS AT HER.

ANDY: Is that confusing you too? Do you think we've landed in the future?

MAGGIE: Shut your face.

(MAGGIE HITS ANDY ON THE ARM AS HE BEGINS TO WALK AWAY AGAIN)

You see, this is why I can never go and speak to that guy because I'm not smart enough for him. He's an intellectual.

ANDY: How do you know he's intellectual? You've never even spoken to him.

MAGGIE: Well, he reads the big papers.

ANDY: Oh, the big papers, sure.

MAGGIE: See, it's always the same, right, if a bloke is really smart I just always worry that I'm not clever enough for him. He's going to want to talk about politics or whatever and I won't know what to say. Like one time, I went out with this bloke and we were in the pub and we were playing the quiz machine and it was for like a fiver and a question came up. 'Who discovered America?' and I just panicked and I said 'Columbo'.

(ANDY LAUGHS LOUDLY)

See you're laughing because I'm . . .

ANDY: (smiling, but kindly) No, it's an easy mistake to make, they sound the same.

MAGGIE: Well, that's what I thought.

ANDY: You should just go and talk to him.

MAGGIE: You think?

ANDY: Yeah, I don't know why you're so shy. Just go and talk to him.

SCENE 11. INT. STUDIO. DAY.

MARK IS SAT READING A BOOK. MAGGIE WALKS TOWARDS HIM, STUMBLING ON SOME SPARE PROPS. SHE SITS DOWN NEARBY AND UNFOLDS A COPY OF THE *FINANCIAL TIMES*. MARK DOESN'T LOOK UP.

MAGGIE: (sighing) The *FT*.

MARK: (looking up at MAGGIE and smiling) Hi.

MAGGIE: Oh, hi.
(SHE SIGHS LOUDLY AND MUTTERS TO GET HIS ATTENTION)
NASDAQ, you twat, what are you like?

MARK: You play the markets, do you?

MAGGIE: Oh, yeah.

MARK: How's it going? Any tips?

MAGGIE: (guessing) Buy high, buy low. Buy low, sell high.
(MARK LOOKS BEMUSED)
What you reading?

MARK: Oh, it's Frank Kermode's book on Shakespeare.

MAGGIE: Oh.

MARK: It's for my new PhD.

MAGGIE: (wittering, trying to sound knowledgeable) Shakespeare, eh?
Oh! Bloody genius, him. *Midsummer Night's Dream*. Bottom.

MARK: (interrupting) Oh, how is your diarrhoea?

MAGGIE: Fine, it's good.

MARK: I'm going to get a coffee, I think.

MAGGIE: I've got to go and call my broker anyway.

MARK: Oh, right, I was going to ask if you wanted to get one.

MAGGIE: Definitely. He's not there anyway, he's away on holiday.

MAGGIE LAUGHS. MARK AND MAGGIE STAND UP AND WALK AWAY
TOGETHER.

SCENE 12. INT. STUDIO. DAY.

ANDY SIDLES UP TO ROSS KEMP.

ANDY: Hiya.

ROSS: (lost in thought) All right.

ANDY: (pointing to the sound stage opposite) They're making a film
over there with Vinnie Jones.

ROSS: (scathing) What's he doing making a film? He's a bloody
footballer.

ANDY: (searching for something to say, looking at film lights in the
other studio) Look at the size of those lights.

ROSS: You reckon they're big lights? If I wanted big lights I could have
big lights. I just don't want big lights, I want small lights if anything.

ANDY: I know an old colleague of yours actually, Shaun Williamson?

ROSS: Shaun?

ANDY: Barry off *EastEnders*.

ROSS: Oh, Barry, yeah, yeah.

ANDY: Yeah, we've got the same agent because I'm a real actor. So if there was a line going in this, just a little bit of dialogue, it would be great for me because I'm, as I say, I'm a proper actor.

OUTSIDE THE STUDIO OPPOSITE, VINNIE JONES APPEARS, TALKING ON HIS MOBILE PHONE.

ROSS: (sidetracked, watching VINNIE) Yeah, well, I hope you're better than him. I mean, he's a bloody footballer.

ANDY: Oh, he's good at what he does, isn't he? The old hard man thing, I suppose, because he actually is in real life so . . .

ROSS: (staring at ANDY) You reckon? You think he's a tough guy? I'd like to see him come at me with all that 'I'm a hard bastard' stuff. I'd say 'Put the baseball bat down, it's just you and me, skin on skin. Stripped to the waist, to the death.'
(ANDY REACTS)
I'm trained. He starts with me, I will destroy him.

ROSS LOOKS BACK OVER AT THE OTHER STUDIO. ANDY STARES AT ROSS, A MIXTURE OF BEWILDERMENT AND CONFUSION ON HIS FACE. AFTER A FEW MOMENTS HE LOOKS AWAY.

ANDY: Okay, well, as I say, if you could put a word in, I could just do a line.

ROSS: Yeah, I'll sort that out for you, no problem. No problem.

ANDY: (surprised) Really? Cheers. I'll see you later.

ANDY GETS UP SLOWLY AND WALKS OFF. ROSS CONTINUES TO STARE
OVER AT THE OTHER STUDIO. ANDY SHAKES HIS HEAD AS HE WALKS AWAY.

SCENE 13. INT. STUDIO. DAY

MAGGIE AND MARK ARE STANDING TOGETHER, TALKING AND LAUGHING.

MAGGIE: I tell you if there's a hag, a washer woman, toothless wench to
be had, it'll be me.
(MARK LAUGHS)
I'm never the one that gets to wear the taffeta dress, it's not fair.

MARK: (feeling MAGGIE's waist) They've padded you up.

MAGGIE: (joking) That's actually me.

THEY BOTH LAUGH.

MARK: I was going to ask, I hope it doesn't seem pushy, but would you like to go for a meal?

MAGGIE: (eagerly) Yeah, I'm starving.

MARK: Oh, not right now, I thought a bit later.

MAGGIE: (laughing) Yeah, no, absolutely yeah, oh, I'd love to.

MARK: Good.

MAGGIE: Okay then.

SCENE 14. INT. STUDIO. NIGHT

ANDY IS WATCHING SOME SPARKS LIGHTING THE SET. AS IF FROM NOWWHERE, GREG APPEARS.

GREG: What you doing here? Still scavenging the bins for food, are you?

ANDY: No, no need. Bloody waiting on a scene I've got to do with Ross Kemp, he asked me personally so . . . Good though.

GREG: (bitter) Yeah, well done. Shame it's only telly but you know . . .

ANDY: Not really.

GREG: It's something. I mean keep at it, you know, you might make it into the films.

ANDY: Yeah, but what I wouldn't do is do a film with Vinnie Jones, he's a footballer, but it's all right . . .

GREG: Well, you say he's a footballer but he's still been in films, hasn't he? With John Travolta and Nicolas Cage.

ANDY LOOKS UNCONVINCED.

ANDY: Yeah, what did he get paid for that by the way? I was going ask, because I was talking to Ross, you know, Ross got a million pounds to go to ITV.

GREG: Yeah, to pretend to be a hard man.

ANDY: Not really.

GREG: Unlike Vinnie. Real-life hard man.

ANDY: Yeah.
(LOWERS HIS VOICE)
On a serious note, Ross explained to me – you know Ross was trained by the SAS – and he said if Vinnie Jones tried his antics on with him, he'd rip him apart, so you might want to warn him that.

GREG: (sceptical) He said that?

ANDY: Yeah. I'm not stirring shit, I don't want to see him get hurt. I don't care about him but I wouldn't want to see him get hurt. I've said my bit so . . .

GREG: I've got to go, I'll see you later.

ANDY: See you later, mate.

SCENE 15. INT. RESTAURANT. NIGHT.

MAGGIE AND MARK ARE SITTING AT A SMALL TABLE TOGETHER, LOOKING AT MENUS.

MAGGIE: You've done so much.

MARK: Not really, I'm probably a bit older than you.

MAGGIE: How old are you?

MARK: Thirty-four.

MAGGIE: Well, I'm actually older than you but thank you very much.

MARK: Oh, well, you don't look it, I thought you were in your twenties.

MAGGIE: (giggling girlishly) You never, did you? I'm not.

MARK: Anything you fancy?

MAGGIE: (flirting) Possibly.

MARK: I meant on the menu.

MAGGIE: I know.

THEY BOTH LAUGH.

SCENE 16. INT. STUDIO. NIGHT.

ANDY IS KILLING TIME, LIKE EXTRAS DO. ROSS KEMP MARCHES UP TO HIM.

ROSS: (angrily) What have you been saying?

ANDY: About what?

ROSS: Why am I hearing that Vinnie Jones is looking for me and he wants to batter me?

ANDY: (lying) I haven't said anything.

ROSS: (nervously) Well, how does he know I've been slagging him off. Who have you been speaking to?

ANDY: No one. You're not scared of him, are you?

ROSS: No. Not with what I could do to him.

ANDY: With your SAS stuff and that.

ROSS: Yeah. I mean, do you know what that stands for?

ANDY: SAS? Special Air Service.

ROSS: What?

ANDY: Special Air Service, isn't it?

ROSS: It doesn't stand for that.

ANDY: Doesn't it?

ROSS: I've talked to actual SAS people, they've told me what it stands for.

ANDY: What does it stand for then?

ROSS: (leaning forward and whispering) Super Army Soldiers.

ANDY LAUGHS, BUT THEN REALISES ROSS IS BEING SERIOUS.

ANDY: Are you sure?

ROSS: Yeah, I mean actual SAS people have told me that. The actual guys themselves and they should know.

ANDY: They weren't winding you up?

ROSS: They wouldn't do that to one of their own.

ANDY: No, I thought it was Special Air Services.

ROSS: (laughing derisively) Special Air Services, I mean, that sounds like Fed Ex or something doesn't it? Registered delivery or whatever.
(ROSS SHOWS OFF HIS MUSCLES)

Do you think a postman needs arms like these? Did I get these muscles lifting jiffy bags?

ROSS KISSES HIS ARM MUSCLE.

ANDY: Definitely not.

ROSS: (serious) If Vinnie Jones comes near me looking for a fight, I will unleash hell.

ANDY: Okay.

SCENE 17. INT.
MAGGIE'S FLAT. NIGHT.

MARK HAS WALKED MAGGIE TO HER DOOR.

MAGGIE: Well, that was fun.

MARK: Absolutely.

MAGGIE: Do you want to come in for a cup of tea?

MARK: I'd love to.

MAGGIE: Okay. Right, just go through.

MAGGIE CLOSES THE DOOR BEHIND MARK. CUT TO: MARK AND MAGGIE LAUGHING AND JOKING TOGETHER IN THE KITCHEN. CUT TO: MARK AND MAGGIE UNDRESSING EACH OTHER IN THE LIVING ROOM. CUT TO: MARK AND MAGGIE, ON THE COUCH, MAKING LOVE. MAGGIE'S FACE SHOWS CONTENTMENT BUT THE MOMENT IS RUINED SUDDENLY BY:

MARK: Come on, love, you're like a dead horse. Put a bit of minge round it.

MAGGIE: (taken aback but carrying on) Okay.

SCENE 18. INT. STUDIO. NIGHT.

ROSS AND ANDY ARE STANDING BEHIND THE SCENES, TALKING. ROSS
IS NOW WEARING HIS FULL LORD NELSON UNIFORM, COMPLETE WITH
TRICORN HAT AND ONE HAND INSIDE HIS JACKET.

ROSS: I head-butted a horse once.

ANDY: He must have really annoyed you.

VINNIE JONES ENTERS DRESSED AS A 1970S FOOTBALL HOOLIGAN.
GREG IS LURKING NEARBY. VINNIE CHARGES UP TO ROSS.

VINNIE: Kemp.

ROSS: All right, Vinnie, how's it going?

VINNIE: (angrily) Never mind the 'All right, Vinnie, how's it going?'
bollocks. What you been saying?

ROSS: What you talking about?

VINNIE: What's all this I've been hearing, some shit about you think
you're harder than me?

ROSS: (nervously) Where have you heard this?

VINNIE: Some extra I've been doing a scene with said he heard it over
here. You been trying to impress the extras by telling them you're
harder than me?

ROSS: I haven't said anything.

VINNIE: You think you're well hard, don't you?
(VINNIE LUNGES TOWARDS ROSS, WHO FLINCHES AND LEANS BACK,
HIS HAT FALLING OFF HIS HEAD)
Are you hard?

ROSS: (quietly) No.

VINNIE: No, you're not. And if I hear you slag me off any more I'll come
over here and I'll show you what really hard is. Do you know what really
hard is?

ROSS: Beating me up and that.

VINNIE: Yeah.
(TO ANDY)
Do you know what really hard is?

ANDY: (quickly) Beating up and that. Kick in the bollocks.

ROSS: No need to be specific.

VINNIE: (pointing at ROSS, angrily) All right. This is the final warning.
(VINNIE WALKS AWAY. TO GREG)
Come on.

GREG SMIRKS AT ANDY BEFORE HE AND VINNIE WALK AWAY. ROSS
PICKS UP HIS HAT AND DUSTS IT OFF SLOWLY. ANDY WATCHES HIM.

ROSS: (quietly) What?

ANDY: Nothing.
(AWKWARD SILENCE)
Why didn't you use your SAS stuff on him?

ROSS: Because I don't know any.

ANDY: What, you don't know kung fu and all the lethal moves?

ROSS: No.

ANDY: Why did you say you did?

ROSS: Why did I say I can hold my breath under water for three and a
half minutes? I can't. I panic in water if anything. I can't get you a line
either, if that's why you're still here.

ANDY: Really?

ROSS: (weakly) I haven't got any power round here.

ANDY: I've told people I've got a line and everything.

ROSS: Sorry.

ANDY: Don't worry about it.

ROSS: Every job I do, I get bullied.

ANDY: Bullied?

ROSS: People calling me names and that. If it doesn't stop soon I think
I'm just going to finish it, end it all. Do what I thought I'd never do.

ANDY: (shocked) Suicide?

ROSS: No, go to *Family Affairs*. I've had an offer. There's no bullying at *Family Affairs*, they're really nice people.

ANDY: Sure.

ROSS: All I want to do is act.

ANDY: And you're good.

ROSS: (eagerly) Am I?

ANDY: (slightly uncomfortable) Yeah, course you are. Put your hat on. (PUTS ROSS'S HAT BACK ON FOR HIM)
Look at that, looks brilliant. Hair and everything.

ROSS: Yes.

ANDY: Look at all these.

(ANDY TOUCHES ROSS'S MEDALS. ROSS FIGHTS BACK TEARS.)
That's shiny, isn't it?

ANDY AND ROSS STAND AWKWARDLY FOR A MOMENT, THEN ANDY
SLOWLY WALKS AWAY.

EXTRAS
EPISODE 2

CAST LIST

Andy Millman RICKY GERVAIS
Maggie Jacobs ASHLEY JENSEN
Goran BORIS BOSKOVIC
Jon STEVE JACKSON
Greg SHAUN PYE

With BEN STILLER

Jackie Greer LIZA SADOVY
Producer JAY VILLIERS
Producer's Wife
ELEANOR MATSUURA
Woman in bar JO WYATT
Boy THOMAS BYRNE
Grip PAUL TRIPP

Written & Directed by
RICKY GERVAIS &
STEPHEN MERCHANT

FILM CLIP: 'DO ANGELS BLEED?'

WE'RE WATCHING A HARROWING SCENE FROM A GRITTY MOVIE
SET IN WAR-TORN BOSNIA. SOLDIERS ARE PUSHING SOME TERRIFIED
VILLAGERS ROUGHLY TOWARDS A WIRE FENCE. GREG (A SOLDIER)
PUSHES ANDY (A VILLAGER) OUT OF THE SHOT.

SCENE 1. EXT. FILM SET
OF WAR-TORN BOSNIA. DAY.

ANDY: (rubbing the back of his neck) Why did you do that?

GREG: It's called acting.

ANDY: Yeah, but why did you have to be quite so rough though?

GREG: Strange, that's what a bird said to me last night. Twenty-five
years old, absolutely gorgeous. We did it five times. Nearly wore me
out. By the end of it, bollocks like a bull dog, I tell you.

THE DIRECTOR CALLS 'CUT'. WE REVEAL IT TO BE BEN STILLER,
STANDING WITH HIS PRODUCTION CREW.

BEN STILLER: Cut! That's it, print that, move to the next one.
Mike, Richard, that's exactly what I was talking about with the
smoke, thank you.

(TO AN ASSISTANT DIRECTOR)
Right, I want to go in tighter next.

MAGGIE, WHO IS DRESSED AS A BOSNIAN WOMAN, LEAVES THE SET
AND WALKS OVER TO ANDY AND GREG.

MAGGIE: (smiling) Did you see me there?

ANDY: It was brilliant.

MAGGIE: Was it?

GREG: You get more money for that.

MAGGIE: Do I?

GREG: You got direction, yeah?

MAGGIE: Yes.

GREG: You get more money.

MAGGIE: Excellent.

GREG: It's called supplementary performance fee, talk to the production manager.

MAGGIE: Brilliant.

GREG: Why do I have to sort everyone's life out?

ANDY: Oh, here we go.

GREG: Talk to the production manager and you'll get a few extra quid. God knows you could do with it.

MAGGIE: These aren't my clothes.

ANDY LAUGHS.

GREG: You could have fooled me.

BEN STILLER IS ROUNDING UP CAST AND CREW.

BEN STILLER: Hey, guys, guys. People, can we gather round, please. Guys. This is Goran, this is the man whose story we're making.

CAST AND CREW APPLAUD.

BEN STILLER: Okay, he's the reason we're gathered here to share his story with the world. A lot of you might be thinking, why am I making this movie? Sure, you guys look at me as one of the world's most successful comedy actors. What does that mean? I mean, yeah, I make *Along Came Polly* and it opens to 32 million dollars. One of the biggest Martin Luther King Junior birthday holiday opening weekends ever. Goes on to gross 170 million worldwide. *Meet the Parents*, double that. But what does the money and the success mean in real terms? If I find a little orphan child in a war zone hiding in a burnt-out building, his parents murdered, persecuted for his race, his religion. What am I going to do? Pop on *Dodgeball* on DVD?

GORAN: It's a funny film.

BEN STILLER: (to GORAN) Thanks.
(TO CROWD)

And I can put on *Dodgeball* and he's going to laugh for an hour and thirty-two minutes, escape reality for a while, but what happens when the film finishes? Back to reality. Still an orphan, still living with fear. How do I help him? Put on *Dodgeball* again? Sure, he's going to laugh again, he'll see things he didn't see the first time, it's layered, it was made like that, but this can't go on indefinitely, all right. At a certain point, you know, after the fifth, sixth, seventh viewing he's still laughing but it's not getting to the root of the problem, okay? How do I help him?

ANDY: (whispering to MAGGIE) Make *Dodgeball 2*?

MAGGIE LAUGHS QUIETLY.

BEN STILLER: Make this movie. Make people think. Change attitudes. So think of that while you're sipping on your frappucinos and . . .
(TO ASSISTANT DIRECTOR)
what are we doing, Mike?

A.D.: Let's have a break.

BEN STILLER: Break time, okay, good. Thank you, thank you very much.

A.D.: Thanks, everyone. Back at quarter past, thank you.

BEN AND GORAN WALK AWAY TOGETHER. THE CROWD BREAKS UP.

SCENE 3. EXT. FILM SET. DAY.

BEN IS STANDING WITH A GROUP OF EXTRAS DRESSED AS SOLDIERS, GIVING THEM DIRECTIONS FOR THE NEXT SCENE. GORAN STANDS NEXT TO HIM. MAGGIE AND ANDY WATCH FROM THE SIDE OF THE SET.

BEN STILLER: And I want you to just be coming straight in, there shouldn't be a blade between when the grenade has gone off and when you guys come around, okay?

GORAN: Ben, is it possible, please: more smoke?

BEN STILLER: Was there more smoke?

GORAN: Yes.

BEN STILLER: (shouting to crew) Okay, can I get more smoke please?

GORAN: Thank you.

BEN STILLER: My pleasure.
(TO THE EXTRAS)
Okay, all right, guys, now while we have the smoke can you come around—

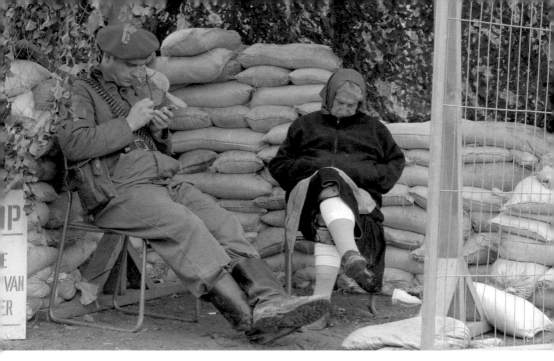

GORAN: The Coke, it's not cold.

BEN STILLER: Sorry, okay, just kill the smoke for a second.
(TO GORAN)
What?

GORAN: My Coke is not cold.

BEN STILLER: Your Coke is not cold? Okay, all right.
(SHOUTS)
Mike?

MIKE: Yeah.

BEN STILLER: Can we get him a cold Coke? Okay? Make sure his Coke
is always cold, okay?

MAGGIE AND ANDY WATCH GORAN.

ANDY: Look at that, he gets anything he wants.

MAGGIE: I know but he's been through a lot, hasn't he?

ANDY: I know he's been through a lot, they're making a film, he's not
a competition winner.
(NODDING TOWARDS GORAN)
That's where the real power lies here.

MAGGIE: (looking at GORAN) I think he's quite attractive actually.

ANDY: Forget it, I know what you're thinking, but never get involved with a man whose wife has been murdered.

MAGGIE: That's awful. Why?

ANDY: Well, for one, he's not going to be a barrel of laughs. Two, you can't compete with her, it's not like the marriage started going downhill and she was boozing and sleeping around, do you know what I mean? She was taken from him at the peak of their love. She's gone out on a high, she's like Marilyn Monroe or Jimmy Dean, you can't compete with it. Never get involved with a man whose wife's been murdered. Rule one. Choose someone else.

MAGGIE: (looking around) Well, who then?

ANDY: It's as easy as that, isn't it, to you?

SCENE 4. INT. PRODUCTION OFFICE. DAY.

THE DOOR IS OPEN. MAGGIE KNOCKS POLITELY. A MAN IS SAT BEHIND A DESK WORKING AT HIS COMPUTER. THIS IS JON. MAGGIE IS STILL WEARING HER COSTUME AND MAKE-UP FROM FILMING. THERE IS A FAKE BULLET HOLE IN THE CENTRE OF HER FOREHEAD.

JON: Yeah, come in, just one second.

MAGGIE: I think maybe I'm owed some money, some supplementary performance money or something, I think?

JON: Right, give me one second.
(JON TURNS TO FACE MAGGIE. HE'S VERY GOOD-LOOKING. THERE'S A LOOK OF MUTUAL ATTRACTION)
Hi.

MAGGIE: Hi.

JON: How can I help?

MAGGIE: (tongue-tied) Yes, the thing, the supplementary acting fee . . .

JON: Right, I'll have to check with the first A.D. really. Let me get your details up.

MAGGIE: Okay.

SHE QUICKLY TOUSLES HER HAIR.

JON: What's your name?

MAGGIE: Maggie Jacobs.

JON: Just take a seat, Maggie.

MAGGIE SITS DOWN ON A SMALL SOFA IN FRONT OF THE DESK. SHE UNDOES THE TOP TWO BUTTONS ON HER BLOUSE TO LOOK MORE SEDUCTIVE.

MAGGIE: Thank you. Oh, I hope your wife doesn't catch me on your sofa, or your girlfriend.

JON: I'm not married.

MAGGIE: Or your girlfriend.

JON: I haven't got a girlfriend.

MAGGIE: Or I suppose your boyfriend.

JON: I'm not gay.
(THEY BOTH LAUGH.)
I should be worried your husband catches you in here.

MAGGIE: I'm not married and I don't have a boyfriend and I'm not a lesbian so, all done, available.

SCENE 5. INT. GORAN'S TRAILER. DAY.

ANDY KNOCKS AND ENTERS. GORAN IS SITTING ALONE AT A TABLE, LOOKING AT SOME PHOTOGRAPHS, LOST IN THOUGHT.

ANDY: Hello. You get on well with Ben, I wondered if you could have a word with him about me because I'm a proper actor. I'm an extra in this but I've done lines . . . You okay?

GORAN: Yes.

ANDY: What you got there?

GORAN: My wife . . . pictures of my wife.

ANDY: (mumbling, sensitive) Oh, yeah, I heard about that, yeah, sorry.

GORAN: Memories, wonderful love.
(HE SHOWS ANDY THE PHOTOS)
This is her, very beautiful.

ANDY: She is.

GORAN: (smiling) Our first holiday. Here she is with my son, one year old.

ANDY: Nice boy.

GORAN: Nice no more. Dead. Dead boy.
(GORAN STARES AT ANDY. ANDY DOESN'T KNOW WHAT HE SHOULD DO.
GORAN SHOWS ANDY ANOTHER PHOTO)
My wife again.

ANDY: Oh, I shouldn't look at that. Is she sunbathing?

GORAN: No, she is dead, lying in the street.

ANDY: Oh, I see now.

GORAN: Dead.

ANDY: Yes.
(PAUSE)
Why did you take a—

GORAN: Why did I take photograph of her?

ANDY: Yes.

GORAN: (angrily) To show the world what must be shown. This is why
I want film to be made by Ben Stiller.

ANDY: Ben Stiller of *Zoolander*, sure.

GORAN: (thrusting photos at ANDY) You look – dead, naked.

ANDY: Yes.

GORAN: You look.

ANDY: I am but I'm only looking at her dead naked face.
(BRIEF PAUSE)
Where did you get these developed?

GORAN: My cousin.

ANDY: I was going to say: it's not the sort of thing you pop into Boots with.

GORAN: Boots?

ANDY: Oh, it's a chain of chemists, high street pharmacies. They don't just do pharmacy now, they do everything. They do gifts, sandwiches, Weight Watchers smoothies, things like that.

GORAN: We don't have Boots.

ANDY: Oh. Oh, you missed a trick. Truprint give you a free film when you get something developed. So you're a mug.
(GORAN BEGINS TO LOOK TEARFUL AS HE STUDIES THE PHOTOS)
Anyway, if you could put a word in to Ben to get me a line . . . in this.
(GORAN BEGINS TO SOB QUIETLY. ANDY FALLS SILENT.)
I'll catch you later.

ANDY GETS UP TO LEAVE.

SCENE 6. EXT. FILM SET. DAY.

MAGGIE AND ANDY ARE SAT IN THE EXTRAS' HOLDING AREA.
MAGGIE IS FLICKING THROUGH A MAGAZINE.

ANDY: He's got photos and everything . . .

MAGGIE: Oh, well, that's not going to help, is it?

ANDY: No. What worries me is I can't push it, I can't go up to him and remind him, go 'Sorry to interrupt you again when you're thinking about your slaughtered loved ones, but that line, have you done anything about it?' Do you know what I mean?

MAGGIE: Might seem a wee bit insensitive, eh?

ANDY: (sarcastic) Yeah, it could do.

MAGGIE: Oh, listen, be warned, Jackie Greer's on the prowl.

ANDY: Why?

MAGGIE: She's having a birthday do.

ANDY: Forget it, I'm not going.

MAGGIE: Well, I'm not going if you're not going.

ANDY: Don't go then.

MAGGIE: No, but I can't not go because she's always really nice to me.

ANDY: Well, have an excuse ready.

MAGGIE: Like what?

ANDY: My standard is 'Oh, my sister's coming down to stay.' And find out exactly when it is and go 'When is it?' This Saturday. 'This Saturday? I can't, my sister's coming down.' You're gutted, you'd loved to have gone but family—

JACKIE APPROACHES MAGGIE AND ANDY. SHE'S LOUD AND OVER-FRIENDLY.

JACKIE: (interrupting) Oh, hello, you two. Oh, I like your hair like that. Isn't she beautiful? Now listen up, no excuses. My birthday this week, I'm having birthday drinks. I'm twenty-one again
(JACKIE LAUGHS. MAGGIE AND ANDY FORCE A BRIEF CHUCKLE)
and I command you both to be there and I won't take no for an answer.

ANDY: Okay.

MAGGIE: Oh, my sister's . . .

ANDY: (stopping MAGGIE, then prompting her)
'When is it?'

MAGGIE: (to JACKIE) When is it?

JACKIE: Friday, after we wrap, it's only local.

ANDY: (prompting) 'This Friday?'

MAGGIE: This Friday?

JACKIE: Yeah, Friday.

MAGGIE: (faking regret) Oh, no, I can't do this Friday, my sister is coming down.

JACKIE: Oh, well, bring her along, I'd love to meet her.

MAGGIE: (MAGGIE stares at JACKIE, stumped) Okay, I'll bring her along.

ANDY: (stepping in) Well, you can't bring her along, can you?

MAGGIE: No.

ANDY: You can't actually physically . . .

MAGGIE: Why?

ANDY: Because you haven't got a sister, no. You've confused her with . . .
(TO JACKIE)
My sister is coming down.

MAGGIE: His sister's coming down.

JACKIE: (to MAGGIE) So you can come?

MAGGIE: Yes, I can come.

JACKIE: (to ANDY) And you, darling?

ANDY: Well, as she said my sister's coming down, so—

JACKIE: And as I said, bring her along.

ANDY: (quiet, earnest) But what she didn't say was she's coming down because she's ill.

MAGGIE: (under her breath) Brilliant.

JACKIE: God, is it serious?

ANDY: We're not sure.

JACKIE: Oh, well, send her my love.

ANDY: I will.

JACKIE: But I will see you there?

ANDY: (smiling at MAGGIE) Definitely.

MAGGIE: Yes. I've got no excuses.

ANDY: Yeah. See you later. Brilliant.

JACKIE BLOWS THEM BOTH A KISS AND LEAVES.

MAGGIE: Oh, my God, you're coming.

ANDY: No, I'm not. What, I've got to be punished because you didn't think on your feet quickly enough? No.

MAGGIE: I can't go on my own.

ANDY: I can't go at all. What if my sister died?

MAGGIE: What's she got?

ANDY: I haven't got a sister.

MAGGIE: (finally understanding) You haven't got a sister?

ANDY: No, I made it up as an excuse.
(PATRONISING)
Are you reading a little magazine there, are you?

MAGGIE: Yes.

ANDY: Do you understand it?

SCENE 7. INT. CANTEEN. DAY.

MAGGIE AND ANDY ARE WALKING TO A TABLE WITH THEIR TRAYS.

MAGGIE: Would you rather have all your food too salty or too sweet?

ANDY: Doesn't matter if it's 'too' anything, it's rubbish, isn't it?

MAGGIE: You see, I would have too salty.

ANDY: Well, no, that would be rubbish, if it's too salty it would be rubbish.

MAGGIE: Yeah, but I like savoury things.

ANDY: Yeah, but you said 'too salty' which means it's horrible.

MAGGIE: I like crisps.

ANDY: Oh, don't ask me any more questions.

MAGGIE SPOTS JON AT A NEARBY TABLE.

JON: Hello again.

MAGGIE: Hey, hello. Oh, this is my friend Andy.

ANDY: Hi.

JON: Hiya, Jon.

MAGGIE: What are you doing here?

JON: Oh, I'm just having lunch.

MAGGIE: (laughing girlishly) Oh, that's what we're doing, aren't we?

ANDY: (sarcastic) Yeah, just letting it cool down here a bit.

MAGGIE: Just having a bit of lunch before we go back to work.
Are you having to work late tonight then?

JON: No, not tonight, I'm going to the drinks do, I don't know if you
know it's Jackie Greer's birthday.

MAGGIE: Oh, my God, I'm going.

(SHE LAUGHS AGAIN)

I'm already going, oh, spooky.

JON: (to ANDY) I'm sure you're welcome to come along as well though.

ANDY: I can't, I'm doing . . . anything else.

MAGGIE: So do you know Jackie Greer very well, good friends?

JON: Not really, no, the producer's going down so he sort of asked us to go along for team bonding or whatever.

ANDY: What, the producer of this?

JON: Yeah, Martin the producer, he's going to be there. He knows Jackie from years back so . . .

ANDY: Yeah, I'll probably . . . I might as well come down for a couple of—

MAGGIE: Yeah, okay, we'll see you later on then for a drink and a bit of a laugh, eh?

JON: That would be great, yeah.

MAGGIE: Yeah, well, I'd better get this down me. Line my stomach. Coq au vin, sounds a bit rude, doesn't it?

ANDY: Not really.

MAGGIE: What have you gone for?

JON: Oh, boring, just three bean salad, spinach and smoothie. I'm on a high-fibre diet.

MAGGIE: (smiling) Oh, no bowel cancer for you then?

JON: (taken aback) Hopefully not, no.

ANDY: Okay.

MAGGIE: See you, bye.

JON: Cheers.

MAGGIE AND ANDY BEGIN TO WALK AWAY FROM JON'S TABLE.

ANDY: 'No bowel cancer for you then?'

MAGGIE: Right.

ANDY: That's a smooth line.

SCENE 8. INT.
GORAN'S TRAILER. DAY.

ANDY KNOCKS AND ENTERS. GORAN IS RELAXING ON A SOFA, READING
HEAT MAGAZINE. ANDY SITS DOWN NEXT TO HIM.

ANDY: Hi.

GORAN: Hello.

ANDY: You all right?

GORAN: Yes.

ANDY: You're not going to . . .

HE MIMES CRYING.

GORAN: No, no, I'm good.

ANDY: Good, well, I got you a gift.

GORAN: Why?

ANDY: Just to say thanks for being part of this amazing project,
you know.

GORAN: Oh, thank you very much.

ANDY: (serious) And to thank you for the line you said you'd get me, do you remember?

GORAN: Did I?

ANDY: Yeah, you probably don't remember because you were crying about your dead family and stuff but you said you'd ask Ben for a line. (STARTS TO TAKE BACK THE GIFT)
Are you going to ask Ben for a line?

GORAN: Yes, I can do that.

ANDY: (handing over the present) I didn't know what to get you, got you vouchers.

GORAN: Vouchers?

ANDY: Yes. Fifteen quids' worth.

GORAN: It's like money?

ANDY: It's exactly like money but you can only spend it at Top Shop, so you'll ask Ben, yeah?

GORAN: Yes, yes.

ANDY: Brilliant. Fifteen quid. See you later.

ANDY GETS UP AND LEAVES THE TRAILER.

FILM CLIP: 'DO ANGELS BLEED?'

A YOUNG NINE-YEAR-OLD BOY IS RUNNING SCARED THROUGH SMOKE, GUNFIRE AND EXPLOSIONS. IT'S ALL VERY DRAMATIC BUT THE BOY STUMBLES FOR A MOMENT AND STARTS TO GIGGLE.

SCENE 9. EXT. FILM SET OF BOSNIAN LANDSCAPE. DAY.

BEN STILLER WALKS ON TO THE SET FROM HIS DIRECTOR'S CHAIR.

BEN STILLER: (to the crew) Cut! Cut! Why is he laughing?
(TO THE BOY)
Why are you laughing?

BOY: I tripped up.

BEN STILLER: What's so funny?

BOY: I tripped up.

THE BOY'S MOTHER WALKS ON TO THE SET AND STANDS BESIDE THE BOY.

BEN STILLER: Okay. All right, do you think this is funny, mm? You think war is funny? Do you think genocide is funny?
(RAISES HIS VOICE)
Huh?
(TO THE MUM)
Are you his mom? Let me ask you this,
(BEN TAKES A GUN FROM THE COSTUME OF A NEARBY EXTRA AND HOLDS IT UP TO THE MOTHER'S FACE)
do you think this would be funny – if I shot your mother right now?

BOY: (almost in tears) No.

BEN STILLER: (in a babyish voice) If I shot your mummy in the face would that make you laugh? Do you think that would be funny, huh? (IN A SERIOUS VOICE)

If I blew your mother's face off right now in front of you would that make you laugh? Okay, so maybe you should think of that next time you trip, okay?

(BEN THROWS THE GUN BACK TO THE EXTRA AND RUNS BACK TO HIS CHAIR. HE SHOUTS TO THE CREW)

Let's do it right now, let's go. Still rolling.

ANDY: (observing the scene, to MAGGIE) And the atrocities continue.

BEN STILLER: And action!

ANDY: (taking out his chest wig and scratching underneath) So itchy, this.

SCENE 10. INT.
TRENDY BAR. NIGHT.

MAGGIE AND ANDY ENTER THE BAR AND WALK OVER TO JACKIE. MAGGIE KISSES JACKIE ON BOTH CHEEKS AND HANDS HER A GIFT.

JACKIE: Oh, is that for me?

MAGGIE: Yes.

JACKIE: Thank you so much.
(TO ANDY)
I wasn't expecting you, I thought your sister was ill.

ANDY: Yes, but it turned out to be not as serious as we first thought. Women's problems. Typical, quite a build-up. I had to get out of the house in the end, I thought she was going to have my face off, a Rottweiler with lipstick.
(ANDY LOOKS AROUND THE CLUB)
Busy though.

MAGGIE: (to JACKIE) You look amazing.

JACKIE: Thank you.

ANDY: Someone said the producer was coming, is that . . .

JACKIE: Oh, yes Martin, he's over there.

JACKIE POINTS HIM OUT.

MAGGIE: (to JACKIE) Look at you, I wouldn't have thought to put that with that . . .

CUT TO MAGGIE WALKING THROUGH THE CLUB ON HER OWN. SHE SPOTS JON. SHE MOVES TOWARDS HIS GROUP OF FRIENDS HESITANTLY, EVENTUALLY SHE CROUCHES BEHIND HIM AND LEANS INTO THE CONVERSATION.

MAGGIE: Hello.

JON: Oh, hello.

MAGGIE: (smiling) Hi.

CUT TO THE PRODUCER TALKING TO TWO WOMEN.

PRODUCER: No, it was Elaine's idea really.

ELAINE: (to the WOMAN) He says that every time, but it was both of us.

ANDY WALKS BEHIND THE PRODUCER AND HIS FRIENDS, TRYING TO MANOEUVRE HIMSELF INTO THE CONVERSATION.

PRODUCER: Anyway, it's a modern retelling of the old stories and we're going to make several of them. It's going to be a little bit like Kieslowski's *Dekalog*.

WOMAN: Oh, yes I know.

ANDY LEANS IN TOWARDS THE PRODUCER.

PRODUCER: Well, you know there's that one character in *The Watcher* and it's a fantastic character, have you read that Kieslowski book?

WOMAN: No, I haven't.

PRODUCER: He wrote later that he was so upset that he left him out of two of the films that he really wished he—

ANDY: (butting in, out of his depth) It's his fault! He should have . . .
(THE PRODUCER AND HIS COMPANIONS NOTICE ANDY)
Do you want a drink? I'm a friend of Jackie's. My round.

PRODUCER: Oh, great, we're on champagne.

ANDY: (hesitant) Three glasses of champagne.

PRODUCER: Oh, just get a bottle.

ANDY: (trying to cover his shock with a laugh, but gutted) Yes, definitely.

ANDY LEAVES TO GO TO THE BAR. THE PRODUCER CONTINUES HIS CONVERSATION.

CUT TO JON AND MAGGIE, SITTING TOGETHER, FLIRTING.

MAGGIE: What do you mean, why have you not seen me around? I've gone red.

JON: No, but have you done other productions? Are you an actress?

MAGGIE: No.

JON: Oh, you look like you should be an actress.

CUT TO THE PRODUCER AND THE TWO WOMEN, NOW SITTING AT A TABLE, STILL DEEP IN CONVERSATION. ANDY RETURNS WITH THE CHAMPAGNE AND PUSHES PAST SOME PEOPLE SO THAT HE CAN SQUEEZE HIMSELF NEXT TO THE PRODUCER. THE CONVERSATION CONTINUES FOR A WHILE UNTIL ANDY LEANS FORWARD AND INTERRUPTS.

ANDY: Hi, Andy.

PRODUCER: Oh, Andy, yeah.
(ANDY POINTS TO THE CHAMPAGNE HE'S BROUGHT)
Oh, cheers.

ANDY: Cheers. Just thinking: what you and Ben are doing in this film, wonderful, it moved me so . . .

PRODUCER: Thank you.

ANDY: No, thank you. Can I ask you something? What was your inspiration?

PRODUCER: Well, obviously the story.

ANDY: Oh, yeah.

PRODUCER: In film terms probably something like the . . . are you a film buff?

ANDY: I adore film.

PRODUCER: Well, I tell you what I rewatched when we were planning this.

ANDY: Oh, please do.

PRODUCER: Andrezej Wadja's *War Trilogy*. They're extraordinary aren't they?

ANDY: (lying) Yeah.

PRODUCER: And I know Ben's been watching – particularly in relation to the battle scenes – a lot of Kurosawa.

ANDY: (no idea) Oh, okay.

PRODUCER: Yeah, particularly in relation to the kineticism of the mise en scene . . .

ANDY: Of the film? Yeah, I see.

PRODUCER: You a fan? Generally . . .

ANDY: Yes.

PRODUCER: . . . Of Japanese cinema?

ANDY: Oh, definitely.

PRODUCER: Kurosawa's obviously a master.

ANDY: Yeah, he's number one.

PRODUCER: I suppose, on a personal level, I'm more a fan of Ozu.

ANDY: Me too, but I think they're both, they're both big boys.

PRODUCER: The aesthetics are completely different.

ANDY: Oh, chalk and cheese . . .

PRODUCER: He tends to knock the camera off—

ANDY: And the other one just lets it on.

PRODUCER: It was Elaine actually who turned me on to Ozu.

ANDY: Oh, congratulations.

PRODUCER: Yeah, I wasn't really a fan before.

ANDY: (faux surprise) Really?

PRODUCER: No.

ANDY: Oh.

PRODUCER: No, I'm sure you've found this. You say to someone, do you like Japanese cinema and they say, 'No, can't get into it, boring.' And you say, 'Well, do you like *The Magnificent Seven*?' And they say, 'Yes.'

ANDY: Oh yeah, they like that.

PRODUCER: And you think, 'Well, it's a remake of the *Seven Samurai*.'

ANDY: Yeah, yeah, course it is! What, they didn't know that? Seven's the clue.

PRODUCER: No, it really upsets me, I want everyone to love the *Seven Samurai*.

ANDY: I love all the number films. Really, *Seven Samurai*, *Ocean's Eleven*, *Dirty Dozen*, which is about as many as I think you can have on screen at once. But seven is perfect for me.

PRODUCER: Apologies for this but I don't really recognise you, what are you doing on the film?

ANDY: I'm an actor, yeah, although at the moment I'm concentrating more on background work, looking out towards getting a speaking role. In anything.

PRODUCER: Right, right.

MAGGIE APPEARS.

MAGGIE: Sorry to interrupt.

PRODUCER: Not at all.

MAGGIE: (to ANDY) Listen, can I have a quick word?

ANDY: Not now, no, just a little bit busy.

MAGGIE: Two minutes.

ANDY: I'm in the middle—

PRODUCER: Don't mind us. We'll be here.

ANDY: Yeah? Okay, all right.

ANDY TAKES MAGGIE TO ONE SIDE.

MAGGIE: I just wanted to let you know that Jon's going on somewhere else and he's asked me to go with him.

ANDY: Fine.

MAGGIE: I know but I wanted to let you know because it was me who dragged you here, I didn't want you to get all annoyed because I'd disappeared and . . .

ANDY: I'm fine, I'm chatting, it's great.

MAGGIE: He's nice.

ANDY: He is, yes.

(ANDY LOOKS TOWARDS JON, WHO IS STANDING BY THE DOOR,
AND NOTICES THAT HE'S WEARING A BUILT-UP ORTHOPAEDIC SHOE)
Foot doesn't bother you?

MAGGIE: Eh?

ANDY: I know you're a deeply shallow person, I thought the foot would
be a problem.

MAGGIE: What do you mean?

ANDY: He's got one leg shorter than the other, look, he's wearing one
of them big shoes.

MAGGIE: Oh my God.

ANDY: You didn't notice that?

MAGGIE: Well, no, it was under the table, wasn't it?

THEY BOTH STARE AT JON'S FOOT.

ANDY: Yes. Must have been a big table.

MAGGIE: No, don't.

ANDY: What?

MAGGIE: I didn't see. Oh, look at him he's lovely, he's a lovely man.
He's funny, he's attractive. Look at him, everybody loves him, life
and soul of the party.

ANDY: Certainly the sole.

MAGGIE: Oh, come on.

ANDY: If you're above it. If you don't mind being known as Maggie, 'Who's Maggie? Maggie, the girl who goes out with the fella with the big shoe,' that's fine.

MAGGIE: But they can do something about it now, can't they?

ANDY: No.

MAGGIE: (looking anxious) Some doctor in China or something—

ANDY: No. That's the weird thing, that's the one thing they can't do anything about. They can give you a new face, new heart, new lungs, new liver, anything, but if you go to a doctor and you say 'Oh, Doc, I've got one leg slightly shorter than the other,' doesn't matter if you've got a million pounds, and they can send you to Switzerland, and all you're coming home with is a big shoe.

MAGGIE: Yes, well, stop it.

ANDY: That's fine, if it's not a problem for you.

MAGGIE: I'm not so shallow that I can't see beyond—

ANDY: Fine.

MAGGIE: Beyond his big shoe.

ANDY: I know you, you'll get involved and it will be a problem. All I'm saying is this. Don't rush off with him tonight, sleep on it, if it's not a problem tomorrow, give him a call.

MAGGIE: In the morning?

ANDY: Absolutely. Why rush into it now?

JON APPROACHES MAGGIE AND ANDY.

JON: Hey.

MAGGIE: Hi.

JON: I'm ready to get going if you are?

MAGGIE: Now? Right now? Er, I don't think I can go right now.

JON: Oh, right, you said you fancied it just then.

MAGGIE: Yeah, but he just reminded me of something . . .

ANDY: Yeah, I just reminded her.

MAGGIE: (meekly) I don't think I can go.

JON: Is it the leg?

MAGGIE: Mm?

JON: (serious) Is it the fact that I've got one leg shorter than the other?

MAGGIE: (quietly, lying badly) I hadn't noticed.

JON: You hadn't noticed?

ANDY: I hadn't.

JON TAKES OFF HIS SHOE AND SLAMS IT DOWN ON THE TABLE IN FRONT OF MAGGIE.

JON: You hadn't noticed that?

MAGGIE: (fake surprise) Oh, no. I hadn't, God, it's a big clumpy one.

ANDY: Don't say clumpy.

MAGGIE: It's like a big Herman Munster . . .

ANDY: Oh, don't say—

MAGGIE SEARCHES FOR SOMETHING TO SAY TO KEEP THE CONVERSATION AFLOAT.

MAGGIE: Do these come in any other styles?

JON JUST STARES AT HER.

ANDY: (trying to help) Do you have to buy a pair and throw one away?

JON: It's been good talking to you.

MAGGIE: Maybe I can phone you tomorrow.

JON: No, no don't worry about it. You've shown your true colours.

JON TURNS AND WALKS AWAY.

MAGGIE: (hitting ANDY on the arm) That was you—

ANDY: That wasn't my fault, how was it my fault?

MAGGIE: That poor man. All his life he's had to deal with people that are so shallow that they can't see beyond his foot thing and he's going to think I'm like that.

ANDY: You are.

MAGGIE: I don't want him to know that.

ANDY: Well, don't say Herman Munster then.

MAGGIE: Well, it just slipped out.

ANDY: (incredulous) Herman Munster just slipped out?
(ANDY AND MAGGIE WALK OVER TO THE TABLE WHERE THE PRODUCER IS STILL SITTING WITH THE TWO WOMEN. THERE'S A FROSTY ATMOSPHERE. TO THE PRODUCER:)
Bit more room. We were having a conversation earlier about films, weren't we?

PRODUCER: Yes.

ANDY: I was going to ask you about this film actually. Are there any parts left to cast?

PRODUCER: No, I'm afraid not.

ANDY: Oh, that's a shame.

WOMAN: Jon seemed quite upset.

MAGGIE: Was he?

WOMAN: I thought you were getting on with him. You seemed to be.

MAGGIE: Yeah, we were.

WOMAN: But you don't want to see him because of his foot?

MAGGIE: I didn't say that.

WOMAN: But it is though, isn't it?

ANDY: Well, it's her private life, isn't it?

WOMAN: Yeah, I'm just saying that I think it's a shame that she obviously goes through life not liking anyone that's different than her.

ANDY: That's not true, she's gets on with anyone, tall, thin, black, white, yellow . . .

(AS HE SAYS ' YELLOW', HE ABSENT-MINDEDLY POINTS AT ELAINE, WHO IS OF JAPANESE ORIGIN)

. . . She's not prejudiced.

ELAINE: Who's yellow?

ANDY: What?

ELAINE: Well, you were just listing racial types, black, white. Who's yellow?

ANDY: (gesturing to the PRODUCER and himself) What we call the Chinese sometimes . . .

PRODUCER: (sceptically) Do we?

ELAINE: Well, one, I'm American and two, my parents are Japanese not Chinese.

ANDY: (tactless) Oh, yes, Japanese, Chinese, I wasn't . . .

ANDY STARES AT HER. A LONG PAUSE AS HE REALISES HIS MISTAKE AND CONSIDERS HIS OPTIONS.

ELAINE: What do you mean, Japanese, Chinese? Both the same to you are they?

ANDY: Well, don't make me sound like a racist, I don't happen to know the intricate differences between Japanese and Chinese people.

MAGGIE: Well, there's that thing that they teach you at school—

ANDY: No.

MAGGIE: (performing the playground rhyme) 'Chinese, Japanese, dirty knees, what are these?'
(MAGGIE PULLS HER EYELIDS UP AND DOWN, AND CLUTCHES HER KNEES AND THEN BREASTS IN TIME TO THE RHYME. THE PRODUCER AND ELAINE SIT SILENTLY IN SHOCK)
Do you remember it?

ANDY: Yeah, it rings a bell.
(TO THE GROUP)
Okay? That's us. Cheers, goodnight.
(NO ONE REPLIES. ANDY AND MAGGIE STAND UP TO LEAVE)

MAGGIE: Are we going?

ANDY: Yeah, do you know why?

MAGGIE: No.

ANDY: Guess.

MAGGIE: Because of the foot.

ANDY: No.

SCENE 11. EXT. FILM SET. DAY.

MAGGIE AND ANDY ARE WAITING ON SET FOR FILMING TO BEGIN. BEN
STILLER IS IN HIS DIRECTOR'S CHAIR, TALKING TO HIS PRODUCTION
CREW, CLEARLY VERY STRESSED.

BEN STILLER: (sharply) I don't need to hear the story of how we got to
this point, I know what point we're at. I'm just wondering when we can
actually shoot it, that's all.

GORAN APPROACHES MAGGIE AND ANDY.

GORAN: Hey.

ANDY: Hi.

GORAN: Good news.

ANDY: Yeah?

GORAN: I got you line.

ANDY: (surprised) Really?

GORAN: I talk to Ben, he say, here, you see, Journalist Two.

POINTING TO A PASSAGE IN THE SCRIPT.

ANDY: (reading) 'Don't go down there, there are snipers down there.'

(PUTTING ON AN EASTERN EUROPEAN ACCENT)
'Don't go down there, there are snipers down there.'

GORAN: What you doing?

ANDY: The accent I was going to . . .
(OFF TO GORAN'S LOOK)
I won't do the accent, that's brilliant.

GORAN: Okay.

ANDY: Excellent.
(GORAN STARTS TO WALK AWAY)
Hold on, sorry, there's two journalists here. Journalist One and
Journalist Two. I'm Journalist Two, but Journalist One's got all
the lines, look,
(TURNING PAGES)
him, him, him, me, snipers, him, him, him. I think I should do
Journalist One, you know.

GORAN: I think someone else already doing that.

ANDY: I know but we could swap. I'd be better.

GORAN: I got you line.

ANDY: I know, but remember the vouchers I got you, the vouchers,
didn't I?

GORAN: (gesturing to his T-shirt) I put them towards this top.

ANDY: Brilliant, doesn't that look good? That looks really good.
Have a word and see if I could do Journalist One.

GORAN: He's busy.

ANDY: Yeah, but he's always busy, just get a quiet moment when he's
not so busy.

BEN WALKS OVER TO A GROUP OF EXTRAS ON THE SET. TWO SOLDIERS
ARE STANDING OVER A LITTLE OLD LADY ON THE FLOOR.

BEN STILLER: Kelvin, go back to one on this, we've got to work this out, all right now . . . Ivan, when you come around—

IGOR: (correcting BEN) Igor.

BEN STILLER: What?

IGOR: Igor.

BEN STILLER: Igor, okay when you knock her down, don't ask her to come down . . .
(BEN BORROWS A RIFLE FROM IGOR AND BEGINS TO MIME ATTACKING THE OLD LADY WITH THE BUTT OF THE GUN)
. . . You smack her in the back of the head, right, and then you come around here and you jam it into her mouth.
(TO THE OLD LADY)
No, you can't put your hand up, okay?
(TO IGOR)

Boom, you jam her in the mouth, okay, break her jaw on the first one, boom, second one, nose, okay, her jaw's broken, she's swallowed her teeth, blood's coming out, all right? Then you smack her again across the side, breaking the neck.
(HE HANDS BACK THE RIFLE, CALLING TO THE CREW)
Okay, can we do this again please?

ANDY: Go and get him now.

GORAN: Okay, I try.
(GORAN APPROACHES A VISIBLY STRESSED BEN STILLER)
Ben.

BEN STILLER: (snappy) Yes.

GORAN: I need to swap the lines.

BEN STILLER: What do you mean, you need to swap the lines?

GORAN: (nervously) For my friend. He wants to—

BEN STILLER: Your friend? No, no I gave your friend a line.

GORAN: Yes, but I want him to have more.

BEN STILLER: (incredulous) You want him to have more? You want him to have more lines?

GORAN: Yes.

BEN STILLER: (sarcastic) I don't understand, are you directing the movie? Or am I directing the movie?

GORAN: No, but this is my story. My memories, my tribute to my dead wife.

BEN STILLER: Would you stop going on about your fucking dead wife? (HIS WORDS ECHO ACROSS THE SET. THERE IS A STUNNED SILENCE) All right, let's do another rehearsal right away please.

MAGGIE: (calling out to BEN, nervously) Ben, that was a bit much.

BEN STILLER: Ben? I'm sorry, what's your name? Oh, wait a minute, I remember. I don't give a shit. Get out of my face.

ANDY: All right, don't have a go at her, she was just worried about Goran.

BEN STILLER: Who are you?

ANDY: Nobody.

BEN STILLER: What's that? Who?

ANDY: Nobody.

BEN STILLER: That's right, nobody. Yeah, and who am I?

ANDY: (pause) It's either Starsky or Hutch, I can never remember.

BEN STILLER: Was that supposed to be funny?

ANDY: You tell me, you were in it.

BEN STILLER: (angrily) Get off my set.

ANDY: Okay.

BEN STILLER: Get off my set.
(PAUSE)
Hey, hey, question: do you know how much *Meet the Fockers* made in its opening weekend?

ANDY: No.

BEN STILLER: No, you don't, do you?
(POINTING TO A CREW MEMBER)
What do you think, huh?

MAN: Don't know.

BEN STILLER: Take a wild guess.

MAN: Twenty million?

BEN STILLER: Way off. Double it, add six, forty-six, three days, seventy million, five days. Five hundred million worldwide. Number-one movie in India right now.

ANDY: Well done. Bye, nerd.

BEN STILLER: Oh, I'm a nerd?

ANDY: Yeah.

BEN STILLER: I'm a nerd?
(BEGINS TO COUNT ON HIS FINGERS)
I've kissed Cameron Diaz, Drew Barrymore, I slapped Jennifer Aniston's butt.

MAGGIE: In films.

BEN STILLER: (angrily) It still counts.
(LOOKS AROUND THE WHOLE SET AND SHOUTS)
It still counts.
(SPEAKS QUIETLY AS HE WALKS BACK TO HIS CHAIR. EVERYONE IS STARING AT BEN)
It still counts. I did it, I actually did it.

ANDY SLOWLY WALKS OFF THE SET.

EXTRAS

EPISODE 3

CAST LIST

Andy Millman RICKY GERVAIS
Maggie Jacobs ASHLEY JENSEN
Agent STEPHEN MERCHANT
Suzanne CHARLOTTE PALMER
Fran FRANCESCA MARTINEZ

With KATE WINSLET

Mike JOHN LIRK
Father KEVIN MOORE
Lisa LUCINDA RAIKES
Old Lady PAMELA LYNE
Spark PAUL PARISER

Written & Directed by
RICKY GERVAIS &
STEPHEN MERCHANT

FILM CLIP: 'SISTERS OF MERCY'

A WORLD WAR TWO DRAMA.

KATE WINSLET IS A NUN HIDING A GROUP OF JEWISH PEOPLE FROM
THE NAZIS IN THE BASEMENT OF HER NUNNERY. MAGGIE IS AMONG
THE EXTRAS IN THE SCENE.

THE SOUND OF GERMAN OFFICERS SEARCHING THE CONVENT DRAWS
CLOSER. GERMAN VOICES GROW LOUDER AND FINALLY THE BASEMENT
DOOR IS KICKED IN BY GERMAN INFANTRYMEN.

ANDY, DRESSED AS A GERMAN SOLDIER, LEANS INTO SHOT. A MOMENT
LATER, THE DIRECTOR YELLS:.

DIRECTOR: Cut!

ANDY: (exasperated) Oh, for fuck's sake.

SCENE 1. INT. FILM SET. DAY.

THE CAST LEAVE THE SET. ANDY WANDERS OVER TO MAGGIE.

ANDY: Was I in it?

MAGGIE: I don't know.

ANDY: No, I wasn't then.
(ANNOYED)
What is the point in getting all tarted up like this if you're not even going to make it to the scene?

MAGGIE: Well, you look quite dapper.

ANDY: It's a Nazi uniform.

MAGGIE: I know. It's quite natty though, isn't it?

ANDY: (laughing) Natty?

MAGGIE: Well, I bet it's more comfortable than this.
(TRIES TO ADJUST HER TIGHTS UNDERNEATH HER COSTUME)
This is riding up my clunge. Oh, can you imagine hiding from the Gestapo for weeks on end dressed like this?

ANDY: (drily) Yeah, it must have been awful.

MAGGIE: (looking at ANDY's costume) Do you know, it's actually very slimming, that.

ANDY: Yeah? I'll wear it out Friday night.

AN ACTRESS, SUZANNE, DRESSED IN A NUN'S HABIT, WALKS PAST AND OVERHEARS THE CONVERSATION.

SUZANNE: (to ANDY) She's right. I can see what she means.

ANDY: (flirting) Yeah? You think I look good in this? You should see me with a white sheet over my head, setting fire to a cross.
(SUZANNE LAUGHS AND STROLLS OFF)
Who's that?

MAGGIE: Not sure.

ANDY: She seems nice. I've got to get out of this, it's doing my back in.

ANDY AND MAGGIE WALK ACROSS THE SET.

SCENE 2. INT. FILM SET. DAY.

A GROUP OF EXTRAS ARE SITTING IN A GROUP BY THE TEA AND COFFEE AREA. MAGGIE AND ANDY SIT DOWN ON CHAIRS NEXT TO EACH OTHER, BOTH WITH A CUP OF TEA.

MAGGIE: Do you know what worries me?

ANDY: Don't know. Where do baby ants go to school? Go on.

MAGGIE: No, all these people going about pretending to be nuns.

ANDY: What do you mean?

MAGGIE: Do you think that's right?

ANDY: It's a film.

MAGGIE: I know but they're all like wandering around as holy ladies, wouldn't that offend God or someone?

ANDY: (laughing) 'Offend God or someone'?

MAGGIE: Well, does it not worry you a bit?

ANDY: No. What, offending God? I'm an atheist.

MAGGIE: What one's that? Is that the one where you haven't decided what you want...

ANDY: No, that's agnostic. I'm an atheist. I firmly believe there is no God.

MAGGIE: Why?

ANDY: The burden of proof is not on me. The burden of proof is on the people who say there is a God. I don't believe in God, I believe in science.

MAGGIE: So do you not believe in anything like ghosts or spirits or anything?

ANDY: No, I don't believe in ghosts or spirits, or elves, certainly not God, no.

MAGGIE: So what do you think happens when you die?

ANDY: Well, if you're buried you go in the ground and you're worm food.

MAGGIE: (wincing) See, I don't like that. I would rather believe that there is a God and your soul just floats away on to eternity and all your friends from school will be there, like all the ones you haven't seen for ages and all your dead pets and just like nice people and you don't have to worry about worms.

ANDY: You believe in God then.

MAGGIE: I think I need to go for a wee. Oh, that's the third one already.

ANDY: Good. Well, keep me posted throughout the week. Maybe keep a journal.

SCENE 3. INT. STUDIO COMPLEX. DAY.

MAGGIE WALKS OUT OF THE STUDIO, AND CATCHES SIGHT OF SOMETHING OFF-SCREEN. SHE STOPS AND LOOKS ANXIOUS. SUZANNE AND FRAN ARE WALKING TOWARDS HER. SUZANNE IS STILL IN A NUN'S HABIT AND FRAN IS LEANING ON SUZANNE'S ARM AS SHE WALKS. MAGGIE IS UTTERLY CONFUSED AND GENUINELY CONCERNED.

MAGGIE: (approaching, worried) Oh God! What, what have you done?

FRAN: What?

MAGGIE: What's happened? Are you all right?

FRAN: (laughing) Oh, no, no, I've got cerebral palsy, don't worry.

MAGGIE: Oh, good. I thought you'd had a fall or something.

FRAN: No, I'm cool really.

MAGGIE: Oh, hello then, I'm Maggie.

SUZANNE: I'm Suzanne and this is my sister Fran.

MAGGIE SHAKES HANDS WITH SUZANNE AND THEN FRAN, AWKWARDLY.

FRAN: Good to meet you.

MAGGIE: Are you in this as well?

SUZANNE: Oh, she's just here to watch.

MAGGIE: I was going to say . . .

FRAN: (drily) Well, I had a bit of spare time, you know, because my tap dancing class was cancelled, so . . .

MAGGIE: (misses the joke) Right.

FRANCESCA: Joke? Tap dancing, me.

MAGGIE: Right. Yeah, yeah.

THEY LAUGH.

SCENE 4. INT. FILM SET. DAY

ANDY IS STILL SITTING ON A CHAIR BY THE TEA AND COFFEE AREA,
MIKE IS SITTING NEXT TO ANDY. THEY'RE CHATTING AND JOKING.

ANDY: I've got a question about your props.

MIKE: Go on.

ANDY: (gesturing to the set) Where does all this stuff come from?

MIKE: You just buy it.

ANDY: What, there's a shop for thirty-foot swastikas, is there?

MIKE: No, I got that from home, it's my nan's.
(THEY BOTH LAUGH. MAGGIE ENTERS AND SITS DOWN NEXT TO MIKE.
MIKE PUTS HIS ARM AROUND MAGGIE)
Here she is.

MAGGIE: All right?

MIKE: (to ANDY) Hey, do you want to have lunch with us later?

ANDY: I can't, I've got to go and see my fool of an agent.

MAGGIE: Still going well, is it?

ANDY: I went in the other day, right, and he said to me, 'Andy,' he said,
'if I don't get a decent client soon I'm going to have to go full time at the
Carphone Warehouse.'
(THEY LAUGH)
Unbelievable.

MIKE: Got to go.

MIKE KISSES MAGGIE AND LEAVES.

ANDY: See you later. Go and move some props around.

MIKE: Will do.

MAGGIE MOVES ON TO THE CHAIR NEXT TO ANDY.

ANDY: Going well, is it?

MAGGIE: Yeah, it's good.

ANDY: That's longer than a day you've been going out with this one, isn't it?

MAGGIE: Three weeks.

ANDY: That has got to be a record for you.

MAGGIE: (admonishing) Cheekiness.

ANDY: No, well done, good bloke.

MAGGIE: Well, I'm glad you like him.

ANDY: Yeah, good.
(THERE'S A PAUSE AND MAGGIE LOOKS INTO THE DISTANCE)
What?

MAGGIE: Nothing.

ANDY: Married?

MAGGIE: No.

ANDY: Gay?

MAGGIE: No!

THEY BOTH LAUGH.

ANDY: It is something, though.

MAGGIE: He likes to talk dirty on the phone. He'll call me up and he's coming out with all this filth.

ANDY: (annoyed and upset) Why would you tell me that? What does he say?
(PAUSE)
What does he say?

MAGGIE: He calls up and says things like
(PUTS ON A HUSKY VOICE)
'What are you doing?'

ANDY: What do you say?

MAGGIE: Well, I didn't know what was going on at first and I was just honest with him and I said, 'Oh, I'm just cleaning out the vegetable drawer of the fridge.'

THEY BOTH LAUGH LOUDLY.

ANDY: He probably thought that was a euphemism. 'Oh, I'm cleaning out my vegetable drawer. Oh, I am scrubbing my front step.' Have you talked dirty back to him?

MAGGIE: No.

ANDY: Have you?

MAGGIE: No, I have not. I don't know what to say to him, it's too embarrassing.

ANDY: Yeah.

MAGGIE: What if I just say something and he just laughs at me, or something and it's too much and he gets all offended?

ANDY: Well, no, it's just all stuff like
(PUTS ON A MOCK-SEXY VOICE)
'Oh, I'm playing with myself.'

MAGGIE LAUGHS. KATE WINSLET IS STANDING BY THE TEA AND COFFEE TABLE AND LOOKS OVER TO MAGGIE AND ANDY.

KATE WINSLET: Ooh, that sounds interesting.

MAGGIE LOOKS MORTIFIED.

ANDY: Hi. Not me, her.

KATE WINSLET: Go on.

ANDY: (quickly, to KATE) Her boyfriend likes to talk dirty on the phone and she doesn't know what to say to him.

KATE WINSLET: Oh, yeah, that can be a bit awkward.
(KATE COMES OVER AND KNEELS DOWN BETWEEN ANDY AND MAGGIE)
Why don't you just start off with something light, you know, like, 'I'd love it if you stuck your willy wonka between my oompa loompas,' you know, something a bit fun, bit jokey and then you can get more hard core. Rattle off the old classics like, 'I'm playing with my dirty pillows. I'm aching for your big purple-headed womb ferret' and then go straight

in hard, like 'Get round here because I'm fudding myself stupid and I'm bloody loving it.' All right?

BOTH MAGGIE AND ANDY LOOK EMBARRASSED AND CONFUSED.

MAGGIE: Yeah.

ANDY: Yeah.

KATE WINSLET: Anyway, better get on. Good luck.

KATE GETS UP AND WALKS AWAY.

ANDY: (calling after her) Love to Sam Mendes.
(TO MAGGIE, WHO'S LOOKING ANXIOUSLY INTO THE MIDDLE DISTANCE)
Kate Winslet just talking dirty to Anne Frank and Joseph Goebells, just another normal day.

SCENE 5. INT. BEHIND THE FILM SET. DAY

SUZANNE IS SITTING ALONE. ANDY APPROACHES HER IN HIS NAZI UNIFORM.

ANDY: (in German accent) Guten tag, Fräulein.

SUZANNE: Oh, hi.

ANDY: (still with accent) 'Oh, hi.' What is this 'Oh, hi'?

SUZANNE: Sorry, is that meant to be German?

ANDY: Yes, that was just a great German sense of humour. You're English, ja? Well then, I have something for you that will make you roll in the aisles.
(ANDY BRINGS OUT A CARROT FROM HIS POCKET AND HOLDS IT IN FRONT OF HIS CROTCH. SUZANNE LAUGHS)
This is funny to you, ja, because it looks like a penis, ja?

(HE PUTS THE CARROT BACK IN HIS POCKET AND DROPS THE ACCENT)

This will make you laugh.
(HE POINTS OUT FRAN, WHO IS WALKING TOWARDS THEM)

SUZANNE: What?

ANDY: Jesus, look, pissed-up nutter over there.
(LAUGHS)
She's had a few. Oh, is she pissed or mental? Oh, here she comes.

SUZANNE: (calmly) That's my sister. She's got cerebral palsy.

ANDY: (back-tracking) No, not her. Another nutter that was, not another nutter, she's not, she's not, she's gone now, the one I meant. Shot on and just shot off again.

FRAN WALKS OVER AND TAKES A SPARE SEAT BY SUZANNE AND ANDY.

SUZANNE: This is my sister . . .

ANDY: (patronisingly loud) Hiya.

SUZANNE: Francesca.

ANDY: You all right?

FRAN: Hiya, you all right? What do you do in this then?

ANDY: (unable to understand) What Judith . . . ?

SUZANNE: No, she said, 'What do you do in this?'

ANDY: (speaking very clearly) Oh, a background artist.

FRANCESCA: Oh, right. And what does that entail?

ANDY: (deciphering) What . . . does that . . . entail? Yeah, just standing round really, although it's not what I do. I'm a real actor, this is just sort of like pocket money.

FRANCESCA: Yeah, well, I bet they all say that don't they?

ANDY COMPLETELY FAILS TO UNDERSTAND SO HE JUST SHRUGS.

SCENE 6. AGENT'S OFFICE. DAY.

ANDY'S AGENT IS SITTING BEHIND HIS DESK, PLAYING WITH A
CALCULATOR. ANDY ENTERS.

AGENT: All right, mate, come and check this out. I just typed in fifty-
eight thousand and eight into a calculator and lo and behold, amazingly,
it comes up 'boobs'.
(HE SHOWS ANDY THE CALCULATOR)
You see that? It's worth knowing, isn't it?

ANDY STARES AT THE CALCULATOR AND THEN AT HIS AGENT,
FROWNING.

ANDY: Good.

AGENT: What can I do—
(THE PHONE RINGS, INTERRUPTING HIM)
hang on, sorry, better get that. Hang on.
(THE AGENT TAKES OFF HIS GLASSES, PICKS UP HIS HANDS-FREE
EAR-PIECE, LOOKS IT OVER, FITS IT TO HIS EAR SLOWLY TAKES IT
OFF AND LOOKS AT IT AGAIN. THE PHONE CONTINUES TO RING)
Oh.

ANDY: (impatiently) Just . . .

THE AGENT EVENTUALLY FITS HIS EARPIECE AND FLIPS OPEN HIS
MOBILE PHONE.

AGENT: Hello? Gone.
(SHUTS HIS PHONE)
Annoying. It's weird that it always happens with that one.

ANDY: Turn it off.

AGENT: Okay, I'll put it on vibrate.

ANDY: (leaning back in his chair, exasperated) You do that.

AGENT: What can I do for you?

ANDY: (looking around in disbelief) You called me in for a meeting.

AGENT: Did I? What was that about?

ANDY: I don't know, you said you wanted to see me.

AGENT: All right, I'll just check on here.

THE AGENT MOVES HIS COMPUTER MOUSE AND SQUINTS INTO THE
MONITOR, CHECKING HIS DIARY. THIS TAKES HIM FOREVER. ANDY
IS GROWING INCREASINGLY ANNOYED.

ANDY: What's the gist of it?

AGENT: It'll be on here.
(CONTINUES TO SEARCH THROUGH COMPUTER SLOWLY)

I've got everything organised on there so it's all . . . I'm looking at the
wrong date. It's the third today, isn't it?

ANDY: Fourth.

AGENT: Fourth. Yeah, I was looking at the wrong date. That's Tuesday,
blank. What does it say here? It just says: today, catch-up meeting.
Just to catch up really with you and find out what's been happening
and tell you about what's coming in and . . .

ANDY: Okay, what's coming in?

THE AGENT STARES AT ANDY THEN LOOKS BACK AT HIS COMPUTER.
MORE INTERMINABLE SEARCHING. ANDY LETS OUT A DEEP SIGH.

AGENT: Nothing's come in according to that.

ANDY: Nothing's come in?

AGENT: No.

ANDY: (sarcastic) Okay, good. Well, that was well worth it. I mean, apart from sitting there and waiting for the phone to ring, what have you done? Have you called, have you sent the script out?

AGENT: What script? Sorry . . .

ANDY: Oh, man, the script I gave you two months ago.

AGENT: Script, that sounds good.

ANDY: The sitcom.

AGENT: Yeah? Funny?

ANDY: You haven't read it?

AGENT: What's it called? Because I can go on to that.

ANDY: 'When the Whistle Blows'.

AGENT: (writing) I'll just write down, 'When the W Blows'.

ANDY: (weary) Don't put 'W' you'll forget what the 'W' stands for. Write it all out.

AGENT: No, 'When the Wind Blows'.

ANDY: Whistle.

AGENT: (writing) I'll put that in. 'W equals Wind.'

ANDY: Whistle!

AGENT: Whistle, it's there. It's in.

ANDY: (sarcastic) That's safe then, is it? That's done, I can forget about that. That's on its way, yeah? I've got my best man on it?

AGENT: Yeah, yeah, yeah.

ANDY: Safe hands. Safe hands.

AGENT: Do you want to put another meeting in?

ANDY: Any point?

AGENT: May as well and then when nothing comes in just phone you up and cancel it.

ANDY: That's a plan.

SCENE 7. INT. FILM SET. DAY.

ANDY IS SITTING WITH MAGGIE, SUZANNE AND FRAN ON AN UNUSED PART OF THE SET.

ANDY: I don't think of him as an agent though. I think of him as a bloke who had some cards printed up in a vending machine in the garage with the word 'agent' on them. That to me is his qualifications. He's got, he sent me up for the lead role in Billy Elliot.
(ALL THE GIRLS LAUGH)
Yeah, right, the man in charge of my career.
(TO FRAN)
I'm glad you're finding this funny.
(TO MAGGIE)
She's laughing at my life.

MAGGIE: (to SUZANNE) It must be lovely to see her laughing.

THIS KILLS THE MOMENT.

SUZANNE: She laughs all the time. She lives to laugh.

FRAN: Well, you have to be able to laugh, don't you? Keeps you sane.

MAGGIE: (seriously, to SUZANNE) I thought she was sane?

FRAN: No, I mean it keeps anybody sane.

MAGGIE: Oh, right, yes. Laughing and . . .

FRAN: You know, don't you reckon if you can laugh you can cope with like anything?

SUZANNE: It's a God-given gift isn't it? Laughing in the face of adversity.

MAGGIE: You're quite religious, are you?

SUZANNE: Yes, we both are.

FRAN: (seriously) We both really believe like that God gives us a struggle and that's the point of life, isn't it?
(MAGGIE AND ANDY LOOK AT EACH OTHER)

You know, to like overcome the difficulties thrown at you and the greatest thing is you know that in heaven everything will be all right. Maggie, do you believe in God or . . . ?

MAGGIE: Yes, I do I think, yes.

FRAN: Oh, great. And what about you, Andy? Do you believe in God? Like, do you believe everything will be okay in heaven?

ANDY: (nodding slowly, lying) Yes.

SUZANNE: What faith are you?

ANDY: What?

SUZANNE: What faith are you?

ANDY: Catholic.

SUZANNE: Oh, really, so are we.

ANDY: Oh, excellent. Lot of us about and I am definitely one of us. Catholicism, the 'C' word. Not the 'C' word, a 'C' word. Heaven, yeah amazing, it's going to be brilliant up there. You're going to have an amazing time, you'll love it. Be like Ibiza or something.

SUZANNE SMILES AT ANDY FOR HIS COMFORTING WORDS.

FILM CLIP: 'SISTERS OF MERCY'

KATE IS IN CHARACTER AS A NUN, PRAYING AT A CHURCH ALTAR.

KATE WINSLET: Please, Lord, let us know that you have seen what we have seen. Please, Lord. You have to let us know that we are not alone.

(SHE BOWS HER HEAD IN PRAYER. LIGHTS FILTERS THROUGH THE STAINED-GLASS WINDOW ABOVE KATE. SHE LOOKS UP INTO THE BRIGHT LIGHT, TEARFULLY)
Thank you Lord.

DIRECTOR: (offstage) Cut!

SCENE 8. INT. FILM SET. DAY.

KATE SNAPS OUT OF CHARACTER. THE LIGHT SHUTS OFF SUDDENLY. THE STAINED-GLASS WINDOW IS JUST A STAND-ALONE PROP. A SPARK HAS JUST SWITCHED OFF A BIG LAMP.

KATE WINSLET: Christ, that's bloody hot.
(GETTING UP)
Oh fuck, my fucking knees. Ow! Can we go again on that? Does it have to be that hot?

SPARK: It's 4k love.

KATE WINSLET: I'm sweating like a bastard. No wonder they lose their rag sometimes.

(KATE HAS HER PICTURE TAKEN BY A CREW MEMBER FOR CONTINUITY. KATE TURNS TO MAGGIE AND ANDY, WHO ARE STANDING BY THE SET)

Oh, hi, you how did it go with your dirty phone call?

A MAKE-UP ARTIST BRUSHES POWDER ON TO KATE'S FACE.

MAGGIE: Oh, I haven't done it yet, I'm working up to it.

KATE WINSLET: Well, here is another one that's always good. Just do all the preliminary stuff and then you go 'Hang on, why is the slut from next door just coming into my bedroom and is taking her bra off?' Then you just pretend you're getting it on with her.

MAGGIE: I couldn't do that.

KATE WINSLET: Course you can, you're an actress.

MAGGIE: No, I'm not. I'm just an extra. You're the actress. A brilliant actress, by the way.

KATE MOUTHS A MODEST 'THANK YOU'.

ANDY: Yeah, she is. I'm an actor as well, if there's a line going in this film I'd love to be part of this because

(FAWNING)

I'd just like to say I think, you know, you doing this is so commendable, you know, using your profile to keep the message alive about the Holocaust.

KATE WINSLET: (laughing) Oh God, I'm not doing it for that. I mean, I don't think we need another film about the Holocaust, do we? It's like, how many have there been? You know, we get it, it was grim. Move on.

(LOWERING HER VOICE)

No, I'm doing it because I've noticed that if you do a film about the Holocaust, guaranteed an Oscar. I've been nominated four times, never won. And the whole world is going 'Why hasn't Winslet won one?'

ANDY: Yeah.

KATE WINSLET: That's it. That's why I'm doing it. *Schindler's* bloody *List. The Pianist.* Oscars coming out of their arse.

MAGGIE: Well, good luck then.

ANDY: It's a good plan.

KATE WINSLET: Thank you. Good luck with your phone calls. See you later.

MAGGIE: Bye.

KATE WAVES AND WALKS AWAY, BACK TOWARDS THE SET.

KATE WINSLET: Can we go again?

SCENE 9. INT. FILM SET. DAY.

TWO EXTRAS STAND ON A STREET SET IN WORLD WAR TWO COSTUMES.

DIRECTOR: (offstage) Yes, let's do it. And action!

ANDY WALKS ON TO THE SET, DRESSED AS A NAZI OFFICER. HE NODS AT THE EXTRAS BUT THEN STUMBLES ON HIS HEEL AND FALLS OFF THE KERB.

ANDY: (grimaces) Sorry, sorry.

SUZANNE SMILES AT ANDY FROM THE OTHER SIDE OF THE SET. ANDY SMILES BACK. ANDY WALKS BACK TO HIS STARTING POINT FOR THE NEXT TAKE.

DIRECTOR: Cut there, thank you. Reset please.

SCENE 10. INT. FILM SET. DAY

ANDY IS TALKING TO FRAN BY THE TEA AND COFFEE AREA.

FRAN: Are you married or single?

ANDY: Why?

FRAN: I think my sister might like you a bit.

ANDY: Really? She's only human.

CUT TO A MUSIC MONTAGE ON SCENES OF SUZANNE AND ANDY LAUGHING TOGETHER AND ENJOYING EACH OTHER'S COMPANY. CUT TO THEM STANDING IN FRONT OF AN OVERSIZED PROP PORTRAIT OF ADOLF HITLER.

SUZANNE: I meant to ask you, actually, a couple of friends of mine are having a get-together tonight. Wondered if you were free, would you like to come along?

ANDY: Yeah, yeah.

SUZANNE: Great.

ANDY: Definitely.
(HE PUTS ON HIS GERMAN ACCENT)
Ja.

THEY BOTH LAUGH.

SCENE 11. INT. ANDY'S BEDROOM. NIGHT.

MAGGIE IS GOING THROUGH ANDY'S WARDROBE.

ANDY: Oh my God, I've got Jeremy Clarkson's clothes. I can't, oh . . .

MAGGIE: Well, what sort of a party is it?

ANDY: Well, she said a get-together with some friends, probably casual, but I want to look good, don't I?

MAGGIE: (spotting something in the corner of the wardrobe) I know you said she was quite a classy, stylish . . .

ANDY: Yes.

MAGGIE: (still in the wardrobe) This, look.

SCENE 12. INT.
CHURCH HALL. NIGHT

A PRAYER GROUP ARE SAT IN A CIRCLE LISTENING TO A WOMAN
RECITING SOMETHING DEVOUT. WE PAN AROUND THE GROUP TO REVEAL
ANDY, DRESSED IN A FLASHY WHITE SUIT AND BLACK SHIRT, HIS HAIR
SLICKED FORWARD. FRAN AND SUZANNE SIT TO HIS RIGHT, AN OLD
LADY TO HIS LEFT. HE'S SCOWLING AND TWIDDLING HIS THUMBS.

LISA: Lead us heavenly father lead us, o'er the world's tempestuous
sea. Guard us, guide us, keep us, feed us, for we have no help but thee.
Yet possessing every blessing if our God our father . . .

OLD LADY: Lovely suit.

ANDY: (whispering) Thanks. I like to look good for a prayer meeting.

LISA: Our God descending, fill our hearts with heavenly joy. Love with
every passion . . .

ANDY: (to SUZANNE) How long is this going to take, out of interest?

SUZANNE: An hour and a half.

ANDY: (shocked) Hour and a half. Oh, time for a drink afterwards?

SUZANNE: Yes.

ANDY: (pleased) Yes?

LISA: . . . nothing can our peace destroy.

FATHER: Isn't that lovely? Thank you Lisa, lovely.

ANDY STARTS TO CLAP BUT STOPS QUICKLY WHEN NO ONE ELSE JOINS IN.

SCENE 13. INT. MAGGIE'S LOUNGE. NIGHT.

MAGGIE SITS ON HER SOFA WEARING A BAGGY JUMPER AND TRACKSUIT BOTTOMS. SHE TALKS INTO A CORDLESS PHONE.

MAGGIE: Hi, it's me. Yeah, no, I'm good. You? Good.

(NERVOUSLY)

Yeah I'm ready, okay.

(TAKES A DEEP BREATH)

I'm not wearing anything. No, you're not wearing anything?

Oh. Hey, both of us are not wearing anything. What am I doing? Yeah.

(READS FROM A BIT OF PAPER)

Er, first off, I'm fudding myself stupid and I'm bloody loving it.

(THERE'S A PAUSE. SHE LOOKS ANXIOUS)

Fudding.

SCENE 14. INT. CHURCH HALL. NIGHT.

ANDY SITS WITH FRAN, SUZANNE AND THE OLD LADY.

ANDY: (to OLD LADY) I think she wanted me to wear my uniform . . .

(TO SUZANNE)

tell her how good I looked in my . . .

SUZANNE: Really nice.

ANDY: Yeah, she really liked it. Do you know what uniform it is? German.

(THE OLD LADY LOOKS DISGUSTED)

I know, yeah. With what they did, you should be ashamed of yourself.

THE CATHOLIC PRIEST APPROACHES ANDY AND SUZANNE.

SUZANNE: I don't think you two have been formally introduced. This is Andy, Father.

FATHER: How are you, son?

(THE FATHER EXTENDS HIS HAND AND ANDY, NERVOUS, TAKES IT AND KISSES IT)

You don't have to do that, I'm not the Pope.

ANDY: No, it's old habits die hard, my old priest used to make me kiss him, on the ring. On his finger, there was none of that going on. That

makes me sick as well, people saying priests are paedophiles and
kiddie fiddlers.
(BEGINS TO RAMBLE)
There's probably, I mean there probably are, I mean you probably know
some but it's no higher percentage of perverts in, but they, you know,
they're in all walks of life, aren't they?
(TO THE OLD LADY)
Not, you know there are nonces everywhere but let's not exaggerate
the issue is what I'm saying. I've never been touched by a priest.
I've been touched by God, not in that way. In the heart, but you know.
(RUNNING OUT OF STEAM, CHANGING SUBJECT)
Or . . . oh condoms. Do we need them? I don't think so. Let the free seed
of love gush forth.

THE PRIEST LOOKS AT ANDY SUSPICIOUSLY.

FATHER: Who was your confirmation saint?

ANDY: Mine?
(STRUGGLING)
Saint Bernard.

FATHER: Saint Bernard? Who was your priest growing up?

ANDY: (lying) Father. Flaa-heer-ty. Father Michael Flatley.

FATHER: Michael Flatley?

ANDY: O'Flatley. Irish fellow.

FATHER: And where was his parish?

ANDY: Just the parish of where I grew up, my town, the (MAKES THE SIGN OF THE CROSS) holy parish of Wokingham.

FATHER: I've done a lot of work in the London and Thames area . . .

ANDY: Oh yeah?

FATHER: And I've never heard of a Father Michael O'Flatley.

ANDY: No, he died. Dead, untraceable. He won't be replaced. Not by me anyway. He was a great man.

FATHER: Can I ask you a personal question?

ANDY: Go for it.

FATHER: And it may seem blunt, but honesty is a cornerstone of the Catholic faith.

ANDY: Amen to that.

FATHER: Are you a Catholic?

ANDY: Am I a . . . ?

FATHER: Are you a Catholic?

ANDY: (chuckling) Am I a Catholic? Well, if you're asking to see some official documentation you're going to be gutted.

FATHER: Have you been confirmed? Have you ever taken communion?

ANDY: (as if surprising himself) No, actually.

FATHER: Did Father Flatley exist?

ANDY: (correcting him) O'Flatley.

FATHER: Did he ever exist?

ANDY: No.

FATHER: Why have you been pretending to be a Catholic?

ANDY: Because it does no harm. Does it? We all want a laugh . . .

SUZANNE: (appalled) Was it just to get close to me?

ANDY: Well, I do fancy you if that's,
(TO THE PRIEST)
even you must think . . .
(PAUSE. TO SUZANNE)
and I thought you might not get off with someone who wasn't Catholic.

SUZANNE: Sorry, I wouldn't get off with you anyway. I don't believe in sex before marriage.

ANDY: (smiling, then realises she's serious) Really?
(TO THE OLD LADY)
In this day and age. Bit annoying, to be honest.

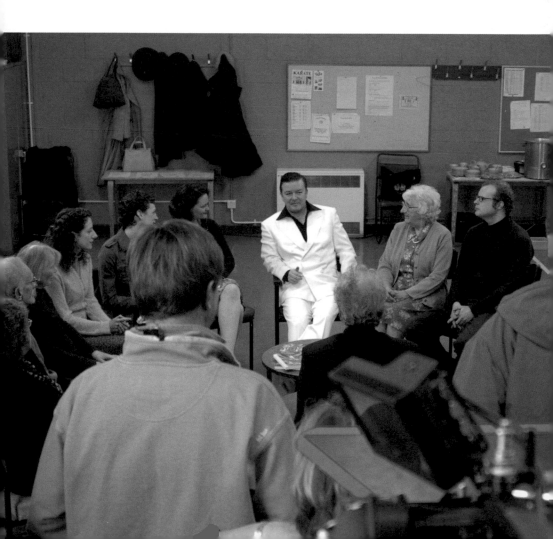

SUZANNE: I can't believe you lied to me just to try and sleep with me.

ANDY: I'd already lied before I tried it on with you, so . . .

SUZANNE: Well, what was the first lie?

ANDY: (pointing to FRAN) I didn't want to upset her.

FRAN: Sorry, what do you mean?

ANDY: (not understanding) Sorry, what the what?

FRAN: (rearticulates) What do you mean?

ANDY: Oh. Oh, well. She was saying the only thing that keeps her going is the thought that one day she'll be in heaven and everything will be all right. And I didn't want to go, 'No you're barking up the wrong tree, love, there's no God, there's no heaven, you're not going to be up there talking normally and running around, legs and playing volleyball and everything,' so I didn't, I said er . . .
(HE LOOKS AT THE OLD LADY)
It's like a white lie, isn't it?

AN AWKWARD SILENCE FALLS ON THE GROUP. AFTER A WHILE, ANDY STANDS UP, PICKS UP HIS WHITE JACKET, WAVES AT THE OLD LADY AND LEAVES.

SCENE 15. INT. FILM SET. DAY.

MAGGIE AND MIKE ARE BY THE TEA AND COFFEE AREA. MIKE HAS HIS ARMS AROUND MAGGIE'S WAIST.

MIKE: Look, if it makes you feel uncomfortable then we shouldn't do it.

MAGGIE: No, but I want to make you happy.

MIKE: I'm happy if you're happy. It's just a silly little thing, isn't it? I mean, it's a bit of fun. If you're not into it so be it, that's cool. I'm going out with you because of you.

MAGGIE: (laughing) My God, really? Do you know what?

MIKE: What?

MAGGIE: You're cool.

SHE LEANS IN AND KISSES HIM.

MIKE: I like to think so.

ANDY ENTERS.

ANDY: Am I interrupting?

MAGGIE: Yes.

ANDY: Good. All right?

MAGGIE: No worries.

ANDY: Good, yeah.

MAGGIE: Oh, how was the date?

ANDY: (sarcastic) The date? Oh, let me just go over some highlights
for you.
(HE BEGINS TO COUNT OFF ON HIS HANDS)
Lied to a priest in front of a room full of Christians, some of them elderly.
Some of them just weird and bewildered. So, insulted them and their
belief system. Made a woman hate me for the rest of her life. Yeah?
Didn't believe in God before, definitely going to hell. I like her as well.

MAGGIE: Oh, here listen, but don't worry. I know someone who'd be
perfect for you. She's desperate and she has real trouble hanging on
to men because she's clinically depressed.

ANDY: (fake enthusiasm) Have you got her number?

MAGGIE: I do actually, I think it's in my phone.

ANDY: I'm being sarcastic, because I don't want to go out with a
psychopath.

MAGGIE: Well, she's quite nice underneath.

ANDY: Oh, she just cuts you if she forgets to take her lithium.

MIKE TURNS TO MAKE TEAS FOR MAGGIE AND ANDY. KATE WINSLET
APPEARS.

KATE WINSLET: Hi, hi.

ANDY: Hi.

KATE WINSLET: How did it go? With the phone?

MAGGIE: (interrupting her quickly) Oh, oh, this is my boyfriend Mike. This is Mike, I don't think you've met before, Mike this is the actress Kate Winslet.

MIKE TURNS TO FACE KATE.

KATE WINSLET: Hi Mike.

MIKE: Hiya, great to meet you.

KATE WINSLET: Yeah, how you doing?

MIKE: Did you want a tea?

KATE WINSLET: No, it's fine.

(MIKE TURNS BACK TO HIS TEAS. BEHIND HIM, KATE MOUTHS 'IS HE THE . . . ?' AND MIMES BEING ON THE PHONE AND MASTURBATING. MAGGIE AND ANDY NOD. MIKE TURNS BACK TO THEM BUT KATE SNAPS OUT OF HER MIME BEFORE HE SEES HER)

So it's the weekend, you all got any big plans? I tell you what we're going to do, we're going to have a big spring clean. Yeah, my husband's going to be rummaging around in my basement while I polish his Oscar.

ANDY: (suppressing laughter) I see what you mean, no, because I'm going to be in the garage probably just cleaning the car. Giving the old girl's headlamps a good soaping up, giving them a good seeing to.

ANDY SMILES SUGGESTIVELY AT KATE, WHO SMIRKS.

MIKE: (to KATE, not picking up the innuendo) Can I just say, I mean you probably get this all the time but can I just say I'm a big fan. I've seen *Titanic* like five times as well.

ANDY MIMES A BLOW JOB TO KATE WHILE MIKE ISN'T LOOKING.

KATE WINSLET: Oh, that's sweet.

MIKE: (to ANDY) Have you seen *Titanic*?

AS ANDY TALKS AND MIKE ISN'T LOOKING, KATE MIMES HOLDING A PHONE, CUPPING HER BREAST AND WRIGGLING HER TONGUE SUGGESTIVELY.

ANDY: Yeah, great, brilliant. A lot of it was er, it's a lot of it is CGI actually, you know that. Half the boat . . .

MIKE: Really?
(LOOKS AT KATE)
What you doing?

KATE WINSLET FREEZES, HOLDING HER MIME FOR A MOMENT, UNSURE WHAT TO DO. SHE MIMES PUTTING THE PHONE DOWN AND PRETENDS TO CHECK HER BREAST.

KATE WINSLET: Just checking that.

MIKE: Is it all right?

KATE WINSLET: Yeah, I think so.

MIKE: (to MAGGIE) So you've told them, have you, about the phone calls?

MAGGIE: No, no, I haven't.

MIKE: You've told them about the phone calls, I can't believe you told other people.
(KATE AND ANDY START TO WALK OFF)
Hey, hey, where you going?

ANDY: Just . . .

MIKE: Well, you know everything anyway so you might as well watch the break-up. This is over.

MAGGIE: (pleading) What? No. Ignore, listen . . .

MIKE: Well, how can I trust you now? Were you really doing anything? When you said you were rubbing it, were you really rubbing it?

MAGGIE: No.

MIKE: I don't know what to do. I don't know what to do, this is such a betrayal, you're just laughing at me behind my back.

MAGGIE: I'm not.

MIKE: Then what's all this with her?

MIKE IMITATES KATE'S MIME.

MAGGIE: I was getting advice.

MIKE: Off Kate Winslet?
(TO KATE)
Are you proud of yourself, are you? You think because you were in the biggest film ever you've got the right to mock the little people?

KATE WINSLET: (like a child being told off) No.

MIKE: So all that stuff about your husband polishing his Oscar, was that supposed to mean wanking?

KATE WINSLET: Yes.

MIKE: And your basement meant?

KATE WINSLET: My fanny.

MIKE: (looking at MAGGIE) Pathetic. Pathetic.

MIKE STORMS OFF.

MAGGIE: (tearful, to ANDY) Thanks very much.

MAGGIE WALKS AWAY. KATE NOTICES FRAN, WHO IS AT THE OTHER END OF THE SET.

KATE WINSLET: I keep seeing her around. What is up with her?

ANDY: She's got cerebral palsy.

KATE WINSLET: (lighting a cigarette) Oh, oh, that's worth remembering. I tell you, that is another way you win an Oscar. Seriously, think about it. Daniel Day Lewis in *My Left Foot*. Oscar. Dustin Hoffman, *Rainman*, Oscar. John Mills, *Ryan's Daughter*, Oscar.

ANDY: Yeah.

KATE WINSLET: Seriously. You are guaranteed an Oscar if you play a mental. See you later.

ANDY: Cheers.

KATE WALKS AWAY, SMOKING A CIGARETTE.

CAST LIST

Andy Millman RICKY GERVAIS
Maggie Jacobs ASHLEY JENSEN
Agent STEPHEN MERCHANT
Bunny GERARD KELLY
Lizzie REBECCA GETHINGS
Shaun SHAUN WILLIAMSON

With LES DENNIS

Simone NICKY LADANOWSKI
Lizzie's Mum LINDA BECKETT
Wishy Washy STEPHEN SWIFT
Dancer STUART RAMSAY
Drunk Woman KATE SMITH
Old Friend SUSAN SCOTT
Staff Member JOANNA BURNETT

Written & Directed by
RICKY GERVAIS
& STEPHEN MERCHANT

SCENE 1. INT. AGENT'S OFFICE. DAY.

ANDY AND HIS AGENT ARE HAVING A MEETING.

AGENT: What's on your mind? Seriously, talk to me.

ANDY: Why am I not getting any acting roles?

AGENT: I've been thinking about this and I'm glad you brought it up. I've got a feeling it could be your shape. It is a very unusual shape and I'm not sure who would be looking for it. Could you maybe do a bit more exercise?

ANDY: Could you maybe do a bit more work?

AGENT: Now, well, we can banter all you like but I mean all I would say is if you insist on remaining, you know, a blob you could maybe at least get a tan?

ANDY: (exasperated) They're looking for a fat bloke with a tan, are they? What's that for, Oliver Stone's *Story of Buddha*? Before I get up and walk out of here, possibly for ever, have you got anything for me at all?

AGENT: Loads of stuff.
(WAVES A BIT OF PAPER, PUTS IN DOWN IN FRONT OF HIMSELF AND STUDIES IT)
Do you fancy panto in Guildford with Les Dennis?

ANDY: No.
(THE AGENT PUTS THE PAPER TO ONE SIDE)
What, that's it?

AGENT: Yeah.

ANDY: You said there was loads of stuff.

AGENT: I thought you'd go with that one.

THERE'S A LONG PAUSE AS ANDY LOOKS DOWN AT HIS FEET AND THINKS. THE AGENT LOOKS AT HIM BLANKLY.

ANDY: What's the role?

AGENT: It is the part of the Genie in *Aladdin*.

ANDY: (sarcastic) Oh, they're happy with a fat bloke for that are they?

AGENT: With a tan ideally.

SCENE 2. INT.
THEATRE STAGE. DAY.

WE FOLLOW ANDY AND HIS AGENT AS THEY WALK ON TO THE STAGE. THEY
APPROACH BUNNY THE DIRECTOR, WHO IS CHATTING WITH LES DENNIS.

BUNNY: I promise you, listen, I've done a panto before.
(TO ANDY)
Aha, Andy Millman this is Les Dennis.

ANDY: Hi, I know you who are.

LES: Good to meet you.

ANDY AND LES SHAKE HANDS.

ANDY: Nice to meet you.

BUNNY: (to LES) Andy is playing our Genie.

LES: (frowns, massively disappointed) Oh no, really? Could Chris
Biggins not do it?

BUNNY: He was busy.

ANDY LOOKS EMBARRASSED.

LES: Biggins was busy? Oh, that's a nightmare. What about John
Thompson off *Cold Feet*?

BUNNY: Well, he was available but he screwed up the audition, very,
very nervous.

LES: Yeah, he can get nervous, that's a shame.

AGENT: Sorry, can I just say, if you're interested in a famous face,
I represent Barry from *EastEnders*.

ANDY: Not for this part though, no. It's too late, isn't it? This part's
taken, isn't it?

THE AGENT MOVES AWAY.

LES: What about Jono Coleman, I thought he was up for it?

BUNNY: Yes, but since he did *Celebrity Fit Club* he's, well, he's just
not fat enough.

ANDY RAISES HIS EYEBROWS. THE AGENT REAPPEARS, WITH HIS
MOBILE PHONE IN HIS HAND.

AGENT: I've got Barry on the phone now, if you just—

ANDY: (angry) No point, is there? No, the vacancy's filled. Remember you took twelve and a half per cent, ring any bells?

LES: This should have been sorted.

AGENT: (back on the phone) Sorry Barry.

LES: No one on the list was available then?

BUNNY: No and in the end we were running out of time and we just got desperate so . . .

POINTS TOWARDS ANDY, WHO SMILES WEAKLY.

SCENE 3. INT. THEATRE STAGE. DAY.

A MUSIC MONTAGE OF BUNNY PUTTING ANDY, LES AND THE CHORUS
LINE THROUGH THEIR PACES.

CUT TO ANDY STANDING AT THE SIDE OF THE STAGE, READING HIS LINES.
LES APPROACHES ANDY WITH AN ATTRACTIVE BLONDE WOMAN IN TOW.

LES: Andy.

ANDY: Hi.

LES: Can I introduce this gorgeous creature?

ANDY: Hello.

LES: This is Simone.

SIMONE: Hi.

LES: Show him your ring. Engagement ring. Cost an arm and a leg.
Didn't want you seeing her and thinking, 'Oh who's that stunner,
I'll make her mine.' Hands off, she's taken.

SIMONE: (giggling) Silly. I'm going to have to get going then, sweetheart,
okay?

LES: Okay.

SIMONE: See you later. Nice to meet you.

SIMONE LEAVES AND WAVES AT LES AS SHE WALKS AWAY.

LES: See you later. Bye. Bye darling.

(SIMONE BLOWS KISSES AT LES, WHO PRETENDS TO CATCH THEM AND
PUT THEM IN HIS POCKET. ANDY LOOKS UNCOMFORTABLE AND TURNS
BACK TO HIS SCRIPT)

Save it for later.

(TO ANDY)

Eh? We asked a hundred people, 'Which comedian is going to land
on his feet and get his end away with an absolute cracker?' You said
Les Dennis, our survey said, ding, top answer, jammy bastard.

ANDY: Yeah, well done.

LES: (suddenly serious) Still, it's about time I had a bit of good luck, isn't it? The stuff that's happened to me, been in the papers.

ANDY: I – I don't know.

LES: You do. Did you watch me on *Celebrity Big Brother*?

ANDY: It was good.

LES: It might have been entertaining for you, but I was at my lowest ebb. The shit that was flying around before I went in. I remember I was sitting there one day thinking, what's the point, eh? What is the point? And I've never really told anybody this before. I even considered suicide.

ANDY: Oh.

LES: Yeah, actually thinking I'm going to end it all. I'm thinking I'll do it here, live on telly, that will show them and as I was thinking about it, Melinda Messenger came in, lovely girl and she was chatting away.

ANDY: Took your mind off it?

LES: (smiling) Yes. I was looking at her tits. Lovely. And I was thinking 'Come on, Les, look at them, life is worth living after all.' I mean, I'd seen them loads of times, you know, in the papers and on the telly but when you're face to face with them . . .

ANDY: Live.

LES: You go 'Yeah, well done.'

ANDY: (murmuring) Yeah, that's a lovely story.

SCENE 4. INT. THEATRE
DRESSING ROOM. DAY.

LES SITS ALONE AT A DRESSING TABLE. HE'S SPEAKING INTO THE
PHONE AND LOOKING AT A MAGAZINE.

HEAT: (from phone) Hello, *Heat* magazine.

LES: Oh, yeah hi, do you deal with the celebrity spotted section?

HEAT: Can do, yeah, why, who have you seen?

LES: Well, I just spotted Les Dennis, the comedian and impressionist
and actor Les Dennis. I just spotted him shopping in New Bond Street.

HEAT: Doubt he can afford much round there, can he?

LES: Well, he can because I just saw him and he was spending a fucking
shit load of cash, all right, so put that in. Make sure you put that in.

LES SLAMS DOWN THE PHONE. ANDY KNOCKS AND ENTERS THE
DRESSING ROOM WITH MAGGIE.

ANDY: Hello.

LES: Hiya.

ANDY: I just wanted to introduce you to my friend Maggie.

LES: Hello Maggie.

ANDY: Les.

MAGGIE: Hello, hi. Pleased to meet you.

LES: Nice to meet you too. What you doing with this reprobate? You two
an item?

MAGGIE: Oh, Christ, no.

ANDY: (slightly offended) All right.

MAGGIE: No, I was just here visiting him, it's the first time he's treaded
the boards.

SHE HUGS ANDY'S ARM SUPPORTIVELY.

LES: Oh, well, theatre.
(ROLLS HIS EYES AND SMILES)
The stories I could tell you. It's where it all started for me, up and down
the country, great to be back. Things have changed a bit, mind. There
was a time when I wouldn't have had to share a dressing room.

(MAGGIE AND ANDY BOTH LOOK AWKWARD)

Back in the day, I'd have had two dressing rooms if I'd wanted.
One for me and one for all the cards and flowers from all the well-wishers. Little presents and things they sent me.

(SMILES FONDLY AND POINTS AT THREE GOOD LUCK CARDS ON HIS DRESSING TABLE)

Don't need a whole dressing room for those three, do you?

THE ROOM FALLS SILENT.

MAGGIE: No.

ANDY: (to MAGGIE, struggling for an excuse) What were you doing? You said you had to . . .

MAGGIE: What?

ANDY: You had to do something, you said.

MAGGIE: Yes, I've got to go to the post office.

ANDY: (to MAGGIE) See you later.

ANDY AND MAGGIE WALK OUT QUICKLY, ANDY SHUTS THE DOOR AS MAGGIE IS STILL SAYING GOODBYE TO LES.

MAGGIE: Yes, really nice to meet you, bye.

LES: Yes, nice to see you, bye.

ANDY: Bye.

LES SMILES AND LOOKS DOWN AT HIS CARDS WISTFULLY.

SCENE 5. INT. THEATRE STAGE. DAY.

ANDY AND MAGGIE ARE SAT IN THE STALLS WATCHING THE DANCERS REHEARSE AS BUNNY DIRECTS THEM.

BUNNY: One and two, three and four, five, six, seven, eight. One and two, three and four, five, six, seven, eight. Oh, right stop, stop, stop. You're missing something. I'm not getting something, what is it, what am I not getting? What am I looking for?

ANDY: (whispering to MAGGIE) I know.

LIZZIE PUTS UP HER HAND.

BUNNY: Somebody else.
(A MALE DANCER RAISES HIS HAND)
Yes.

DANCER: A hundred and ten per cent.

BUNNY: You should be giving me a hundred and ten per cent all the time, but that is not what I was thinking of. What am I looking for?
NO ONE ELSE PUTS THEIR HAND UP. BUNNY RELUCTANTLY TURNS TO LIZZIE.
Okay.

LIZZIE: 'T and T'.

BUNNY: Correct. 'T and T', and what is 'T and T'? Come up here and show them.

(LIZZIE QUICKLY MOVES TO THE FRONT, SMILES AND STICKS OUT HER CHEST)

'T and T'. 'Tits and teeth', yes. 'Tits and teeth' and before any of you have me up on sexism charges, do not forget this is my daughter.

BUNNY LAUGHS AND TAPS LIZZIE ON THE BOTTOM AS SHE RUNS BACK INTO POSITION.

MAGGIE: (recognising LIZZIE) I know that girl.

ANDY: Hold on, his daughter? But he's definitely gay.

MAGGIE: Well, he can't be gay if he's got a daughter.

ANDY: Oscar Wilde was married with two kids.

MAGGIE: Well, he couldn't have been gay.

ANDY: What, Oscar Wilde?

MAGGIE: Yes.

ANDY: I've got to stop hanging around with you.

BUNNY: (to the dancers, wrapping things up) Okay, back at two o'clock.

THE DANCERS ALL LEAVE THE STAGE. LIZZIE LEAVES THE STAGE AND WALKS PAST MAGGIE. HER EYES WIDEN AND SHE LOOKS DELIGHTED.

LIZZIE: Oh hi!

MAGGIE: Oh, hiya . . .

LIZZIE: Maggie. Do you remember me, Lizzie Bunton?
(CALLS TO BUNNY)
Daddy, we worked on that BBC kids' show together, *The Orphans of* . . .

MAGGIE/LIZZIE: (simultaneously) *Penny-Farthing Lane.*

ANDY: Brilliant, that.

LIZZIE: (to BUNNY) Daddy, this is my friend Maggie, we worked on *Orphans* together.

BUNNY WALKS OVER TO THE STALLS AND OFFERS HIS HAND.

BUNNY: Hello, nice to meet you. Ian Bunton, everyone calls me Bunny.

LIZZIE: Oh, already started your lunch I notice.

MAGGIE: It's a banana.

LIZZIE: (singing) 'Food glorious food, hot sausage and mustard.'

BUNNY/LIZZIE: (singing together) 'While we're in the mood, cold jelly and custard.'

ON THE WORD 'CUSTARD' LIZZIE IS SLIGHTLY OFF KEY. BUNNY IS NOT HAPPY.

BUNNY: (correcting her) No, no, no, no, 'Custard.'

LIZZIE: (tries again) 'Custard.'

BUNNY: (annoyed) No come on, 'Custard.'

LIZZIE: (no longer smiling) 'Custard.'

BUNNY: 'Custard.'

LIZZIE: (weakly) 'Custard.'

ANDY: Don't worry about it.

BUNNY: No, come on.

LIZZIE: 'Custard.'

BUNNY: 'Custard.'

LIZZIE: (hits the right note) 'Custard.'

BUNNY: There, see, if something's worth doing it's worth doing correctly. Must dash.

HE SLAPS ANDY ON THE WRIST AND SCUTTLES AWAY.

LIZZIE: I'll catch up with you later then.

MAGGIE: Yes.

ANDY: Definitely.

LIZZIE: Bye, bye.

LIZZIE LEAVES. THERE'S A PAUSE.

ANDY: Cheers.
(TO MAGGIE, SARCASTICALLY)
Oh, where have you been hiding her?

MAGGIE: Oh, she's really lovely but she's a wee bit mental.

ANDY: Of course she's mental, her dad's a gay.

MAGGIE: He can't be gay.

BUNNY IS BACK ON THE STAGE, TALKING TO A MALE DANCER IN A VERY CAMP VOICE.

BUNNY: Hee hee hee, Smarties! Yum, yum, yum.

ANDY LOOKS AT MAGGIE.

SCENE 6. INT.
THEATRE STAGE. DAY.

ANDY IS WANDERING ACROSS THE STAGE WHEN HE SEES TWO PEOPLE IN THE SHADOWS. HE LOOKS CLOSER. IT'S LES'S FIANCÉE, KISSING ONE OF THE STAGE HANDS. ANDY HEARS WHISTLING. IT'S LES, APPROACHING ACROSS THE STAGE, HOLDING A LITTLE CARRIER BAG. ANDY GLANCES AGAIN AT THE INFIDELITY THEN RESOLVES TO PROTECT LES FROM IT.

ANDY: Les, you all right, mate?

SIMONE QUICKLY BREAKS AWAY FROM THE STAGE HAND. LES HASN'T SEEN HER KISSING THE STAGE HAND.

LES: Hiya.

ANDY: You all right?

LES: Yes.

ANDY: Oh, what have you got in your little bag?

LES: Oh, it's the local paper. Don't want to blow my own, not with my back, but there's a little article in here.
(TO SIMONE, AS SHE APPROACHES LES)

Hi, darling, listen to this,
(READING)
'*Family Fortunes* loser Les Dennis is on the come-back trail thanks to a starring role in *Aladdin*. Things are looking up for Les, 50, who recently announced his engagement to beautiful fiancée Simone Lewis, 26. With an age gap of a quarter of a century Dennis is clearly punching above his weight again but insists they are very much in love.'

ANDY: (looking at SIMONE with disdain) Ah, marriage, faithfulness.

LES: Do you want to get some lunch, darling?

SIMONE: I can't, sweetheart, I promised I'd meet a friend.

ANDY: A friend.

LES: Oh, do you want some money?

SIMONE: Yes please.

LES: Fifty okay?

LES TAKES OUT HIS WALLET, SIMONE QUICKLY TAKES THE FIFTY-POUND NOTE HE HANDS TO HER.

SIMONE: Yeah.

ANDY: Bit much for lunch, isn't it?

SIMONE: Bye.

LES: Bye.
(SIMONE LEAVES. TO ANDY)
Alone again?

ANDY: (looking at LES with pity) Yes.

LES: Do you want to get some lunch?

ANDY: I can't, I've already eaten.

LES: Yes?

ANDY: But I'll come for a coffee with you.

LES: Yeah.

ANDY: Yeah, course I will, course I will.
(ANDY HUGS HIM)
If that's what you want.

LES: (bemused) Yeah. Thanks.

ANDY: Oh, come on then, what shall we have?

SCENE 7. INT.
BACKSTAGE CORRIDORS. DAY.

MAGGIE IS WANDERING AROUND, LOST. SHE PASSES AN OPEN
DRESSING-ROOM DOOR. A VOICE CALLS OUT.

LIZZIE: Oh, Maggie!

LIZZIE COMES OUT OF HER DRESSING ROOM.

MAGGIE: Oh, hello, oh, it's you.

LIZZIE: Hello.

MAGGIE: I'm trying to find my way out of here, it's like a blooming maze.

LIZZIE: Come in, come in.
(LIZZIE PULLS MAGGIE INSIDE HER DRESSING ROOM QUICKLY)
This is my dressing room.

MAGGIE: Oh, look at it.

LIZZIE: I share this with the other girls in the chorus.

MAGGIE: Where are they?

LIZZIE: Oh, I think they've all gone to lunch. Sometimes they forget
to invite me.

MAGGIE: Right.

LIZZIE: Oh, what are you doing on Sunday?

MAGGIE: What, this Sunday?

LIZZIE: I'll tell you what you're doing. You're coming to my party . . .

MAGGIE: (trying to find an excuse) My sister might be—

LIZZIE: It's going to be my birthday on Sunday and I'm having a party so I'm going to be twenty-nine, it's very important and I'm just inviting my very best friends like you.

MAGGIE: Yeah?

LIZZIE: It's going to be brilliant. Oh, my parties are always great.

MAGGIE: Yeah?

LIZZIE: Please come. There will be entertainment there and everything.

MAGGIE: Oh, well . . .

LIZZIE: (putting on a silly voice) Please, please.

MAGGIE: Oh, I'm just thinking—

LIZZIE: You must . . .

MAGGIE: Okay then.

LIZZIE: (hugging MAGGIE) Brilliant. Let me just check with Daddy that that's okay.

MAGGIE: Yeah, you'd better check with him first.

LIZZIE TAKES MAGGIE'S HAND AND PULLS HER OUT OF THE ROOM AND DOWN THE CORRIDOR TOWARDS BUNNY'S ROOM, SKIPPING AS SHE GOES. LIZZIE KNOCKS ON THE DOOR.

BUNNY: (through the door) Do not come in!

LIZZIE: Daddy, it's Lizzie.

BUNNY: I won't be a minute. Do not come in. I'm just finishing up a meeting.

(FROM INSIDE THE ROOM WE HEAR HUSHED VOICES SQUABBLING. BUNNY EVENTUALLY OPENS THE DOOR AND A YOUNG MAN SCURRIES OUT)

Okay, we've finished. This is an old friend. Bye Paul.

(TO MAGGIE)

An old friend.

LIZZIE: Daddy.

BUNNY: Yes.

LIZZIE: Can Maggie come to my party, please?

BUNNY: Of course dear, of course.

(DISTRACTED)

The little bastard's pinched my watch.

LIZZIE: He's nicked your watch?

BUNNY: It's fine it's—

LIZZIE: Well, call the police.

BUNNY: (sternly) Do not call the police. And don't tell your mother, she'll, she'll only worry.

LIZZIE: That happened before, didn't it? With your mobile phone?

BUNNY: (to MAGGIE) The crime rate's through the roof.

MAGGIE: Yes.

SCENE 8. INT. THEATRE DRESSING ROOM. NIGHT.

ANDY IS SAT, LOST IN THOUGHT. LES WALKS OUT OF THE SHOWER ROOM, WITH A TOWEL WRAPPED AROUND HIS WAIST.

LES: You all right?

ANDY: Yeah.

LES: Cheer up. Turn that frown upside down. What's the matter with you?

HE BEGINS TOWELLING HIMSELF OFF.

ANDY: Nothing.

LES: Is everything okay? You look a bit down.

ANDY: No, I'm fine.

LES: If you're worried about the audiences, don't be. They're always a bit thin early on in the run but they'll pick up as we get towards Christmas. We've got the press in tonight, they'll rave about it. You know it's a good show.

ANDY: Oh, it is, yeah.

LES: Can I ask your opinion on something?

ANDY: Yeah.

LES: What do you make of Simone?

ANDY: She's fine.

LES: Beautiful girl, isn't she?

ANDY: Yes.

LES: Lovely girl, I'm very lucky.

ANDY: You are, yes. When is the wedding?

LES: We're thinking June, July.

ANDY: Oh, summer wedding. That will be good if it – when it happens, I suppose. Congratulations again.

LES: Oh, cheers, mate, cheers.
(THEY SHAKE HANDS. PAUSE)
I can't marry her.

ANDY: Why, what have you heard?

LES: Nothing. What do you mean?

ANDY: No, what did you say?

LES UNDOES HIS TOWEL AND LIFTS IT UP TO DRY HIS SHOULDERS.
ANDY DOESN'T KNOW WHERE TO LOOK.

LES: Oh, it's just that I've been doing a bit of thinking and I just don't
think I can marry her. It's not fair. I mean, don't get me wrong . . .

TO DISTRACT HIMSELF FROM LES DENNIS' NETHER REGIONS, ANDY
EXAMINES A SMALL SWITCH ON THE WALL.

ANDY: Funny little switch . . .

LES: . . . There's nothing wrong physically.

ANDY: I'm sure.

LES: And the sex is extraordinary, some of the stuff she dreams up.

ANDY PLAYS WITH THE SWITCH ON THE WALL.

ANDY: What is that for?

LES: (drying his crotch) She likes to video us and we watch it back
together and sometimes I can't believe it's my arse going up and down.

(HE THRUSTS HIS HIPS BY WAY OF ILLUSTRATION)
I'm getting excited just thinking about it.

ANDY: (looking up at the ceiling) Well, think about something else then.

LES: It will break her heart but now I'm back on the up and up, this in the papers is just the beginning.

ANDY: I know.

LES: I'll be in the full glare of the media spotlight again. I can't put her through that.

ANDY: No.

LES: She's young.

ANDY: Yeah.

LES: Yeah, she can't take that pressure.

ANDY: Probably not.

LES: I mean, who knows what this will lead to? More TV, maybe even Hollywood.
(ANDY LOOKS DOUBTFUL)
I just think I'm better off letting her go now before she falls in love with me any deeper.

ANDY: I think you're making the right decision and I'm so glad you said this because it's a weight off my mind. I saw her getting off with the stage hand and that's who she's with now.

LES: What?

ANDY: Well, I wasn't going to say anything but you,
(LES DROPS HIS TOWEL)
oh, I wish I hadn't . . . but you were going to finish it anyway and I . . .
(LES SITS DOWN IN A CHAIR, COMPLETELY HEARTBROKEN)
You're not upset, are you?

A STAFF MEMBER APPEARS.

STAFF MEMBER: The house is open, gentlemen.

ANDY: Okay.

STAFF MEMBER: Sorry.

THE STAFF MEMBER LEAVES QUICKLY.

ANDY: Les, cover it up, mate.

LES: Yeah.

LES PUTS HIS HANDS OVER HIS GROIN. THE ROOM IS SILENT.

ANDY: I'll shut the door.

ANDY GETS UP AND SHUTS THE DOOR.

SCENE 9. INT.
THEATRE STAGE. NIGHT.

LES IS ON STAGE DRESSED AS ALADDIN, PERFORMING TO A HALF-EMPTY THEATRE. AN ACTOR PLAYING WISHY WASHY IS ALSO ON STAGE. LES PICKS UP THE MAGIC LAMP PROP.

LES: Look, Wishy, what's this? It looks like the magic lamp. What do you think I should do?

WISHY WASHY: Just leave it here.

LES: (loudly, to the audience) What do you think, gang? Should I just leave it here or should I give it a rub?

AUDIENCE: (weakly) Give it a rub.

LES: What? Can't hear you!

AUDIENCE: (a little louder) Rub it.

LES: Rub it?

AUDIENCE: Yes.

LES: Okay. If you say so, I'll rub it. Here goes.

LES RUBS THE LAMP. THERE'S A FLASH OF LIGHT AND A PUFF OF SMOKE. ANDY APPEARS ON STAGE DRESSED AS THE GENIE, WEARING A LOT OF FAKE TAN.

LES: Blimey, what a big poof.

ANDY: (very camp) Cheeky.

LES: Who are you?

ANDY: Well, I'll be anyone you want me to be, but you can call me Genie.

LES: How does somebody as big as you fit into this tiny lamp?

ANDY: Don't worry about it, I'm used to squeezing myself into tight holes. Oooh! No pain, no gain.

MILD LAUGHTER.

WISHY WASHY: Can you help us? We're in danger, the evil Abunaza is after us.

ANDY: What makes you think that?

WISHY WASHY: We heard him say he wants to get Aladdin.

ANDY: Don't we all?
(LES REMAINS SILENT AND STARES INTO THE MIDDLE DISTANCE. ANDY PROMPTS HIM)
'Abunaza has a glorious ring.'

LES: (wearily) I know the line. What's the point though, eh? They don't care, look at them.

(TO THE AUDIENCE)
You lot enjoying yourselves?

AUDIENCE: (cheering weakly) Yeah.

LES: (sneering) Yeah, well, tell your faces. And maybe some of your friends as well, get them along. The empty seats aren't laughing much are they?

BOY: (calls out from the audience) Get on with it.

LES: (angrily) You bloody get on with it. Ignorant. How many of you are thinking of leaving at half time? Be even less people here then, won't it? Even more embarrassing for those that have stayed.

THERE'S A LONG AWKWARD SILENCE.

ANDY: (whispering to LES) Where do you want to go from?

LES: How about 1992?

ANDY: No, where do you want to go from in the script?

LES: I don't know, just do some more of the queer shit. Let's just get through it, shall we?

ANDY: (to the audience, in a camp voice) Oh, I've been in that lamp so long I'm bent out of all recognition.

SCENE 10. EXT.
SUBURBAN HOUSE. NIGHT.

MAGGIE RINGS THE DOORBELL OF THE HOUSE. LIZZIE ANSWERS THE DOOR AND MAGGIE STEPS INSIDE.

LIZZIE: Hello.

MAGGIE: Hi.

LIZZIE: Come in, look at you.
(TAKES MAGGIE INTO THE SITTING ROOM)
Everyone this is Maggie.

THE LIVING ROOM IS FULL OF GUESTS THAT ARE SIXTY-PLUS YEARS OLD – CLEARLY THEY'RE ALL NEIGHBOURS OR OLD FAMILY FRIENDS.

WOMAN: Oh, hello Maggie.

LIZZIE: You know Dad. That's Maureen and John and Barbara and Len and that's Nana.

LIZZIE'S MUM ENTERS.

MUM: We're just waiting for Frank and Jean. They said they'd be here by eight. What time is it, dear?

BUNNY: (looking at his wrist but realises he's still missing his watch) Er, about eight. Irene, fetch the Glade, Nana's let off again.
Why don't you sit next to Nana?

BUNNY, MUM AND LIZZIE LEAVE THE ROOM. MAGGIE SITS DOWN NEXT TO NANA AND THEN QUICKLY HOLDS HER BREATH.

WOMAN: Hello dear.

MAGGIE: Hi.

AN AWKWARD SILENCE.

SCENE 11. INT. PUB. NIGHT.

LES IS SAT AT A TABLE. ANDY SITS DOWN WITH SOME DRINKS.

ANDY: There you go.

LES: Thanks. Thanks for doing this tonight on your only night off.

ANDY: Well, it's not a chore.

LES: I was scared to be alone tonight. Bit worried about what I might do on my own.

ANDY: Well, you're not alone.

LES: No.
(BITTERLY)
We asked a hundred people 'Will Les Dennis ever hang on to a bird?' Our survey said
(MAKES A BUZZER NOISE)
We asked a hundred people 'Do you want to go out tonight and watch Les Dennis in panto?' Our survey said
(BUZZER NOISE)
Why don't people want to come out and see Les Dennis?

ANDY: They do.

LES: Why don't twice as many?

ANDY: Well, because you're competing with a lot these days aren't you? Internet, DVDs.

LES: Where did it all go wrong, eh?

ANDY: Can I ask you something?

LES: Yes.

ANDY: You're a comedian, right?

LES: Yes.

ANDY: I haven't seen you make a joke for five years.

LES: What do you mean?

ANDY: When you're on telly and stuff, when you're on chat shows or in *Big Brother*. You're talking to the chickens but you're moaning about stuff.

LES: (interrupting wearily) It's the way they cut it.

ANDY: All you do, there you go, moaning about stuff. Make a joke about it, make a joke. I mean, what was that impression you used to do?

LES: Impressions. I did loads.

ANDY: What was it?

LES: Mavis Riley, *Coronation Street*.

ANDY: Do that.

LES: No, I'm not doing that.

ANDY: Do it.

LES: No!

ANDY: Go on.

LES: (doing the impression) 'I don't really know.'

ANDY: That's great.

LES: Yeah, I know, it is good, yeah.

ANDY: You need another one, she hasn't really been on telly for fifteen years, but good.

LES: Correct me if I'm wrong but I'm famous for more than a Mavis Riley impression and *Family Fortunes*.

(ANDY LOOKS UP AT THE CEILING)

I am famous for other things, aren't I?

ANDY: Um . . .

LES: *The Les Dennis Laughter Show. Russ Abbot's Madhouse.*

ANDY: Were you in that?

LES: Yes.

ANDY: Well then, if you . . .

LES: (bitterly) You don't remember. Nobody remembers. That's why I'm in a shitty little panto where the only people laughing were that bunch of gays.

ANDY: Nothing wrong with gays.

LES: Yeah, I know. But they'll laugh at anything. No victory making a bunch of gay fellas laugh, they'll laugh at anything. Look at that Graham Norton.

ANDY: He's all right, isn't he?

LES: Is he? Is this funny, is it?
(HE PUTS ON A HIGH-PITCHED IRISH VOICE)
'Oh, look at this website about cocks and fannies, oh, Jackie Collins, what lovely tits. Do you like a cock up your arse? Oh!' . . . Is that funny?

ANDY: It is quite funny when you do it, but keep it down a little bit because we're in a pub.

LES: What is that? I want to do something more highbrow. Oscar Wilde or something.

ANDY: Yeah, definitely. He was gay.

LES: I know, but not in the same way, he was clever. Would this have been funny, him going through customs: 'I have nothing to declare but my genius . . .
(HE PUTS ON THE CAMP IRISH ACCENT AGAIN)
. . . Oh, and this vibrating tongue for pleasuring fannies.' Oh, is that funny?

ANDY: Again, quite funny when you do it, but it's Sunday, can you keep the fannies down to a minimum?

SCENE 12. INT.
SUBURBAN HOUSE. NIGHT.

MAGGIE COMES UP THE STAIRS AND APPROACHES LIZZIE'S BEDROOM BUT STOPS IN HER TRACKS WHEN SHE OVERHEARS TALKING. LIZZIE AND BUNNY ARE HAVING A HEATED DISCUSSION IN HER BEDROOM.

LIZZIE: Why can't I just stay in this?

BUNNY: Because that is not the costume we said you'd wear. Olivia Newton-John wouldn't be seen dead in that. Look, just do as you're told, will you?

BUNNY LEAVES LIZZIE'S BEDROOM. MAGGIE DUCKS DOWN SO SHE'S NOT SEEN. BUNNY SLAMS LIZZIE'S BEDROOM DOOR AND THEN HIS OWN. MAGGIE WALKS UP THE STAIRS AND KNOCKS ON LIZZIE'S DOOR.

LIZZIE: (from inside) I'm changing, I'm changing.

MAGGIE: It's me, it's Maggie.

LIZZIE: (opening the door) Hi.

LIZZIE'S ROOM LOOKS LIKE IT HASN'T CHANGED SINCE SHE WAS EIGHT YEARS OLD.

MAGGIE: Your mum said I had to come up and have a look at all your awards and cups and . . .

LIZZIE: (pointing) Oh, yeah, here they are.

MAGGIE: Oh, look at that, gymnastics. Second, second, lots of photographs of your dad there, doing his – whatever he's doing. I don't see any photographs of you with your friends. Have you got any friends your own age?

LIZZIE: Yeah, you, you're my best friend.

MAGGIE: (laughing nervously) Apart from me?

LIZZIE: Well, all the friends downstairs, they're all friends, they're all old friends.

MAGGIE: They are old friends, they look like the cast of *Last of the Summer Wine* down there.

LIZZIE: Dad said when I'm famous that I'll have all the friends I'll need. He said I'd have too many friends.

MAGGIE: Do you enjoy all this though? I mean, really like all this dressing up and performing?

LIZZIE: Yeah, I love it.

MAGGIE: Do you though? I mean, is this what you want to do or is it what your dad wants?

LIZZIE: But Dad knows what's good for me. Well, I've been doing this since I was two, it's in my blood.

MAGGIE: Ah, but it wasn't your ambition when you were two, was it? I mean, oh, I don't know, I think you seem to be missing out on a whole load of stuff, just, I think he's suffocating you a bit.

LIZZIE: You're making me sad and it's, it's my birthday.

MAGGIE: Sorry.

CUT TO THE LIVING ROOM. MAGGIE IS SITTING WITH THE ELDERLY FRIENDS, AWAITING SOME KIND OF PERFORMANCE.

A SPANGLY CURTAIN HAS BEEN SET UP AT THE BACK OF THE ROOM. MUSIC
BEGINS. LIZZIE APPEARS THROUGH THE CURTAIN AND BEGINS TO SING.

LIZZIE: 'Anything you can do I can do better.'

BUNNY'S HEAD APPEARS ABOVE LIZZIE'S.

BUNNY: (singing) 'I can do anything better than you.'

LIZZIE: 'No you can't.'

BUNNY: 'Yes I can.'

LIZZIE: 'No you can't.'

BUNNY: 'Yes I can. Yes I can, yes I can.'

LIZZIE AND BUNNY EMERGE FROM BEHIND A CURTAIN. BUNNY IS
SQUEEZED INTO LEATHER TROUSERS ABD A TIGHT WHITE T-SHIRT.
THEY BEGIN A DANCE ROUTINE. THE ELDERLY FRIENDS NOD ALONG TO
THE MUSIC. MAGGIE SITS WITH HER MOUTH OPEN, SILENTLY APPALLED.

LIZZIE: (singing) 'Tell me more, tell me more, was it love at first sight?'

BUNNY: 'Tell me more, tell me more, did she put up a fight?'

BUNNY/MAGGIE: (singing together) 'Aha, aha, aha, aha, aha, aha, aha,
aha . . . You've got to speed it up and then you've got to slow it down,
because if you believe that a love can hit the top you've got to play around
(BUNNY MIMES SQUEEZING LIZZIE'S BREASTS AND MAGGIE LOOKS
HORRIFIED)

and soon you will find that there comes a time
(BUNNY TEARS OFF LIZZIE'S VELCROED SKIRT, À LA BUCKS FIZZ)
for making your mind up. For making your mind up. For making your
mind up.'

LIZZIE FINISHES THE SONG TOO EARLY. HER FATHER THROWS HER A STERN LOOK AND TRIES TO COVER HER MISTAKE.

BUNNY: For making your mind up.

THERE IS SOME WEAK APPLAUSE. BUNNY MOVES TO THE STEREO TO TURN OFF THE MUSIC. LIZZIE FOLLOWS HIM APPREHENSIVELY.

LIZZIE: Sorry Dad.

BUNNY: Don't apologise to me. Apologise to the audience who thought that you ruined it. That was bad. It was bad because we did not do enough rehearsal.

LIZZIE: I was getting ready for my birthday.

BUNNY: We were all getting ready for your birthday but some of us found time to practise and some of us didn't because you were too busy worrying about your stupid bloody dress and now you have let down your public. What is the golden rule?

LIZZIE: Never let down your public.

BUNNY: Never let down your public. Well, you have let them down and you've let me down and you've let yourself down. Enjoy the rest of the day, maybe next time listen to your silly old dad, eh?

LIZZIE: (breaking down) Maggie was right.

BUNNY: Why? What did Maggie say?

LIZZIE: This is weird.

MAGGIE: (to the other guests) I didn't say weird.

LIZZIE: I should have friends my own age, like she said. You do look like the cast of *Last of the Summer Wine*.

MAGGIE: (to the other guests) Great show.

LIZZIE: I want to start living my own life. Do you know what I want to do in life? No, because you've never asked me.

LIZZIE RUNS OFF. MAGGIE IS LEFT, SMILING POLITELY.

BUNNY: (venomously) Well, well, well, it seems quite a poisonous element has entered our little home. Quite a nasty little piece of work.

MAGGIE: Can I just say—

BUNNY: I think that you should go, you have done quite enough damage.

MAGGIE: (laughing) Oh God, this is daft, this is . . .

OLD FRIEND: It's his house, if he wants you to leave you should leave.

MAGGIE: Bye Nana, bye everybody.
(MAGGIE IS ALMOST OUT OF THE DOOR WHEN SHE TURNS BACK)
Oh, I just want to say, do you mind if I take a couple of sandwiches for the train? I haven't eaten since four o'clock and I've got no food in the house. Didn't think I was going to get chucked out of the party.

BUNNY: (angrily) Well, you should have thought of that before you fucked up my daughter's life, goodnight.

MAGGIE: Yes, okay.

SCENE 13. INT. PUB. NIGHT.

LES IS LOST IN MELANCHOLY THOUGHT. ANDY NURSES HIS DRINK.

LES: 'When the laughter stops, when the audience departs, when the make-up has been removed, what is left of the clown?
(ANDY LOOKS AT HIS WATCH)
Nothing but an empty costume.' I should have listened to that. Do you know who said that?

ANDY: Jean-Paul Sartre?

LES: Bobby Davro. Davvers took me aside, he said, 'Beware, Les, you won't always be riding high.' But I wasn't even listening, I was too busy telling him some of the funny answers we get on *Family Fortunes*. Have I ever told you any of those? Like I said to this woman, 'Name something red. She said—'

ANDY/LES: My cardigan.

LES: (laughing) How could that have been up there? I mean we survey a hundred people, how would they know? 'Name a domestic pet', this fella said 'Leopard'.

ANDY: That's not domestic, is it?

LES: No.

ANDY: No way.
(NODS TOWARDS A WOMAN AT THE BAR)
What about her?

LES: No, I'm not interested in birds any more. They just bleed you dry and then they're off out the door, bye, bye.

ANDY: She's been looking at you all night.

LES: She's pissed up, She's a pissed-up slapper. I'm not about to have a one-night stand with a pissed-up slapper just to make myself feel a bit better. I've still got some dignity.

CUT TO LES IN BED, MAKING LOVE UNDER A DUVET.

SCENE 14. INT. ANDY'S LIVING ROOM. NIGHT.

ANDY IS LYING ON THE SOFA, WATCHING TELEVISION. THE PHONE RINGS. ANDY ANSWERS WITHOUT GETTING UP.

ANDY: Hello?

CUT TO MAGGIE ON THE OTHER END OF THE PHONE, IN HER OWN LIVING ROOM. SHE'S ALSO LYING ON THE SOFA, WATCHING TV.

MAGGIE: Would you rather have a bionic arm, or a bionic leg?

ANDY: Good question. Um, bionic leg, so I could hop to work.

MAGGIE: So would I. I'd have a bionic leg, but it would be for kicking.

ANDY: (laughing) Actually, I tell you what, a bionic arm would come in useful some nights.

MAGGIE: How do you mean?

ANDY: Doesn't matter.

MAGGIE: I'm starving, have you eaten anything?

ANDY: No.

MAGGIE: Shall I come over and cook you something?

ANDY: It's half eleven. And you can't cook.

MAGGIE: Fair point. Well, see you tomorrow then?

ANDY: Yeah.

MAGGIE: Bye.

ANDY: Bye.

ANDY PUTS DOWN THE PHONE AND CONTINUES WATCHING TELEVISION, SMILING.

SCENE 15. INT. LES'S BEDROOM. NIGHT.

LES IS STILL IN BED WITH A WOMAN, HAVING SEX.

WOMAN: Is that good? Is that good?

LES: (doing his Mavis impression) 'I don't really know.'

WOMAN: What?

LES: (using his *Family Fortunes*' catchphrase) 'If it's up there I'll give you the money myself.'

WOMAN: (sternly) Get off me.

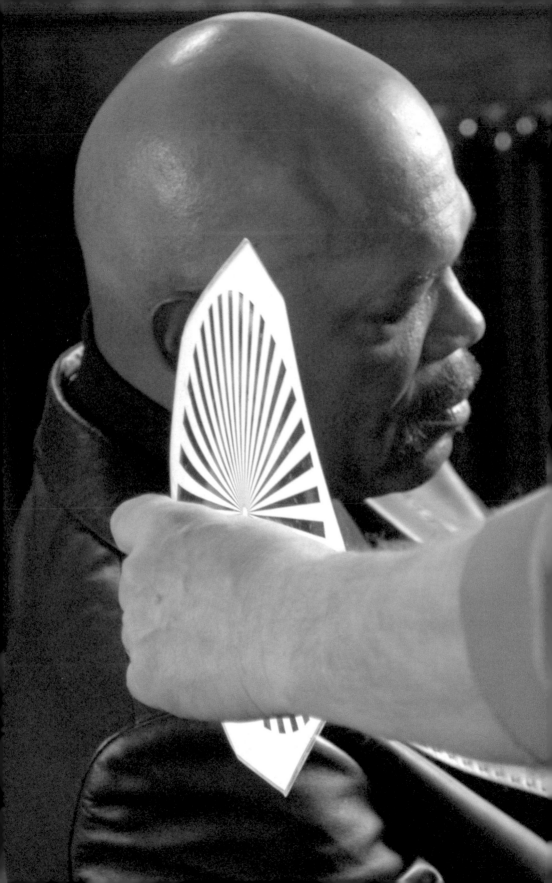

EXTRAS
EPISODE 5

CAST LIST
Andy Millman RICKY GERVAIS
Maggie Jacobs ASHLEY JENSEN
Dullard STEVE SPEIRS
Danny MICHAEL WILDMAN
Minister PATRICK MALAHIDE

With SAMUEL L. JACKSON

Actress GRACE KINGSLENE
A.D. DAVID RICARDO-PEARCE
Waiter NICK BALL

Written & Directed by
RICKY GERVAIS
& STEPHEN MERCHANT

FILM CLIP: 'FATAL ERROR'

WE ARE IN SOME KIND OF BRITISH GOVERNMENT BUILDING. A MINISTRY MAN IS STOOD BEHIND A DESK BARKING AT SOMEONE OFF-SCREEN. ALSO IN THE SCENE IS DANNY, A HANDSOME BLACK GUY, HOLDING A FILE.

MINISTRY MAN: (angrily) For God's sake, you bloody Yanks are all the same. You walk round like you're John Wayne and leave us to clean up your mess. I've got three embassies baying for blood. I've got two dead diplomats and a partridge in a bloody pear tree. Whitehall's running round like a bunch of headless chickens. What exactly am I supposed to tell the Prime Minister?

WE REVEAL THAT THE MAN HE'S BEEN SPEAKING TO IS SAMUEL L. JACKSON. THE CAMERA TRACKS INTO A BIG CLOSE-UP OF SAM, WHO TAKES A DRAG ON A CIGAR.

SAM: (exhaling cigar smoke) Tell him Uncle Sam's in town.

DIRECTOR: (off-screen) And cut there, thank you, check the tape, we're moving on.

SCENE 1. INT. FILM SET. DAY.

ANDY AND MAGGIE ARE BOTH DRESSED AS POLICE CONSTABLES.
ANDY IS MAKING MAGGIE LAUGH BY PRETENDING TO TALK INTO
HIS WALKIE-TALKIE.

ANDY: Sarge, these lads keep saying 'Afternoon Cun . . . stable'
but making it sound like you-know-what. What do I to do them?
Can I hit them?

(MAGGIE SHUSHES ANDY, LAUGHING. ANDY THROWS ON HIS
POLICEMAN'S HAT WITH A FLOURISH)

If I was a real copper though, I'd get ready like that, I would and
I'd have . . .

(ANDY PRETENDS TO USE HIS PEPPER SPRAY ON MAGGIE)

it's all right it's only hairspray. I want my prisoners to look good.

DANNY WALKS PAST. MAGGIE QUICKLY INTERCEPTS HIM.

MAGGIE: (flirtatious) Excuse me, can I just say I thought you were
really brilliant in that scene.

DANNY: Oh, thank you. I didn't really do anything, I just had to hold
this folder.

MAGGIE: (flirting) Which you did brilliantly, didn't drop it or anything.

DANNY: Well, that's three years of drama school for you.

MAGGIE BURSTS INTO FITS OF OVER-THE-TOP LAUGHTER.
ANDY WATCHES HER.

MAGGIE: I'm Maggie by the way.

DANNY: Dan.

MAGGIE: Hi Dan.

DANNY: Hi Maggie.
(THEY SHARE A MOMENT. ANDY LOOKS ON, SMILING)
Look, I can't really talk now I have to . . .

MAGGIE: Oh, no, sorry. You go, go and do your thing, I just wanted
to say that.

DANNY: Thanks.

MAGGIE: Bye.
(DANNY LEAVES. ANDY LOOKS AT MAGGIE, SMIRKING)
What?

ANDY: What?

MAGGIE: What?

ANDY: (laughing) Just a normal conversation. He just held the file well, that's all you wanted to say to him.

MAGGIE: (hits ANDY with her hat) I'm going to put my pumps on.

ANDY: Don't leave me here.

MAGGIE: Why?

ANDY: (pointing to a group of extras sitting in a corner) What if one of them talks to me?

MAGGIE: Well, they're only human.

ANDY: (pointing to an odd-looking extra reading a puzzle magazine) He's not.

MAGGIE: (laughing) It'll take me two minutes, right.

ANDY: Hurry up. Hurry up.

MAGGIE LEAVES. ANDY GLANCES AT THE CROWD OF EXTRAS. HE MOMENTARILY CATCHES THE EYE OF ONE OF THEM, A BIG, OVER-FRIENDLY DULLARD WHO NODS AND SMILES AT ANDY. ANDY LOOKS AWAY QUICKLY BUT IT'S TOO LATE. HE'S UNWITTINGLY MADE A NEW FRIEND. ANDY MOVES OVER TO THE TEA AND COFFEE AREA, TRYING TO SEEM PREOCCUPIED BUT THE BIG GUY WANDERS OVER AND STARTS A CONVERSATION.

DULLARD: (leaning in towards ANDY) Quite incredible, eh?

ANDY: Huh?

DULLARD: Mr Samuel L. Jackson in our midst.

ANDY: No, I'm not Sam Jackson. I can see the confusion we look alike but—

THE DULLARD LAUGHS HYSTERICALLY.

DULLARD: I've hit gold, eh? I've found the joker in the pack.

ANDY: I don't know about that.

DULLARD: No, I tell you what, seriously, that is great that is, mate. That is brilliant. That's a gift that is, the gift of laughter. You remind me of a mate of mine, Pete Shepherd, he used to run the Londis near me, and God, we used to have a laugh together.

ANDY: (not interested) Did you?

DULLARD: Oh, he'd have me in hysterics every time I saw him. He was a Chelsea fan, I was a Spurs fan and when we'd meet we'd always have a chat and a laugh.

ANDY: Yeah. Why are you telling me this?

DULLARD: Oh, we used to have a laugh, you know, we'd have a chat and a laugh every time.

ANDY: Oh good.

DULLARD: And one day a couple of kids, right, they were messing around in his shop
(SUDDENLY SERIOUS)
and they chucked bleach in his eyes and blinded him. I went to visit him in the hospital, tears were coming out of his bandaged, frazzled, useless eyes. And he went, 'I don't think I'll ever laugh again.' Do you know what?

ANDY: (taken aback) What?

DULLARD: I don't think he has. I stopped going to visit him in the end, to be honest.

ANDY: Did that cheer him up?

DULLARD: Got too depressing, you know. I only used to hang out with him because he was a laugh but he just got boring.
(ANDY RAISES HIS EYEBROWS)
He was miserable, blind, not my cup of tea. 'My eyes, my eyes . . .'

AN ASSISTANT DIRECTOR APPEARS.

A.D.: Sorry to interrupt.

ANDY: (relieved) No, please don't apologise.

A.D.: (to DULLARD) I need someone to do a few lines, sometime next week, probably not until Tuesday, it's an officer in an ID parade. Interested in that?

DULLARD: I don't mind. I don't mind. Oh, hang on though, I was already seen. I was on the desk when Samuel Jackson walked past.

A.D.: Oh, yeah. No, I can't use you then, sorry, mate. I need someone who hasn't been seen.

DULLARD: (pointing at ANDY) He hasn't been seen.

ANDY: (eager) I haven't been seen.

A.D.: All right, you fancy that?

ANDY: Yeah.

A.D.: Sam Jackson comes in, you're joking around with him and then you go, 'Ten to one he's going to pick Sergeant Harris again'.

ANDY: With Sam Jackson?

A.D.: Yeah, you want to have a stab at that?

ANDY: (quickly) Yeah.

A.D.: Yeah?

ANDY: Yeah.

A.D.: All right. Well, I'll let you know when we're doing it. It won't be today though.

ANDY: Okay, cheers mate.
(THE A.D. WANDERS OFF. ANDY TURNS TO DULLARD)
Oh, bloody hell, a line with Sam Jackson, cheers for that.

DULLARD: Eh?

ANDY: I owe you one.

DULLARD: Hey, a favour's a favour. Don't worry.

(PAUSE)

Just take me out one night.

ANDY: What?

DULLARD: Take me out, on the town, one night.

SCENE 2. EXT. CATERING BUS. DAY.

MAGGIE AND ANDY ARE BOTH HOLDING LUNCH TRAYS. MAGGIE IS SIDE-TRACKED, WATCHING DANNY, WHO IS EATING HIS LUNCH ON THE ACTORS' BUS.

MAGGIE: Let's go and eat on the other bus.

ANDY: Why?

MAGGIE: Nothing, no reason, don't need a reason. Just let's do something out of the ordinary once in a while.

ANDY SCANS THE BUS AND SEES DANNY SITTING DOWN.

ANDY: (smiling) Yeah, all right.

MAGGIE: Bit of a break from the old routine.

MAGGIE AND ANDY START TO CLIMB ABOARD THE ACTORS' BUS. THE A.D. IS SITTING IN THE DRIVING SEAT.

A.D.: Whoa, where are you going? You can't come on here, it's actors only.

ANDY: I am an actor.

A.D.: No, you're background. This bus is for actors.

ANDY: I am an actor.

A.D.: No, your voucher is green, that means you're background.

ANDY: Right, okay. So you're judging my entire career on the colour of my voucher.

A.D.: (sarcastic) No, I'm sure you've had major roles in other things.

MAGGIE: He hasn't.

ANDY: (quickly, to MAGGIE) Shut up.

A.D.: I can't let you on here.

ANDY: Sure. There's no one on though, can I just eat it and go? I'll be five minutes.

A.D.: I can't allow that.

ANDY: No, you can't allow it.

WHILE THIS ARGUMENT CONTINUES A BLACK ACTRESS CLIMBS ON BOARD, SQUEEZES PAST THEM, AND WALKS DOWN THE BUS TOWARDS DANNY. SHE SITS DOWN NEXT TO HIM AND THEY BEGIN TO TALK. MAGGIE WATCHES THEM, ANXIOUS AND A LITTLE JEALOUS.

A.D.: (to ANDY) You can't come on here, okay, that's the rule. You've got a perfectly good bus over there. This bus is for actual actors.

ANDY: (sarcastic) Yeah, yeah, don't know why I asked, mental. As if I could go on a bus meant for other people.

ANDY WALKS AWAY TO THE OTHER BUS.

MAGGIE: (to A.D.) I don't really know him. Can I come on?

A.D.: No.

MAGGIE: Okay.

(MAGGIE FOLLOWS ANDY BUT WHEN SHE FEELS SHE'S AT A SAFE DISTANCE, SHE TURNS BACK TO THE A.D.)

Pig.

SCENE 3. EXT. CATERING BUS. DAY.

ANDY IS STANDING BY THE LUNCH TABLE. HE SPOTS THE DULLARD AND ROLLS HIS EYES, QUICKLY TURNING AWAY. THE DULLARD APPROACHES ANDY.

DULLARD: Got any more jokes?

ANDY: I haven't, no.

DULLARD: Come on, eh?

ANDY: What's E.T. short for?

DULLARD: Dunno.

ANDY: He's only got little legs.

DULLARD: (laughing too loud) My uncle was like you.

ANDY: Was he?

DULLARD: Oh, very funny guy . . .
(SUDDENLY SERIOUS)
. . . Not towards the end though, not so much of a laugh towards the end. Lost both his legs, you see. Thrombosis. There was very little to laugh about when he knew he was stuck downstairs, no legs and he could hear his wife upstairs with another man, having it off. Oh, despite the morphine he could still hear her up there, at it. Reckon he died from a broken heart in the end. Still, it's a wonderful gift that, laughter.

SILENCE. ANDY STARES AT HIM.

ANDY: Yeah. The gift that keeps on giving. Anyway, I've got to go and slash my wrists, I'll see you later, all right?

DULLARD: Hey, what are you doing Saturday afternoon?

ANDY: Why?

DULLARD: Well, I thought, you know, you could come round my place, couple of lads, open a couple of cans. I've got a new DVD. Do you know what it is? *Vera Drake*.

ANDY: Tempting. I've got to watch the game, it's Chelsea/Man U, so see you later.

ANDY STARTS TO WALK AWAY, BUT THE DULLARD STOPS HIM IN HIS TRACKS WITH A QUESTION.

DULLARD: Hey, when we going to go for that night out?

ANDY: What?

DULLARD: I know a lovely little restaurant.

ANDY: Well, yeah, you said, 'Shall we go for an evening out?' and I didn't say no.

DULLARD: You're not going back on your promise, are you?

ANDY: Well, it's not a promise, is it?

DULLARD: It was.

ANDY: No, well, you did me a favour, which I thanked you for, but I don't think it warrants, you know, a whole evening out, a candlelit meal.

DULLARD: What's wrong with going for a meal with me?

ANDY: Nothing but . . . bit weird.

DULLARD: What's wrong with a couple of mates having a meal together?

ANDY: Well, we're not really friends—

DULLARD: Yes, but that's how we'll become friends, you see, we'll go for a meal.

ANDY: But I go out for meals with people that are already friends. I don't go up to people willy nilly and go, 'All right, mate, I don't know you from Adam but do you want to go to Butlins for the weekend? You might be a mental case but let's find out.' It's mad, do you know what I mean?

DULLARD: No.

THE DULLARD LEAVES, UPSET. ANDY LOOKS GUILTY.

SCENE 4. EXT. OUTSIDE THE STUDIO. DAY.

MAGGIE IS LEANING AGAINST THE WALL BY THE DOCK DOORS AS DANNY WALKS OUT.

DANNY: Hello.

MAGGIE: Oh hello, Maggie.

THEY SHAKE HANDS.

DANNY: Yeah, Dan.

MAGGIE: Hi again. So how long have you been in this lark then?

DANNY: I've only been acting for a couple of years. You know, done a couple of plays. I'd like to do more films but they're hard to come by so I'm just trying to get into TV.

MAGGIE: (nodding her head) Sure.

DANNY: I mean, to be honest, there's not a lot of black faces needed on television.

MAGGIE: No.
(THINKS)
Crimewatch?

DANNY: What?

MAGGIE: (earnest) The reconstruction of *Crimewatch*, they always need black actors.
(REALISING HOW THIS SOUNDS)
Or white actors. They need black actors and white actors depending on who's committed the crime that day. I mean there's criminals, black criminals, certainly there's white criminals as well as black criminals . . . oh God, I've just remembered I've got to go and, yeah, what was it again . . .
(BEGINS TO MUMBLE)

. . . The bag, yeah . . . I'll see you later.

MAGGIE HURRIES AWAY. DANNY LOOKS BEMUSED.

SCENE 5. INT.
EXTRAS' CATERING BUS. DAY.

MAGGIE AND ANDY SIT TOGETHER AT A TABLE, TALKING AS THEY
EAT LUNCH.

MAGGIE: Well, why don't you just tell him you don't want to be his friend?

ANDY: I can't, it's too damning, you can't say that to someone. That is
saying that you fundamentally have a problem with their personality.

MAGGIE: Well, what are you going to do?

ANDY: The only honourable thing I can do.

MAGGIE: What?

ANDY: Add him to the long list of people that I have to avoid for the rest
of my life. You can never have that time back. I remember I sat through
a whole evening of Comic Relief once because I was—

MAGGIE NOTICES THE BLACK ACTRESS FROM BEFORE CLIMBING ON
TO THE BUS. MAGGIE QUICKLY GETS UP AND BLOCKS HER WAY.

MAGGIE: Sorry, excuse me. Are you an actress in this film?

ACTRESS: Yes.

MAGGIE: Well, you can't come on here.

ACTRESS: Sorry?

MAGGIE: You're not allowed on this bus. This bus is for supporting
artists only and you are an actress.

ACTRESS: What are you talking about?

MAGGIE: You've got your own bus there and we've got our own bus. I'm not allowed on yours, you're not allowed on mine . . .

(AN EXTRA, WHO HAPPENS TO BE WHITE, CLIMBS ON TO THE BUS. TO THE EXTRA)

. . . You can come on, on you go.

ACTRESS: (trying to push past MAGGIE) This is pathetic.

MAGGIE: I know, it is pathetic, isn't it, but you can't come on.

ACTRESS: Get out the way.

MAGGIE: Look, I don't make the rules here.

THE ACTRESS GIVES UP AND WALKS OFF TOWARDS THE ACTORS' BUS.

ACTRESS: You're a child.

MAGGIE: (calling after her) Yes, well, that's as maybe. We'll stick to our own, you stick to your own and then we're all happy.

AS SHE SAYS THIS SHE NOTICES THAT DANNY IS WATCHING THE INCIDENT. HE LOOKS QUIZZICAL. MAGGIE REALISES HOW THE EXCHANGE MUST HAVE SOUNDED AND LOOKS HORRIFIED.

SCENE 6. INT.
EXTRAS' CATERING BUS,
MOMENTS LATER. DAY.

MAGGIE IS SITTING BACK AT THE TABLE WITH ANDY.

ANDY: He doesn't think you're a racist.

MAGGIE: He does, he's just seen me say to a black woman, 'You're not allowed to sit on this bus.' It's like that whole racism-on-a-bus incident all over again.

ANDY: What, the Rosa Parks incident?

MAGGIE: It wasn't in a park, it was on a bus.

ANDY: (rolling his eyes) Sure. He doesn't think you're a racist, and even if he does, which he doesn't, he's wrong because you're not. Don't worry about it.

MAGGIE: (anxious) I know, but what if I am and I don't know it? What if, like subconsciously, I'm a little bit racist?

ANDY: Well, there is that test I can give you.

MAGGIE: What test?

ANDY: (winding her up) The racism test. The one they give you when you join the council to make sure you're not a racist, it's . . .

MAGGIE: I've never heard of this.

ANDY: Yeah. Do you want to do it? Just ten questions.

MAGGIE: Go on then.

ANDY: (getting out his police-costume notebook) Yes. Right you've got to answer just totally honestly, okay? Just relax, you've got nothing to worry about . . . unless you are a racist. Question one. Question one is: who would you rather see with their shirt off? Brad Pitt or Sir Trevor McDonald?

MAGGIE: Brad Pitt, obviously.

ANDY: (making a face) Obviously?

MAGGIE: What?

ANDY: No, I can't say anything until the end. Right, question two is about racial awareness because often you catch out a real racist because they don't know or care about any black issues. Who is the Prime Minister of Great Britain?

MAGGIE: Tony Blair.

ANDY: Correct. Who is the Prime Minister of Namibia?

MAGGIE: (worried) I don't know.

ANDY: You knew the white one. Okay, good.
(MAKING A NOTE IN HIS BOOK)
Okay, who is the Queen of England?

MAGGIE: Queen Elizabeth II.

ANDY: Correct. Who is the president of Dijibouti?

MAGGIE: This is ridiculous. I've never even heard of blooming Dijibouti.

ANDY: Oh, please do not ridicule the totally valid African language, please. Right, next question. Who would you rather have waiting for you when you got home tonight? Johnny Depp or O.J. Simpson?

MAGGIE: Johnny Depp, because of the murder thing.

ANDY: Because of the murder thing? I think you'll find that Mr O.J. Simpson was acquitted, but in your eyes because he's black he's still guilty.

MAGGIE: People still think he is guilty.

ANDY: Racist people still think he's guilty.

MAGGIE: I'm not a racist.

ANDY: Well, I'm just going by the test.

MAGGIE: Listen to me, I'm trying to get off with a black person.

ANDY: Yes but, according to you, you wouldn't want him waiting for you in your house when you got home tonight.

MAGGIE: Only because I would go, 'How did you get in here?'

ANDY: (fake outrage) Oh, now he's breaking and entering as well. Fascist.

MAGGIE: Right, I'm going to go and ask him out now.

ANDY: Well, I'd . . . hold on.

MAGGIE: (getting up and leaving the bus) Watch.

ANDY: Tell him you had a 'hate rating' of nine-point-eight, one more than Hitler.

MAGGIE: Watch, I'm going now.

CUT TO ANDY SCRAPING HIS PLATE INTO THE BIN OUTSIDE THE BUS. MAGGIE RUSHES OVER.

MAGGIE: He said yes. He is so lovely and totally amazing and I'm going out for a drink with him.

ANDY: When?

MAGGIE: Tonight.

ANDY: Well done.

MAGGIE: Actually I'm a little bit nervous about this date.

ANDY: Racist!

THEY LAUGH.

SCENE 7. EXT. STREET. DAY.

MAGGIE AND ANDY ARE WALKING ALONG THE STREET OUTSIDE THE STUDIO.

MAGGIE: Would you rather die of the cold or die of the heat? Would you rather be trapped in a freezer or trapped in a microwave?

ANDY: How would you ever get trapped in a microwave?

MAGGIE: Well, a giant—

THE DULLARD SUDDENLY JOGS UP BEHIND THEM.

DULLARD: Hiya.

ANDY: (annoyed) Oh!

DULLARD: You going up the station?

ANDY: No.

DULLARD: Going back into town?

ANDY: No.

DULLARD: Where you going then?

ANDY: We're just . . .

THEY ARE PASSING A GRAVEYARD.

MAGGIE: (pointing to the graveyard) We're going in here.

DULLARD: Really?

ANDY: Yeah so . . .

MAGGIE: We're going to visit his mum's grave. Taking her some flowers and stuff.

DULLARD: You haven't got any flowers.

ANDY: (quickly) No, I've taken her some flowers, collecting the dead flowers. From all the other visits so . . .

DULLARD: That's a bit of a coincidence, isn't it, you know. She's buried here right in the graveyard next to the studio we work at.

MAGGIE: Handy. That's why we're going.

ANDY: We'll see you later.

DULLARD: Do you mind if I come with you?

ANDY: (sarcastic) Why would I? Come on.

(THEY WALK INTO THE GRAVEYARD TOGETHER. CUT TO ANDY, MAGGIE AND THE DULLARD WANDERING AMONG THE GRAVESTONES)

You don't have to wait around, mate. I'll be about half an hour and I get quite emotional so . . .

DULLARD: Oh, that's all right, that's not a worry. That's not a problem, mate, no, no. I spend a lot of time by graves, I'm used to it. You take your time, enjoy.

(ANDY ROLLS HIS EYES AT MAGGIE)

Which one is it anyway?

ANDY: Which one?

MAGGIE: (pointing at a nearby gravestone) That one.

ANDY: That one.

MAGGIE: The one with the . . .

ANDY: Yeah. There she is.

DULLARD: (looking closely at the gravestone) Rebecca Leibovitch?

ANDY: Mum!

DULLARD: Sounds Jewish. I didn't know you were Jewish.

ANDY: Didn't you?
(PUTTING ON A YIDDISH ACCENT)
Oy. Yeah. Oish.

DULLARD: Good God, died in 1953. How old does that make you then?

ANDY: (quickly calculating in his head) At least fifty-two. Fifty-two.

DULLARD: You're fifty-two?

MAGGIE: You don't look it one bit.

ANDY: No, thanks. Hard to believe, isn't it? It's just like it's hard to believe I was just passing my dead mother's grave, who is Jewish.

DULLARD: (reading the gravestone) She was born in 1893. So she died when she was sixty?

ANDY: In childbirth. They warned her, they said, 'Becky, you, cannot have a kid at your age', but old Ma Leibovitch didn't listen.

MAGGIE: No.

ANDY: So here I am.
(SARCASTIC, TO MAGGIE)
Fifty-two and Jewish.

MAGGIE: Yeah.

ANDY: Okay.

DULLARD: Why did you change your surname then?

ANDY: Well, fed up with the persecution, usual story, isn't it? Enough is enough, proud race and religion.

DULLARD: Is your dad round here too?

MAGGIE: He's still alive.

DULLARD: Really?

ANDY: (shrugging) Apparently.

DULLARD: How old is he then?

ANDY: Hundred?

MAGGIE: He's doing well though . . .

ANDY: Yeah.

MAGGIE: . . . For a hundred.

DULLARD: (looking at ANDY) Do you like taking the mickey out of me? This is fun for you, is it?

ANDY: What?

DULLARD: That is not your mother's grave.

ANDY: (looking at the gravestone, faking shock) Oh, no.

DULLARD: And I don't think you're Jewish.

ANDY: No, she pointed to that . . .

DULLARD: Why do you keep lying to me?

ANDY: I don't keep lying to you.

DULLARD: Yes, you do. You said that we were going to go for a nice meal, then you went back on that. I mean, do you think I haven't got any feelings or something?

ANDY: I know you've got feelings which is why I thought I would avoid the issue because I don't want to go for a meal with someone . . .

DULLARD: You won't go for a meal, right , because you hate me.

ANDY: I don't hate you.

DULLARD: You hate me so much that you can't bear to sit opposite me—

ANDY: I don't hate you at all—

DULLARD: And have a little nibble on a bit of food in my company—

ANDY: I could have a meal with you . . .

DULLARD: Yeah, well, I know I'm not the joker of the pack.

ANDY: That's nothing to do with it.

DULLARD: Yeah, all right I might not be able to do that. I'm reliable. I'm reliable, if I say I'll be somewhere I'm there.

ANDY: I know and I'll quite happily have a meal with you.

DULLARD: No, you're just saying that now because, you know . . .

ANDY: No, I'd like to have a meal with you.

DULLARD: Well, when then?

ANDY: Any time.

DULLARD: What, tonight?

ANDY: Not tonight.

DULLARD: Well, see what I mean?

ANDY: Okay, tonight. Tonight will be fine. Let's have a meal tonight, okay? I'm looking forward to it.
(MOUTHS TO MAGGIE 'THAT'S YOUR FAULT')
Oh, come on.

THEY ALL WALK AWAY FROM THE GRAVE.

SCENE 8. INT. RESTAURANT. NIGHT.

ANDY AND THE DULLARD ARE SAT AT A SMALL TABLE, FACING EACH OTHER. THE DULLARD IS SHOWING ANDY PHOTOS OF HIS CHILDREN.

DULLARD: (smiling) Louise, thirteen; Karen, ten.

(SUDDENLY SERIOUS)

Haven't seen either of them in three months.

(ANDY REACTS)

Word of advice, never get married and if you do get married don't let your wife go to the greengrocer's on her own. Right? She was going out three, four times a week getting fresh fruit and veg. I said to her, 'Why don't we do one big shop?' No, she wasn't having that, she was always down there. I got suspicious, you know, my wife's going out at eight o'clock at night buying cauliflower.

(HE LOOKS AT THE MENU)

Right then, what we having? Shall I order us some champagne?

ANDY: (quickly) No, it's not appropriate. We'll have a lager, we'll have a lager each, down it and go home and watch telly . . .

(RAISING HIS VOICE SO THAT THE WOMEN AT A NEARBY TABLE CAN HEAR)

. . . in our separate homes.

DULLARD: I don't, I don't . . . what are you going to have? I don't know what to have.

ANDY: I don't know.

DULLARD: We just can't decide. We're a tragic couple, we are.

ANDY: (loudly, to the nearby women) We're not a couple. His wife left him and I'm out shagging regular as clockwork.

SCENE 9. INT. BAR. NIGHT.

MAGGIE AND DANNY SIT ON BAR STOOLS NEXT TO EACH OTHER,
LAUGHING AND TALKING. DANNY STROKES MAGGIE'S HAIR. CUT TO
MAGGIE'S LIVING ROOM. MAGGIE AND DANNY ARE SITTING ON THE
SOFA, ENJOYING EACH OTHER'S COMPANY.

DANNY: There's this stallion of a horse – being brought on to set – and
who's got to ride it? Me. Okay, right.

(AS MAGGIE LISTENS TO DANNY TALK, SHE NOTICES A GOLLIWOG TOY
ON HER SHELF. PANIC SETS IN)

So, okay, I big up my chest and I say, 'Right, I'm going to ride this horse.'
I get on the horse—

MAGGIE: I have to go to the toilet.

DANNY: (a little taken a back) Yeah, yeah, sure.

(MAGGIE GETS UP AND WALKS TO THE DOOR, GRABBING THE GOLLIWOG
AS SHE PASSES AND PUTTING IT BEHIND HER BACK)

What you got there?

MAGGIE: Nothing.

DANNY: (smiling) No, you've got something, what is it?

MAGGIE: No, it's fine.

DANNY: Let me see.

MAGGIE: Oh, it's nothing.

DANNY: Come on, let me see. What have you got?

MAGGIE SLOWLY BRINGS THE DOLL OUT FROM BEHIND HER BACK.

MAGGIE: (showing him the doll) It's just a gollyiw—toy. A golly toy.

DANNY: A what?

MAGGIE: A golly toy, oh don't worry about that though, I mean I have had Sam—
(CORRECTING HERSELF QUICKLY)
– Sinbad since I was about six or seven, he's been in the family for years, so I mean, that's harmless. You know, I think if I was a racist I wouldn't be about to do what we were about to do. Not that I know what we were about to do, but whatever you want to do I'm up for it.

DANNY: Why were you trying to hide it?

MAGGIE: I wasn't hiding it, I was just, I was putting it there because it puts me off, well, it doesn't put me off. I was putting them all together, all the toys together. Because all the toys are equal,
(SHE PICKS UP A BARBIE DOLL AND STARTS NERVOUSLY ACTING OUT A SCENE BETWEEN THE TWO DOLLS)
'Oh, hello, how are you?' 'Hello there.' 'Hello there.' 'How are you?'
'I'm fine, I'm not a racist, in fact I think I fancy you.'

MAGGIE'S MIME TURNS X-RATED AS THE DOLLS START HAVING SEX, WITH THE APPROPRIATE NOISES. DANNY JUST STARES AT HER.

DANNY: I think I'm going to shoot off.

MAGGIE: No, really? Sorry.

DANNY: No, it's totally cool, I just think the black thing's getting in the way here.

MAGGIE: No, it's not, it's not.

DANNY: Don't worry, I don't think you're a racist or anything. I just think that, you know, it's on your mind and you can't get past it so, you know, we should just relax and rewind things a bit.

MAGGIE: Okay. Oh, look, can I just say something? The black thing, it's not an issue really, I hardly notice it really.

DANNY: Maggie, it's fine, it's cool. Let's do something next week, shall we? We'll go out Friday, yeah, dinner, dancing?

MAGGIE: Definitely. I love dancing, me. Do you, are you a good dancer? Not that there's any reason why you should be a good dancer.

DANNY: I have to, I'm going to go, I'll speak to you tomorrow, yeah?

MAGGIE: Yeah, okay.

DANNY: All right. See you. See you, okay. Thanks again for the wine and everything, yeah, all right?

MAGGIE: Okay, bye.

DANNY: See you.

DANNY LEAVES. MAGGIE SHUTS HER EYES AND THINKS ABOUT WHAT SHE'S DONE, MORTIFIED.

SCENE 10. INT.
RESTAURANT. NIGHT.

ANDY AND THE DULLARD ARE EATING THEIR STARTERS.

DULLARD: (offering a spoonful of food to ANDY) This is delicious, try that.

ANDY: (recoiling) No, what are you doing?

(HE LOOKS OVER AT ANOTHER DINER WHO IS SLURPING SOUP)
Jesus, listen to that.

DULLARD: What?

ANDY: (angrily) Oh, listen to this, right.
(HE SIPS HIS OWN SOUP SILENTLY)
Nothing. I'm two feet away. Now listen to him.
(THEY LISTEN AS THE OTHER DINER SLURPS LOUDLY)
Oh, it's driving me mental.

DULLARD: You really are Mr Grumpy Boots tonight, aren't you, eh?

ANDY STARES AT THE DULLARD. LONG PAUSE.

ANDY: (putting down his soup and leans back in his chair)
Oh, I can't do this, sorry. I can't go through with this. I am so fed up.

I'm forty-three years old and most people my age are out with their
wives or their girlfriends. I'm sat here having dinner with another
middle-aged man because I felt sorry for you and, don't take this the
wrong way, I looked at you and I thought, what a pathetic loser.
And I took pity on you and that's why I came and I'm worse off than
you in many ways. I'm lower on the chain than you, how do you think
that makes me feel? And I'm not having a go at you because I'm sure
you're a nice bloke. I know you're a nice bloke but I've got to go, mate,
because I'm actually depressed.

HE MAKES TO LEAVE.

DULLARD: Wait, I'd just like, I understand, I know what you're saying
and look, I got you this as a surprise. I was going to give it to you later,
but you might as well have it now.

THE DULLARD PUTS AN ENVELOPE ON THE TABLE.

ANDY: What is it?

DULLARD: (smiling) That is two tickets for the Ben Elton musical
We Will Rock You.

(ANDY LOOKS AT THE ENVELOPE THEN UP AT THE DULLARD.
HE CONSIDERS HIS OPTIONS.
THEN LEANS OVER THE TABLE AND PLUNGES HIS FACE INTO
HIS BOWL OF SOUP)

What are you doing?

ANDY RE-EMERGES. HE LOOKS AT THE DULLARD, SOUP DRIPPING
FROM HIS FACE . . . AND GOES BACK IN AGAIN.

HE RE-EMERGES FOR A SECOND TIME, STARES AT THE DULLARD AND
THEN GETS UP AND LEAVES, SOUP STILL DRIPPING FROM HIS FACE.

ANDY: See you later. Cheers.

SCENE 11. INT. FILM SET. DAY

ANDY AND MAGGIE ARE AGAIN DRESSED AS POLICE CONSTABLES,
STANDING IN THE TEA AND COFFEE AREA.

ANDY: (dejected) I've really had it with this. I am so fed up.

MAGGIE: It'll be all right.

ANDY: What will? People always say that. What will be all right?
When will it be all right? I'm forty-three. I've got nothing.

MAGGIE: No, listen, things are looking up. You've got a line with Samuel
L. Jackson, haven't you? It's a start. Oh, please don't be like this.

ANDY: Oh, it's just after last night. How was your evening, any better?

MAGGIE: Word of advice, if you get the most amazing, gorgeous, good-looking black guy in the world back at your house, don't leave your golliwog lying around.

ANDY: (laughing) That's remarkable advice, cheers.

MAGGIE: Oh, and then he caught me trying to hide it, which made matters worse.

ANDY: Why did you try and hide it?

MAGGIE: I didn't want to offend him and he was right, the black thing was on my mind. I didn't know whether to talk about black things or to not talk about black things. I ended up talking about what I thought he wanted to hear.

ANDY: Well, don't pander to him just because he's black. If he says, 'I like reggae' and you don't then say you don't. It's not being racist, it's having an opinion.

MAGGIE: I'll go and have a wee word with him now, eh?

ANDY: (in Scottish accent) Aye, go and have a wee word with him.

MAGGIE APPROACHES DANNY. ANDY LISTENS IN.

MAGGIE: Hi.

DANNY: Hey.

MAGGIE: Can I have a quick word?

DANNY: Yeah, of course.

MAGGIE: I just wanted to say that I hate reggae.

ANDY THROWS UP HIS HANDS IN DESPAIR.

DANNY: (confused) Sorry?

MAGGIE: I hate reggae, I hate it. It's slow, everything sounds the same, it's boring, I can't be doing with it. What do you think?

DANNY: Well, I don't particularly like reggae either.

MAGGIE: Right. Well, even if you did like it I would still hate it. What sort of music do you like?

DANNY: Well, I like jazz.

MAGGIE: I hate jazz, I hate it. In fact, do you know who I really hate in jazz? You know that big fat black man, him with the big fat puffed-out cheeks
(MAGGIE PUFFS OUT HER CHEEKS LIKE LOUIS ARMSTRONG)
and his bulging-out eyes and everything, he's like trumpet man. Sass . . . Sasquatch.

SAMUEL L. JACKSON WALKS UP BEHIND MAGGIE AS SHE'S TALKING.

SAM: Sachmo. Louis Armstrong.

MAGGIE: (meekly) Yeah, hi.

SAM: Hi. Do you hate all jazz?

MAGGIE: Yeah, well, that's just my opinion, it's not based on anything else other than the music, because I hate anybody doing it, you know, black or white.

ANDY LEAPS IN.

ANDY: Sorry, we were just having a conversation about music and she wasn't . . . she doesn't hate jazz—

MAGGIE: Yeah, I do, but I like lots of other things, white or black.

ANDY: Yeah . . .

MAGGIE: (to SAM) I like you for example, I think you're great.

SAM: (smiling) Thank you.

MAGGIE: I don't normally watch films more than once but I thought *The Matrix*, I loved it, it was amazing.

SAM: It was a good film.

ANDY: (realising her mistake and trying to cover for her) A good film, that's all she's saying.

MAGGIE: And you were brilliant in it.

SAM: I wasn't in that one.

ANDY: Wasn't in it.

MAGGIE: Yeah, you were.

ANDY: (to MAGGIE) He should know.

MAGGIE: Yeah, you were in *The Matrix*, you were the main one.

SAM: (smiling) No, no, no I can assure you I was not in *The Matrix*, but Laurence Fishburne was, maybe that's why you're confused.

ANDY: I know what you're thinking, she doesn't think you all look alike.
(SAM LOOKS AT ANDY)
If that, if that's what you were thinking. No, I'm just saying she doesn't, she's not racist. No way, she's not a racist. In fact she's been trying to get a black guy to shag her for a few weeks, so I don't think—

MAGGIE: (pointing at DANNY) That one . . .

ANDY: . . . specifically but I mean it's open to all, not all, but I mean you definitely, I know you're married but if you wanted to you could be up her like a rat up a drainpipe.
(ANDY DOES THE REQUISITE SOUND EFFECT AND CORKSCREWS HIS FINGER UP INTO THE AIR. THERE IS SILENCE AS EVERYONE LOOKS AT ANDY. MAGGIE LOWERS ANDY'S FINGER)
Yeah, okay.

(ANOTHER AWKWARD SILENCE)
Pulp Fiction!

SAMUEL L. JACKSON STARES WEARILY AT ANDY.

SAM: (calling out to the crew) Are we ready for the next shot?

ANDY: Yeah, are we ready yet? What are they doing? What are they . . . keeping you waiting.

SAM AND DANNY WALK AWAY. THE A.D. APPROACHES ANDY.

A.D.: I think you'd better leave.

ANDY: Yeah, we're off, we're off.

MAGGIE: Yeah, but we can't because you've got the line with Samuel L. Jackson.

ANDY: I think that's the point, I haven't got a line. I haven't got a line with Samuel L. Jackson because of the line 'Rat up a drainpipe.'
(ANDY CALLS OUT TO EVERYONE ON THE SET)
Okay, well, cheers everyone, thanks.

MAGGIE AND ANDY LEAVE THE SET TOGETHER.

ANDY: Another good day being friends with you.

EXTRAS
EPISODE 6

CAST LIST
Andy Millman RICKY GERVAIS
Maggie Jacobs ASHLEY JENSEN
Agent STEPHEN MERCHANT
Greg SHAUN PYE
Shaun SHAUN WILLIAMSON

With PATRICK STEWART

Damon Beesley MARTIN SAVAGE
Iain Morris GUY HENRY
Female Extra MICHELLE TERRY
Male Extra MARLON BULGER
Film Director MICHAEL VIVIAN
Secretary NAOMI TAYLOR

Written & Directed by
RICKY GERVAIS
& STEPHEN MERCHANT

FILM CLIP: 'THE TEMPEST'

PATRICK STEWART STANDS IN THE MIDDLE OF A WOODLAND SET,
GIVING A POWERFUL PERFORMANCE AS PROSPERO IN *THE TEMPEST*.

PATRICK: 'To the dread rattling thunder
Have I given fire, and rifted Jove's stout oak
With his own bolt; the strong-bas'd promontory
Have I made shake, and by the spurs pluck'd up
The pine and cedar. Graves at my command
Have wak'd their sleepers, op'd, and let 'em forth
By my so potent art.'

SCENE 1. INT. SET. DAY.

MAGGIE AND ANDY, IN PERIOD DRESS, ARE WATCHING THE
PERFORMANCE.

MAGGIE: Here's one. What would you rather be?

ANDY: Is now the best time to do this?

MAGGIE: (whispering) Right. Would you rather be you with your face
and your legs and brain of a chimpanzee?

ANDY: Brilliant.

MAGGIE: Or would you rather be a chimpanzee but with your brain?

ANDY: I can't answer that, it's too inane even for you. That's the worst
one yet.

PATRICK: 'And deeper than did ever plummet sound.
I'll drown my book.'

DIRECTOR: And cut! Good. Very good. Patrick, happy?

THE FILMING STOPS, THE CREW RELAX. GREG APPEARS AND SITS DOWN
NEXT TO ANDY.

ANDY: (annoyed at the sight of GREG) Oh, for . . .

GREG: All right?

ANDY: Yeah.

GREG: (pointing to PATRICK) Now that is acting.

ANDY: Yeah, I know what acting is, Greg.

GREG: Well, you know what *watching* acting is. Actually you can watch me later. I've got a line. 'All's lost. To prayer, to prayer, all's lost.'

ANDY: That's embarrassing.

GREG: Yes. You don't know what it means, do you?

ANDY: Not the way you did it, no.

GREG: But you don't know what it means?

ANDY: No, I don't care what it means so you—

GREG: You've no idea?

ANDY: No, because while you were at school swotting up on Shakespeare I was out living a real life, shagging birds.

MAGGIE: (earnest) Really? You told me you didn't have sex until you were twenty-two.

ANDY: Why are you joining in?

GREG: Interesting, this is interesting.

ANDY: Not interesting, no, it's not, no.

MAGGIE: It is a bit interesting because you said your mum wouldn't let you bring girls home.

ANDY: Why are you still joining in?

GREG: The plot thickens.

ANDY: No, the plot doesn't thicken, because I could have been lying to her, so like—

GREG: All right, calm down.

MAGGIE: If you were lying, why did you say that you lost your virginity to a woman that looked like Ronnie Corbett?

GREG: (laughs, imitating Ronnie Corbett) 'And it's goodnight from me.'

ANDY: Rubbish.

GREG: I've got to go, that's great. Good luck. I hope you have better luck with the acting than you clearly have had with the ladies.

ANDY: You don't know anything.

GREG: See you later.

GREG LEAVES.

MAGGIE: Bye.

ANDY: (angrily) Oh, I'd love to show him.

MAGGIE: Oh, don't worry, you will get off with another woman.

ANDY: (very annoyed) No, I mean my acting career. I get off with birds all the time.

MAGGIE: (laughing) Sorry.

ANDY: Why did you tell him about the Ronnie Corbett woman?

MAGGIE: I don't know.

SCENE 2. EXT. PATRICK STEWART'S TRAILER. DAY.

ANDY KNOCKS, HOLDING A SCRIPT.

PATRICK: Enter.

ANDY: Oh, hi. I'm probably going to get fired for even being here. I'm an extra in this but I'm an actor really and, well, I'm desperate and as I say, I'm really sorry but—

PATRICK: Oh, come on, don't apologise. Sit down.
(ANDY SITS DOWN NEXT TO PATRICK)
You're hustling. Acting is a noble profession, but it's a tough one. So how are you getting yourself out there?

ANDY: Well, I'm getting my face around in anything I can, I suppose I'm networking, but I've written a script . . .

PATRICK: Writing. You see, that's the key. I'm writing myself at the moment.

ANDY: Right.

PATRICK: You see, as actors, the only choice we have is 'yes' or 'no'. Whereas if you're writing your own material, you're creating your own opportunities.

ANDY: Well, this is my thinking, yes.

PATRICK: I'm writing this screenplay and I find the whole process absolutely exhilarating.

ANDY: What's yours about, if you don't mind me asking?

PATRICK: Well, how best to explain it? You've seen me in *X-Men*?

ANDY: Yes.

PATRICK: The character I am – Professor Charles Xavier – if you remember, he can control things with the power of his mind.

ANDY: Yes.

PATRICK: Make people do things and see things. So I thought, what if you could do that for real? I mean, not in a comic book world but in the real world.

ANDY: Oh, right.

PATRICK: So in my film, I play a man who controls the world with his mind.

ANDY: Right. That's interesting.

PATRICK: (earnest) Yes. For instance, I'm walking along and I see this beautiful girl and I think I'd like to see her naked and so all her clothes fall off.

ANDY: All her clothes fall off?

PATRICK: (deadpan) Mm, yes and she's scrabbling around to get them back on again but even before she can get her knickers on I've seen everything. I've seen it all.

ANDY: (frowning) Okay. It's a comedy, is it?

PATRICK: No. It's about what would happen if these things were possible.

ANDY: What's the story though? What's the . . .

PATRICK: Well, I do other stuff. Like, I'm riding my bike in the park and this policewoman says, 'Oy, you can't ride your bike on the grass' and I go 'Oh, no?' and her uniform falls off and she goes 'Argh' and she's trying to cover up but I've seen everything. Anyway and I get on my bike and I ride off . . .

(A PAUSE. PATRICK POINTS AT ANDY TO EMPHASISE)
. . . on the grass.

ANDY: So it's mainly you, sort of, going round seeing ladies' tits?

PATRICK: Mainly. And I do other stuff, like I go to the World Cup Final and it's Germany versus England and I wish that I were playing and suddenly I am and I score the winning goal and they carry me into the dressing room and there's Rooney and Beckham and then Posh Spice walks in and—

ANDY: Her clothes fall off?

PATRICK: Instantly.

ANDY: Sure.

PATRICK: And she doesn't know what's happening.

ANDY: No.

PATRICK: But I've seen—

ANDY/PATRICK: (simultaneously) . . . everything.

PATRICK: Again.

ANDY: Good. Is there a narrative at all, is there like a story in the film or is it just . . . ?

PATRICK: Well, I'm a sort of James Bond figure.

ANDY: Right.

PATRICK: And I have to go to Iraq to rescue these hostages and I get there and I rescue them but they're all women and they're naked because their clothes had rotted off, but I get them into the helicopter and I'm flying the helicopter but I can still sneak a look in the mirror and I can see everything. You know, one of them's bending over, two of them are kissing.

ANDY: They've turned lesbian?

PATRICK: Yes, because they'd been in the camp so long.

ANDY: It can happen. Well, look, good luck with that, I've just written a sitcom, but I wonder if you could give it to anyone you know in film or TV.

PATRICK: (serious) Is there any nudity in it?

ANDY: Any?

PATRICK: Any nudity in it?

ANDY: Not really.

PATRICK: (disappointed) Oh.

ANDY: Well, there could be.

PATRICK: Men or women?

ANDY: Either.
(PATRICK LOOKS UNHAPPY AT THIS IDEA)
Well, just women.

PATRICK: (nodding, smiling) Right.

ANDY: I'd need to rewrite but in the meantime if you could give it to anyone that you know in TV or film or . . .

PATRICK: Yes, definitely. I will 'make it so'.

(PATRICK POINTS AT ANDY AS HE USES HIS *STAR TREK* CATCHPHRASE. ANDY LOOKS BACK BLANKLY)

You've seen *Star Trek: The Next Generation*, have you?

ANDY: I haven't, no.

PATRICK: What, your wife won't let you have it on?

ANDY: I'm not married.

PATRICK: Oh, your girlfriend then?

ANDY: I haven't got a girlfriend, I live alone.

PATRICK: You're not married and you haven't got a girlfriend and you don't watch *Star Trek*?

ANDY: No.

PATRICK: (serious) Good lord.

SCENE 3. INT. AGENT'S OFFICE. DAY.

ANDY IS IN A MEETING WITH HIS AGENT. SHAUN 'BARRY OFF *EASTENDERS*' WILLIAMSON SITS ON A LITTLE STOOL IN THE CORNER, LICKING ENVELOPES.

AGENT: Well, you're probably wondering why I called you in for an unscheduled meeting.

ANDY: Got the wrong day?

AGENT: No, not at all, no. These are exciting times. I know you've been busy. I've been busy as well, generating a lot of heat about your sitcom script.

ANDY: Really?

AGENT: Yeah. Took the liberty of sending the script to a little production company called Picard Productions. They in turn sent it on to the comedy department at the BBC who have been in touch and apparently there's a lot of buzz.

ANDY: What, the BBC have called you?

AGENT: Yeah, yeah, they've been in touch and they just said we love the script, we'd like to get you in and just have a meeting, a chat and brainstorm everything.

ANDY: Brilliant.

AGENT: Yeah.

ANDY: Who's the production company?

AGENT: Well, you wouldn't have heard of them, it's a little production company called Picard Productions. Set up by Patrick Stewart and I just sent it to them and I just said—

ANDY: You sent this to Patrick Stewart?

AGENT: I just said, 'This is dynamite stuff, this is—'

ANDY: What, recently?

AGENT: Well, about two months ago and I just said—

ANDY: (interrupting angrily) No, you didn't. I gave it to him on set.

SILENCE. THE AGENT KNOWS HE'S BEEN CAUGHT OUT. ANDY STARES AT HIM.

AGENT: (pathetically) Even if I haven't done anything towards this, please can I still have my twelve and a half per cent?

A PAUSE.

ANDY: (sarcastic) Yeah, why not?

AGENT: Yeah? Thank you. That sort of is the way it's done, so . . . have you thought about who could play the main character?

ANDY: I'm playing the main character.

AGENT: Really? Are you sure? Because you're sort of a bit of a nobody, I'm not sure they'd cast a nobody in the main role.

ANDY: Well, we'd insist.

AGENT: Because I think the obvious choice is right under your nose. Barry.

ANDY: Yeah. No offence Shaun, I'm playing the lead character.

AGENT: Are you sure though, because he's really versatile.

ANDY: Yeah, I'm sure he is.

AGENT: You know, I mean, I'm not sure what it is you can do, but you know Barry can do all sorts.
(TO SHAUN)
Do your serious.

SHAUN: (serious) 'You do love me, Janine, you do, I know you do.'

AGENT: Yeah. Do your comical.

SHAUN: (laughing) 'Pat, you've trodden on my foot, get off.'

AGENT: He's a singer as well.

SHAUN: (singing at full blast) 'Mustang Sally—'

ANDY: Loud, isn't it?

AGENT: Loud? He did a gig once without a microphone.

SHAUN: There wasn't a microphone there.

AGENT: Nothing was there. No, he just turned up for this gig, there was no PA system, nothing.
(TO SHAUN)
Tell him what happened.

SHAUN: They were going to cancel the gig, I said, 'You're having a laugh, aren't you? I don't need a microphone, microphones are for wimps.'

AGENT: He said, 'Microphones are for wimps.'

SHAUN: And I belted it out, just like that, in front of, what, hundred and forty-odd people.

AGENT: Yeah, and they were really spread out because it was a thousand-seater venue. Lot of empty seats, didn't phase him, didn't bother him, just went for it. Go on do it.

SHAUN: (singing loudly) 'All you want to do is ride around Sally'
(TO THE AGENT)
. . . sing it with me now. . .

AGENT: (also singing loudly) 'Ride, Sally ride—'

ANDY: What are you doing?

AGENT: Just having a little sing-song.

ANDY: I'm doing the lead in this, okay, I'm playing the lead character. That's it, I don't want to discuss it.

AGENT: Are you sure though?

ANDY: (annoyed) Yes.

AGENT: I don't know, you know I just – you've never struck me as a funny bloke.

ANDY: Sorry?

AGENT: Well, you always come in here and you're really negative and a bit . . .

ANDY: Doesn't that tell you something?

AGENT: Well, I know what you're trying to say but I don't get Barry any work and he's happy.

SHAUN: Not entirely happy.

AGENT: All right, Bar, calm down, mate, giving it all this in front of another client. If you've got an issue have a private meeting with me but don't...

(HE POINTS AT ANDY, STILL TALKING TO SHAUN)

you've been hanging around with him too much, giving it this.

(OPENS AND CLOSES HIS HAND IN A TALKING GESTURE)

THE AGENT ROLLS HIS EYES AT ANDY, WHO LOOKS AWAY.

SCENE 4. INT. BBC OFFICE. DAY.

ANDY AND HIS AGENT ARE BEING SHOWN INTO THE OFFICE OF IAIN MORRIS, HEAD OF BBC COMEDY. IAIN OFFERS HIS HAND.

IAIN: Hi, hi, hello. Iain Morris, Head of New Comedy.

ANDY: I'm Andy, this is my agent.

AGENT: Darren Lamb, nice to meet you.

IAIN: Hello. Nice to meet you. Good. Okay, well, take a seat.

THEY SIT DOWN.

ANDY: Thank you.

IAIN: Okay, well, we're just waiting for one more person. I want you to meet Damon Beesley, he's a producer here but he's also a great writer, he's a script editor and I'd like to—

OUTSIDE THE DOOR WE HEAR SOME MUTTERING AND A HIGH-PITCHED CAMP LAUGH.

DAMON: (entering the office, extremely camp) Room for a small one? Cheeky, started without me, not for the first time. What's he been saying? It's all lies.

IAIN: Lucky for you I haven't said anything at all. Andy, this is Damon.

ANDY: Hi.

DAMON: Oh, bloody hell . . .

(BOWS IN MOCK-WORSHIP TO ANDY)

. . . we're not worthy, we're not worthy. *Je t'aime* your script, I wet myself laughing. At last, some real talent at the BBC.

ANDY: Cheers.

AGENT: (to ANDY, about DAMON) He's happy.

DAMON: Where are we?

IAIN: (to ANDY) Well, I just wanted to find out where you see this project going.

AGENT: BBC 1.

ANDY: No, I don't actually.

AGENT: BBC 3?

ANDY: No, BBC 2. I think that's really good for comedy and I think if you come up with a new project on BBC 1 you've got to really water it down, do you know what I mean? I don't want a laughter track.

AGENT: No laughs.

ANDY: There'll be laughs.

AGENT: There'll be big laughs.

ANDY: But I just want it to be, I don't want it to be a comedy aimed at people without a sense of humour, if you know what I mean, I want people to be able to think about it. I don't want it filmed in front of a live studio audience.

AGENT: Unless you guys disagree with that in which case we can change all that and just do whatever you want to do.

ANDY: No.

IAIN: No, no, no, there's no need to do that, no. What I would say though is, because this is your first project, I would like you to initially write with someone else.

AGENT: He will write with anyone.

ANDY: I won't work with anyone.

AGENT: He will not write with anyone, that's a deal breaker.

ANDY: (to AGENT) No. Ssh.
(TO IAIN)
I'd like to write it myself just because it's based on my own experiences really. The character is based on a boss I used to work for and I just generally think the best things are auteured.

AGENT: (giggling) Turd.
(THE AGENT LOOKS AROUND, EXPECTING BIG LAUGHS. HE IS MET WITH SILENCE)
No?

ANDY SHAKES HIS HEAD IN SILENT DESPAIR.

IAIN: All right, well, I'm happy for you to write it yourself, but I would feel happier getting Damon here just to work with you as script editor, you know someone to bounce ideas off, just tidy up the first script. I think it's a little bit flabby.

ANDY: Yeah, it's a bag of ideas at the moment but yeah. Fine.

IAIN: Okay, well, I think the best thing to move this forward is to get you two together in a little room . . .

AGENT: (innuendo) Oh!

ANDY: Sssh . . .

IAIN AND DAMON STARE WEARILY AT THE AGENT.

AGENT: Inappropriate at a meeting at the BBC, that.

ANDY: Okay, that would be, that would be great.

IAIN: Okay.

AGENT: Okay, let's talk cash, because as you know this script is piping hot. So we're looking for big bucks on this one.

ANDY: No, we don't need to talk cash now.

AGENT: We need to talk a little bit about cash, just get some money up front for, you know, supplies, pencils.

IAIN: I could probably find you a computer.

AGENT: Are you happy with a computer?

ANDY: Yes.

AGENT: Yeah? He's happy with a computer. We'll just go with that.

IAIN: Okay, good.

AGENT: You sure you're all right?

ANDY: Yes.
(THEY ALL STAND AND SHAKE HANDS)
Well, thank you very much.

IAIN: Great. Thank you very much.

SCENE 5. INT. FILM SET. DAY.

A GROUP OF EXTRAS, INCLUDING MAGGIE AND GREG, ARE WAITING
OFF-SET, DRESSED IN PERIOD COSTUME. ANDY ENTERS WITH A BOTTLE
OF CHAMPAGNE.

ANDY: (singing , showing MAGGIE the champagne) 'Celebrate good
times, come on.'

MAGGIE: Did you get it?
(MAGGIE LEAPS UP EXCITEDLY AND HUGS ANDY)
Oh, brilliant.

ANDY: Oh, yes.

GREG: Someone's celebrating. What, a wealthy old relative popped her
clogs, has she?

ANDY: No. So, why are we celebrating? Could be because of the TV show
the BBC have just given me?

GREG: (sceptical) TV show?

ANDY: Yeah, pilot for a sitcom. So—

GREG: What sitcom?

ANDY: The sitcom that I wrote.

GREG: You're not funny.

ANDY: (laughing) Well, the BBC beg to differ.

GREG: What's it about?

ANDY: It's just about my old boss I used to work for. Write about what you know. And I'd just like to say I've got something for everyone just to say thanks for all the great times.

(HE SHOWS THEM ALL THE CHAMPAGNE. THE OTHER EXTRAS MAKE
APPRECIATIVE NOISES)
Just a few crumbs from the table, share the wealth. I am devastated
really to be leaving you lot behind . . .
(TO LUCY)
. . . especially you, Julie.

LUCY: Lucy.

ANDY: Whatever. Shouldn't you be in costume?

LUCY: (deadpan, not getting the joke) I am in costume.

ANDY: Yeah? Why did we never . . . And you . . .
(POINTS TO A FAT EXTRA)
Will you please call me?

FAT EXTRA: I haven't got your number.

ANDY: Yeah, 079 . . .

ANDY BEGINS TO MUMBLE NUMBER INCOHERENTLY.

FAT EXTRA: 07 . . . what?

ANDY: 079 then a four, all the threes, put them all in otherwise it doesn't work and in a particular order. Get them off Julie if you can't—

LUCY: Lucy.

ANDY: Whatever.

LUCY: I haven't got your number.

ANDY: Haven't you? I'll text it to you.

LUCY: You haven't got my number.

ANDY: (smiling) I know but I'll work it out, and then we'll all have it, won't we? And we can arrange the camping trip we've always talked about.
(TO MAGGIE)
Anyway I'll see you later.

MAGGIE: Yeah, okay, bye.

ANDY STARTS TO WALK AWAY.

ANDY: (to GREG) See you later, man. You all right? You look a bit pale.
(CALLING OUT)
Could you get some rouge for Greg?

GREG: I'm fine.

ANDY: You all right? You look a bit sick.

SCENE 6. INT.
BBC OFFICE. DAY.

A MONTAGE OF SCENES FEATURING ANDY AND DAMON WORKING ON
THE SCRPIT, BRAIN-STORMING IDEAS AND WORKSHOPPING SCENES.
PERIODICALLY, DAMON LAUGHS HIS HYSTERICAL, HIGH-PITCHED
LAUGH AND ANDY WINCES. THEN INTO:

DAMON: I think structurally we're all higgledypiggledypew and I think we can get to the boss coming in quicker and set him up straight away.

ANDY: Well, we could start with him actually walking in to work, in the first scene he just actually comes in and that's when you see him. The real Ray used to come in to work every day without fail, he'd just walk up to someone and say something like 'Have you done the invoices?'

And they'd go 'No'. And he'd go
(ANDY PUTS ON A GRUFF VOICE AND PULLS A FACE)
'Is he having a laugh? Are you having a laugh?'

DAMON LETS RIP WITH YET ANOTHER HIGH-PITCHED LAUGH.

DAMON: (hysterical laugh) Brilliant. We're having that. That's super, that's funny. Do it again.

ANDY: That's what he used to do, just go up to someone and go, every time, 'Is he having a laugh? Are you having a laugh?'

DAMON: That's great, that will be a catchphrase.

ANDY: Well, I'm not sure about catchphrases.

DAMON: No, no, it'll be great. People can say it. 'Is he having a laugh? Are you having a laugh?'

ANDY: I just think catchphrases are too easy.

DAMON: 'Are you having a laugh?'

ANDY: Yeah, I think it could get a little bit annoying after a while.

DAMON: Do you fancy a coffee? I haven't had one in about, oh, twenty minutes. Shall I get one from upstairs or do you fancy one from Costa's? It might take me a bit longer.

ANDY: That one then.

DAMON: (laughing) 'Are you having a laugh?'
(HE EXITS. AS HE DOES, MAGGIE COMES IN)
Oh, hello. Can we help?

ANDY: Hi,
(TO DAMON)
it's my friend Maggie.
(TO MAGGIE)
Come in. This is Damon.

DAMON: Oh, you cow, I love your bag.

MAGGIE: Oh, thank you.

DAMON: I'm just off on a cappuccino run, do you want one?

MAGGIE: No, it's fine, I'm just here for a wee minute.

DAMON: Okay, well, lovely to meet you. See you again hopefully.

MAGGIE: Yes.

DAMON: Bye for now.

MAGGIE: Bye.

DAMON: (spotting someone in the corridor) Oy, Bowker, you poofter!

ANDY WELCOMES MAGGIE IN. SHE SITS DOWN IN DAMON'S CHAIR.

MAGGIE: Look at you.

ANDY: Take a seat. Take a letter.

MAGGIE: (pretending to type) I will.

ANDY: Are you well?

MAGGIE: Yeah, well, you know, got my health. Listen, how's it going here?

ANDY: He's doing my head in.

MAGGIE: Who?

ANDY: Who? Who? Who do you . . . the owner of this monstrosity.
(HE HOLDS UP A PINK FLUFFY PEN)
Quentin Crisp. He's just skipped down the corridor going 'I want
a cappuccino'. Oh, he's too gay, he's too gay.

MAGGIE: What do you mean, 'He's too gay'?

ANDY: No one needs to be that gay.

MAGGIE: What do you mean, 'He's too gay'?

ANDY: He's a cliché of a gay. If I was doing *Give Us A Clue* and the clue came up 'a gay bloke', I'd do him. Unbelievable.

MAGGIE: Well, that's just a wee bit homophobic.

ANDY: It's not homophobic. No, I don't care how much arse sex he has . . .
(THEY BOTH LAUGH)
. . . but do you have to be that camp? Screaming and clapping, when does that happen? When do you suddenly think, well, I prefer a nice little savaloy to a battered cod, so I'd better walk like this.

MAGGIE: I liked him.

ANDY: Course you do. Women like you love the gays.

MAGGIE: What do you mean, women like me?

ANDY: Wrong side of thirty, six out of ten for looks, you've got someone to go to the disco with, haven't you? And you walk in with him and you go, look, I'm not shy, I think I've got a bloke. But if a bloke comes up that you fancy you go 'Oh, him, oh, he's just my gay friend'. Perfect, it's a safety net.

MAGGIE: Six out of ten?

ANDY: Yeah.

MAGGIE: Is that all I get? Six out of ten.

ANDY: I don't know—

MAGGIE: Look me in the eye and say six out of ten.

ANDY: So, look you in your wonky eye or your good eye?

SCENE 7. INT.
BBC CORRIDOR. DAY.

DAMON IS RETURNING WITH SOME COFFEES. MAGGIE PASSES HIM.

DAMON: See you.

MAGGIE: Bye.
(STRUCK BY AN IDEA)
Oh, I was going to ask you, how are you getting on with Andy?

DAMON: Oh, he's lovely, isn't he? He's very talented. Very funny script.

MAGGIE: You've not run into his funny little ways?

DAMON: No.

MAGGIE: Well, he can be quite odd sometimes. I just wanted to let you know that he is like that with everybody.

DAMON: How do you mean?

MAGGIE: Well, like noise. He's got this thing about noise. Like I've seen him at a restaurant, somebody at the table nearby is cutting their meat too loudly and he's like getting himself all annoyed about it.

DAMON: Oh, note to self. Cut meat quietly.

THEY BOTH LAUGH.

MAGGIE: Yes. And you might find you might want to just tone it down a little bit.

DAMON: Tone what down?

MAGGIE: (trying to be helpful) Well, you're quite camp which is great, but I think maybe sometimes he thinks you're too gay.

DAMON: (suddenly serious) Did he say that?

MAGGIE: Yeah, but I mean he wasn't being nasty about it. I just think, oh no, I've said the wrong thing, I shouldn't have, should I?

DAMON: No, no, I'm fine. I'm glad you told me.

MAGGIE: Oh, good, thank God for that, I thought I'd put my foot in it by telling . . .

DAMON: Not at all.

MAGGIE: Okay. Well, it was lovely to meet you then.

DAMON: Absolutely.

MAGGIE: Yes.

DAMON: Lovely to see you.

MAGGIE: See you again.

DAMON: I'll take it on board.

MAGGIE: Bye.

MAGGIE AND DAMON WALK AWAY IN OPPOSITE DIRECTIONS.

SCENE 8. INT. MAGGIE'S FLAT. DAY.

MAGGIE ENTERS HER FLAT. WE SEE THAT IT'S VERY UNTIDY, WITH OLD MAGAZINES AND CLOTHES EVERYWHERE. SHE PICKS UP HER POST AND PLAYS HER ANSWERPHONE MESSAGES.

ANSWERPHONE: You have one message. Message one.

DAD: Hello, dear, it's your daddy here with your mummy. Nothing important.

MUM: Oh, give it to me. Hello, dear, great news about Andy, we're so pleased for him and it just got us thinking that maybe you should try and do something with your life.
(MAGGIE ROLLS HER EYES)
I mean your dad and I aren't expecting anything spectacular, we were just thinking maybe a wee job you could be proud of.
(MAGGIE CLENCHES HER FISTS)
You know we love you so much, we hate to think of you growing old and being poor and living in squalor and dying a spinster. So just give us a call to put our minds at rest that you're not just frittering your life away, would you? Okay? And if things get any worse you can always come back home, we've still got your room.

MAGGIE LOOKS DEFLATED.

DAD: Well, it's sort of my study now.

MUM: Oh, we could easily squeeze in a tiny wee single bed. All right then, give us a call, sweetheart, bye for now.

DAD: Bye dear.

MAGGIE: Bye.

THE ANSWERPHONE CLICKS OFF. MAGGIE SITS ALONE IN HER SILENT FLAT.

SCENE 9. INT.
IAIN'S OFFICE. DAY.

ANDY, IAIN AND DAMON ARE SITTING IN IAIN'S OFFICE, HAVING A
SCRIPT MEETING.

IAIN: Okay, great. Well, I love the changes, I think this is looking great,
well done.

ANDY: Oh, thank you.

ANDY SMILES AT DAMON, WHO LOOKS AWAY.

IAIN: I think we're ready to move things forward a stage. My thought
is I'd like to shoot a non-broadcast pilot with a view to making a series.

ANDY: (huge smile) Oh, okay, thank you.

IAIN: All right.

ANDY: Brilliant.

IAIN: So are you happy with the way things have gone so far?

ANDY: Definitely.

IAIN: You happy working with Damon?

ANDY: Definitely.

IAIN: No problems in your working relationship? Nothing you want
to discuss?

ANDY: No.

DAMON: (bitterly) Okay. I'm not too gay for you then?

IAIN: Damon.

DAMON: I'm sorry, I said I wasn't going to say anything but he's lying through his teeth. Excuse me.

DAMON FLOUNCES OUT.

IAIN: Your friend, Maggie, is it? She told him what you said about him.

ANDY: What did I say about him?

IAIN: That he's too gay.

ANDY: (anxious) Oh, no, she's an idiot. She's an idiot.

IAIN: So you didn't say that?

ANDY: Yes, but he wasn't meant to hear it.

IAIN: Well, what concerns me is if you're so homophobic you couldn't work with a single gay person—

ANDY: No, no, no, no I'm not homophobic. In fact I actually said to her, I said, I don't care how much arse sex he has,
(HE REALISES HE'S CROSSED THE LINE AND LOSES HIS TRAIN OF THOUGHT)
. . . he's just too . . . what was it . . . I can't remember what I said.

IAIN: You're aware that I'm gay?

ANDY: Well, no, you don't make a song and dance about it. You don't go 'Ooh . . .'
(HE PUTS ON A CAMP VOICE AND BENDS HIS WRIST BUT VERY QUICKLY REALISES THIS IS INAPPROPRIATE)

IAIN: I'll stop you there.

ANDY: Go on.

IAIN: What concerns me is we've all got to work together and if this is where we are when we've only just started, where the hell are we going to be a month or so down the line?

ANDY: (nervously rambling) It won't be a problem because I'll just apologise to Damo and just, everybody gets wound up with the people they work in close proximity with. Little things wind you up, so it doesn't matter. It's not a case of being straight or gay, it's my neuroses and I'll just you know–

IAIN: Well, do you think you could put your hang-ups and your neuroses on hold?

ANDY: Yes.

IAIN: He won't be around for long.

ANDY'S FACE DROPS.

ANDY: What, Aids?

IAIN: Sorry?

ANDY: Is it Aids?

IAIN: No, I mean the pilot will only take a couple of months.

ANDY: Oh, yeah. Oh.

IAIN: Right, listen, talk to Damo, I'll talk to him, we'll see where we are and if we feel we can go forward with this project or not.

ANDY: Oh, we can. Oh, okay, I'll talk to him, I'll talk to him now.

IAIN: Okay, good.

ANDY: Okay. Okay, I'll go and talk to him.

ANDY GETS UP AND LEAVES QUICKLY.

IAIN: All right, bye.

ROUTE
DO NOT
OBSTRUCT

SCENE 10. INT. MAGGIE'S FLAT. DAY.

MAGGIE OPENS THE DOOR TO ANDY.

MAGGIE: Hello.

ANDY: (angrily) Hi. Do me a favour, stay out of my business.

ANDY STARTS TO WALK AWAY BUT MAGGIE PULLS HIM INSIDE.

MAGGIE: Andy, what? Come in, come in.

ANDY: I may have lost the pilot thanks to you.

MAGGIE: Why?

ANDY: (raising his voice) Why? Because you stuck your nose in once again where it wasn't needed. Telling Damo I thought he was too gay. What were you thinking?

MAGGIE: I was thinking that you were stressed and I just wanted to help you.

ANDY: What, that's helping me, is it? I just can't believe the stupidity sometimes–

MAGGIE: (upset) Oh, Andy, don't be like this, I can't cope. I'm having a bad time at the moment.

ANDY: (very angry) Sorry. What's a bad time for you? Tie-dyed the wrong T-shirt? You lost a kookie brooch? I was just about getting to where I wanted to be and you may have fucked it up. I've been grovelling all day at the BBC.

MAGGIE: What do you mean?

ANDY: I've got a meeting there at four o'clock, right. They may pull the plug. Imagine if they pull the plug, how am I going to look you in the face again?

MAGGIE: Do you want me to say something?

ANDY: You're not listening.

MAGGIE: I'm sorry. I'm sorry, Andy, I don't know what you want me to say. I was just trying to help you.

ANDY: I don't want you to help me any more. I want you to stop living like a child, just floating through life like everything's okay until it actually affects someone, okay? So really my advice to you is, is you've got to grow up.
(HE POINTS TO HER FLAT)
Clean up, just sort your own mess out before you get involved in my life, really.

ANDY LEAVES. MAGGIE SLOWLY CLOSES THE DOOR AND WANDERS
INTO HER LIVING ROOM, LOOKING AT THE CLUTTER OF HER FLAT.

SCENE 11. INT.
BBC FOYER. DAY.

ANDY SITS WAITING. A SECRETARY APPEARS.

SECRETARY: Do you want to follow me?

ANDY: Yeah.

CUT TO ANDY, IAIN AND DAMON ALL IN IAIN'S OFFICE.

IAIN: It's unfortunate we've ended up in this position, Andy. I'm not going to speak for Damon. Damon, do you want to . . .

DAMON: Well, things were said that were very hurtful.

ANDY: Yeah.

DAMON: But your apology means a lot to me. So if you're happy to work with me then I'd like to carry on working with you.

ANDY: (humble) Definitely. Definitely, yeah.

DAMON: I'm such a huge fan of this project.

ANDY: I'm a big fan of yours so . . .

DAMON: Great.

IAIN: Happy?

ANDY: (relieved) Definitely.

DAMON: Water under the bridge.

IAIN: Wonderful. Okay, let's get some dates sorted and get the ball rolling on his project.

DAMON: (standing up and approaching ANDY with his arms outstretched) Come on, silly, huggy bears. Okay?

ANDY AND DAMON HUG AWKWARDLY. ANDY MOVES TOWARDS IAIN WITH HIS ARMS OPEN.

ANDY: Do you want one?

IAIN: No.

ANDY: Just normal?

IAIN: Yes.

IAIN AND ANDY SHAKE HANDS.

ANDY: Okay.

IAIN: Okay.

ANDY: Brilliant. Okay, thanks. Cheers.

ANDY LEAVES THE OFFICE. IAIN PATS DAMON ON THE BACK.

SCENE 12. INT. MAGGIE'S FLAT. DAY.

MAGGIE IS CLEANING HER FLAT, PACKING AWAY HER SOFT TOYS AND CHILDISH NICK-NACKS, TAKING DOWN HER POSTERS.

CUT TO MAGGIE IN HER FRESHLY DE-CLUTTERED FLAT, CAREFULLY STRAIGHTENING HER HAIR.

SCENE 13. INT. FILM SET. DAY.

DIRECTOR: Cut, thank you.

CREW AND ACTORS BEGIN MOVING AROUND THE SET. CUT TO MAGGIE, OUT OF COSTUME, LEAVING THE STUDIO. SHE OPENS THE DOOR FOR ANOTHER EXTRA AND BEGINS TO WALK AWAY.

MAGGIE: See you.

MAN: Okay, I'll see you soon.

MAGGIE: Yeah, bye.

ANDY IS SITTING ON SOME STEPS BY THE DOOR.

ANDY: (calling out to catch her attention) Maggie.

MAGGIE WALKS TOWARDS ANDY TENTATIVELY.

MAGGIE: Hi.

ANDY: You all right?

MAGGIE: Yeah. And you?

ANDY: Yeah.
(ANDY SPEAKS INTO HIS MOBILE PHONE)
Okay, now.
(HE HOLDS THE PHONE UP TO MAGGIE. IT'S ON SPEAKERPHONE. PATRICK STEWART STARTS TO SPEAK)

PATRICK: Hello Maggie.

MAGGIE: (unsure) Hello?

PATRICK: This is Patrick Stewart here. And the reason you're hearing my rich, sexy voice is that Andy is not man enough to apologise himself, even though he knows he's in the wrong, that's why he's asked me to do it for him. Please look at his fat, expressionless face.
(MAGGIE LOOKS AT ANDY AND GIVES HIM A SMILE)
He doesn't mean any of the things he said and he knows that you don't have a malicious bone in your body and was just trying to help.

MAGGIE: Thank you.

PATRICK: If you can find it in your heart to forgive him then please 'make it so'.
(PAUSE)
Have you seen *Star Trek: The Next Generation*?

MAGGIE: Er, no, I haven't actually.

PATRICK: Never mind. Incidentally Maggie, are you an actress? Because I'm writing a film and I'd love you to be in it.

ANDY: (interrupting him and hanging up) Okay. No, she can't, okay, thanks, cheers.

MAGGIE: What was that about a film?

ANDY: You don't want any part of it, trust me.
(THERE'S AN AWKWARD SILENCE. THEY LOOK AT EACH OTHER)
Your hair looks really nice.

MAGGIE: Shut your face.

ANDY: What? It does.

MAGGIE: Well, thanks.

ANDY: The pilot's fine by the way.

MAGGIE: Thank God for that.

ANDY: Yeah.

PAUSE.

MAGGIE: I just wanted to let you know that I have taken on board all that stuff that you were saying about growing up.

ANDY: (feeling uncomfortable and guilty) Oh, don't, please, shut up.

MAGGIE: Well, I have.

ANDY: Oh, don't.

MAGGIE: Well, you know what I mean.

ANDY: Well, I'm mortified actually.

MAGGIE: No, I know, I know, but you were right.

ANDY: I wasn't right. You're about the most grown-up person I know.

MAGGIE: Sort of the only person you know.

ANDY: You win by default.
(MAGGIE LAUGHS)
Correct.
(TAKING MAGGIE'S HAND)
I'm really sorry.

MAGGIE: (smiling, looking over to the car park) Can you let go of my hand, please?

ANDY: (letting go of her hand) Of course. That would ruin everything, wouldn't it?

MAGGIE: He's quite a nice one though, isn't he?

ANDY: He's fine.

MAGGIE: I've been working up to say hello to him for the last couple of days.

ANDY: Sure.

MAGGIE: What do you think?

ANDY: You know what I think.

MAGGIE: What?

ANDY: I think you're a tart. Go on then. Work your magic.

MAGGIE: Yeah, I will.

ANDY: I'll see you later, yeah?

MAGGIE: Mm, see you.

ANDY: See you.

ANDY AND MAGGIE BOTH WALK AWAY. MAGGIE HEADS IN THE DIRECTION OF THE MAN SHE'S BEEN LOOKING AT BUT AT THE LAST SECOND CHANGES DIRECTION AND JOINS ANDY.

ANDY: That was quick.

MAGGIE: I couldn't think of anything witty to say. He was on the phone anyway.

ANDY: Sure. What would you rather do . . .

MAGGIE: Go on then.

ANDY: . . . Wake up and your teeth have sort of fallen out or wake up and your hair's fallen out? Or wake up and your toes have fallen off?

MAGGIE: (laughing) What, has my hair gone for good?

THEY STROLL OFF THROUGH THE STUDIO LOT.

EXTRAS
Episode 1

CAST LIST
Andy Millman RICKY GERVAIS
Maggie Jacobs ASHLEY JENSEN
Agent STEPHEN MERCHANT
Shaun SHAUN WILLIAMSON
Iain Morris GUY HENRY
Damon Beesley MARTIN SAVAGE
and KEITH CHEGWIN

Guest Starring ORLANDO BLOOM

Defence Lawyer SOPHIA MYLES
Rita LIZA TARBUCK
Kimberley SARAH MOYLE
Gobbler ANDREW BUCKLEY
Brains JAMIE CHAPMAN
Louise KATHERINE JAKEWAYS
Judge COLIN WAKEFIELD
Make-Up Woman SARAH PRESTON
Sitcom Director TOBY WALTON

Written & Directed by
RICKY GERVAIS &
STEPHEN MERCHANT

FILM CLIP:
'REJECTION OVERRULED'

A COURTROOM SCENE. ORLANDO BLOOM IS ADDRESSING THE JURY, ONE OF WHOM IS MAGGIE.

ORLANDO: Maybe I'm stupid, maybe the jury's stupid, so many things don't add up – you say you were in a restaurant, you ate alone, but no one remembers you. And the flowers, the flowers . . . it seems very odd that you would send your wife flowers and not include a card. Whenever I sent my wife flowers I always wrote a card.

THE FEMALE DEFENCE LAWYER RISES TO HER FEET.

DEFENCE LAWYER: Objection! When did you ever send me flowers?

ORLANDO: I sent you flowers . . .

DEFENCE LAWYER: Name me one occasion when you sent me flowers.

ORLANDO: After your mother died.

DEFENCE LAWYER: A wreath doesn't count!

ORLANDO: Of course it does.

DEFENCE LAWYER: (to JURY) Does that count?
(TO JUDGE)
M'Lud, does that count?

ORLANDO: It's still flowers. You asked when did I ever send you flowers. Let's stick to the facts, shall we?

DEFENCE LAWYER: Shove your facts and your flowers—

JUDGE: (hitting gavel) Order! Order! I order you . . . to kiss and make up!

ORLANDO/DEFENCE LAWYER: M'lud?

JUDGE: You heard me!

THEY LOOK AT EACH OTHER SUSPICIOUSLY BUT SUDDENLY THEIR ICY PROFESSIONAL EXTERIORS MELT AND THEY MOVE IN FOR A BIG HOLLYWOOD KISS. THE JURY CHEER. THE TOUGH-LOOKING DEFENDANT WEEPS WITH JOY.

DIRECTOR: (off screen) And cut there. Thank you everybody, thank you very much guys.

SCENE 1. INT. COURTROOM FILM SET. DAY.

THE SCENE BREAKS UP. THE FEMALE JURORS CROWD ROUND ORLANDO, ASKING FOR AUTOGRAPHS AND PICTURES. HE OBLIGES. MAGGIE'S PHONE RINGS.

MAGGIE: (into phone) Hello?

CUT TO ANDY ON THE SET OF HIS SITCOM.

ANDY: All right?

MAGGIE: Hey, how you doing?

ANDY: Nervous.

MAGGIE: Why?

ANDY: Big night, isn't it?

MAGGIE: Why, why, what's happened?

ANDY: Filming the sitcom.

MAGGIE: What sitcom?

ANDY: My sitcom. You're coming down!

MAGGIE: Oh, yeah, I thought that was next week.

ANDY: No, it's tonight, seven-thirty. Then every Thursday for six weeks. Put it in your diary.

MAGGIE: I haven't got a diary.

ANDY: It's a figure of speech.

MAGGIE: You doing a speech?

ANDY: (sarcastic) Well, this has been helpful, I'm glad I called.

MAGGIE: All right, listen, let me know how it goes, hey?

ANDY: You're coming down!

MAGGIE: Oh, all right then. What time does it start?

ANDY: Seven-thirty!

MAGGIE: All right then. Bye.

ANDY: All right, cheers.

ANDY HANGS UP, SHAKING HIS HEAD.

SCENE 2. INT.
COURTROOM FILM SET. DAY.

MAGGIE IS THE ONLY ONE WHO DOESN'T ASK ORLANDO FOR A PICTURE OR AN AUTOGRAPH. ORLANDO NOTICES THIS AS HE POSES FOR PICS WITH THE OTHERS. HE LOOKS AT MAGGIE. SHE SMILES AND ROLLS HER EYES. HE NODS BACK. THE EXTRAS DISPERSE.

ORLANDO: All right, see you later, bye, yeah.
(TO MAGGIE)
Hiya.

MAGGIE: Hi.

ORLANDO: What were you rolling your eyes at?

MAGGIE: Just all that lot, all 'Oohh,' fawning all over you. That must get a bit exhausting, hey?

ORLANDO: Yeah, it can be pretty exhausting, yeah.

MAGGIE: Well, especially 'cause they're just doing it 'cause you're famous.

ORLANDO: Well . . . They're not doing it just because I'm famous though.

MAGGIE: Well, it is though, isn't it?

ORLANDO: No, it's my looks as well.

MAGGIE: Hmm, I just don't think that they would be acting like that if you weren't a film star.

ORLANDO: Yeahhhh, they pretty much would, yeah. I've always had attention.

MAGGIE: Well, all I'm saying is, like, if you were the prop boy you'd just get ignored.

ORLANDO: (smiling) What, with this face? I wouldn't get ignored. I'll tell you who does get ignored. Johnny Depp. On the set of *Pirates of the Caribbean* the birds just walk straight past him. 'Get out the bloody way, whoever you are, we want to get to Orlando.' They're round me like flies round shit.

MAGGIE: They ignore Johnny Depp?

ORLANDO: Yeahhhh. They're going, 'Oh Orlando, who's that freak over there that we didn't notice?' I'm going, 'It's Johnny Depp.' They're going, 'Who cares, you know? You were Legolas in *The Lord of the Rings*!'
(DOING AN IMPERSONATION OF JOHNNY DEPP, WAVING HIS HANDS IN THE AIR)
'Ooh look at me, I make art-house movies, ooh I've got scissors for hands.'
(HE STARES AT MAGGIE.)
Willy Wonka? Johnny Wanker.

MAGGIE REACTS.

SCENE 3. INT. SITCOM SET. DAY.

ANDY'S AGENT APPEARS.

AGENT: Hey, buddy! All right, how's it going, all set?

ANDY: (serious) I'm not sure I'm doing the right thing.

AGENT: No?

ANDY: This is not the comedy I set out to do. I wanted something real that people would relate to and it's all changed because people have stuck their nose in.

AGENT: Yeah, I'm hearing you, all right, but do you know what? This is typical first night nerves, all right? I know what you're thinking, you're thinking, 'Oh, the script's not funny, it's crass, it's lowest common denominator'. And you know, you're right. But don't worry about it because people will watch anything, all right? Particularly if it's on after *EastEnders* and they haven't got to change the channel. Those sort of morons will help us win the ratings war and ratings in the end are what count. And merchandise.

ANDY: Well, it's not what counts for me, all right? I wanted to write a good, credible comedy that would stand the test of time.

AGENT: Yeah, I know, okay. Well, I agree and I was just saying that 'cause that's what I thought you wanted me to say.

ANDY: Well, don't, tell the truth.

AGENT: Well, I will and the, the truth is, if you're not happy I'm right behind you.

ANDY: Right.

AGENT: And I've got the perfect replacement.

ANDY: For what?

AGENT: For you, for your character, it's only Barry.

SHAUN WILLIAMSON APPEARS.

ANDY: All right, Shaun.

AGENT: He's all set, knows all the lines, he's ready to go, can step in. What's your character's catchphrase?

ANDY: It's not a catchphrase, it's something the real Ray used to actually say.

AGENT: What was it?

ANDY: 'Are you having a laugh? Is he having a laugh?'

THE AGENT REMAINS STONY-FACED.

AGENT: Look at that, nothing, stony-face. And I love a giggle, me. I love a laugh, don't I?
(TO SHAUN)
You do it.

SHAUN: 'Are you having a laugh? Is he having a laugh?'

THE AGENT FALLS ABOUT IN HYSTERICS.

AGENT: (laughs) It's good, isn't it? I don't know how he comes up with it.

ANDY: He didn't come up with it.

AGENT: Yeah. The thing about Barry is, and I've noticed this, right, people will laugh at him, they never laugh with him, it's extraordinary. Look at that face, there's a sort of undercurrent of tragedy to it, isn't there?
(TO SHAUN)
Do it.

SHAUN: (as RAY) 'Are you having a laugh? Is he having a laugh?'

AGENT: (laughing) I love it because he's desperate.

ANDY: Yeah, the role's taken, cheers.

HEAD OF COMEDY IAIN MORRIS AND PRODUCER DAMON BEESLEY APPEAR ON SET.

IAIN: Pardon us. Hello, how's it going? All right?

ANDY: Yeah, everything all right?

IAIN: I think so. Damon?

DAMON: Yeah, everybody's in. Rehearsals should kick off about twenty-past.

ANDY: Right.

DAMON: Er, just one tiny incy winsy little hiccup. Paul Shane's dropped out.

ANDY: Why?

DAMON: He was worried it was a little bit too broad.

ANDY: (incredulous) Paul Shane thinks this is too broad? Right.

DAMON: Well, it's only a little part, isn't it? We've got a replacement, Keith's on his way.

ANDY: Keith?

IAIN: Keith Chegwin.

ANDY: Keith Chegwin? Can he act? He's a TV presenter, isn't he?

IAIN: We thought that'd add a nice little bit of extra kitsch value.

ANDY: Yeah, great.

AGENT: You see that does annoy me a little bit.

DAMON: Why?

AGENT: Well, if you're looking for a podgy fella who'll do anything to get on the telly – Barry.

ANDY: You were trying to get him my part a minute ago.

AGENT: Well, he's versatile. He's multi-talented. You never even saw his one-man version of *Romeo and Juliet*, it was extr—
(TO SHAUN)
Well, do a bit for them, it was brilliant.

SHAUN: (playing both parts, very earnestly)
(AS ROMEO)
'O, wilt thou leave me so unsatisfied?'
(AS JULIET, WITH HIGH-PITCHED VOICE)
'What satisfaction canst thou have to-night?'
(AS ROMEO)
'The exchange of thy love's faithful vow for mine.'
(AS JULIET)
'Oh I gave thee mine before thou didst request it: And yet I would it were to give again.'

ANDY REACTS. HE GLANCES AT THE AGENT, WHO IS ALMOST IN TEARS.

AGENT: Always gets me, that bit. Well done.

SHAUN: All right, okay.

THE AGENT AND SHAUN HUG. ANDY ROLLS HIS EYES.

SCENE 4. INT.
COURTROOM FILM SET. DAY.

MAGGIE IS WAITING ON SET. AN ATTRACTIVE, WELL-GROOMED WOMAN
IN EXPENSIVE CLOTHES BOTHERS HER.

LOUISE: Maggie. Hello . . .

MAGGIE: Oh, hi.

LOUISE: You're not still an extra, are you? Oh God, that must do your
head in. You know I'm an actress now? How long have you been an extra?

MAGGIE: Supporting artist.

LOUISE: How long have you been doing that now? 'Cause I only did
it for about eighteen months and then I was plucked out of the cesspool.
No disrespect.

MAGGIE: None taken.

LOUISE: I've got a scene later with Orlando Bloom. He's gorgeous.

MAGGIE: Well, I just did a scene with him.

LOUISE: No, but yeah, I mean I've got an actual scene with dialogue,
not just a fuzzy blob in the background. No disrespect.

MAGGIE: None taken, again.

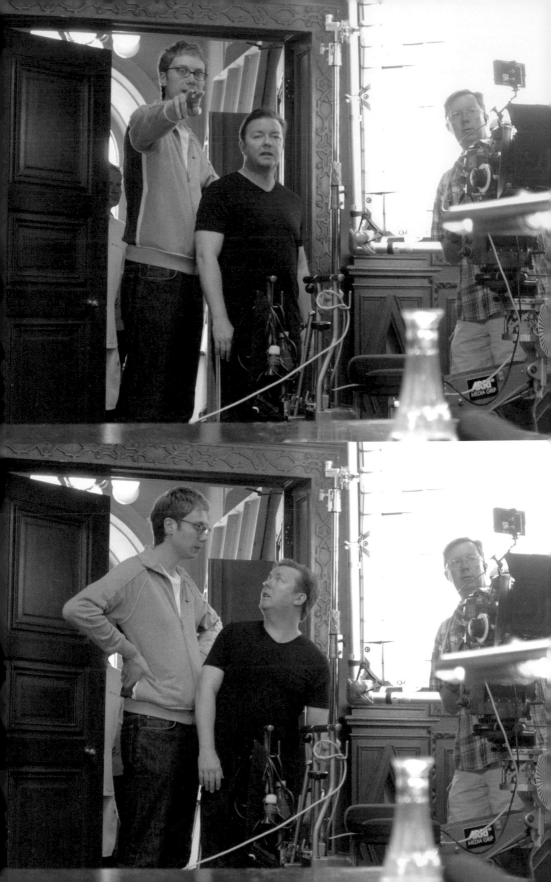

LOUISE'S MOBILE PHONE RINGS.

LOUISE: (checking caller ID) Oh, hang on. Oh, it's Matty Bowers.
I've just got to take this.
(INTO PHONE)
Hello, darling.
(LAUGHS HYSTERICALLY)
Listen, listen, no, Matt, can I just call you back? Sorry, I'm just with
a friend . . .

MAGGIE: (trying to extricate herself) It's all right. I'm all right.

LOUISE: Yes, she is female . . .
(LAUGHING, THEN TO MAGGIE)
Oh, he says can I take a picture of you?

MAGGIE NODS. LOUISE TAKES AIM WITH HER CAMERA-PHONE.

LOUISE: Hold on a sec, hang on.
(INTO PHONE)
I'll text it to you. You're a dirty old man, bye.

SHE FLIPS HER PHONE SHUT AND TEXTS AS SHE TALKS.

LOUISE: He's not old, he's twenty-eight and he's got his own yacht.

MAGGIE: Oh.

LOUISE: Mmm, he's quite a catch.

MAGGIE: Oh.

LOUISE: So, where you living at the moment? Have you got your
own place?

MAGGIE: Yes, I've got my own place.

LOUISE: Oh, 'cause you were renting before – that grotty little council
place behind Londis.

MAGGIE: Yeah, I'm still there.

LOUISE: You're well though.

MAGGIE: Surprisingly.

LOUISE: Yeah, well, that's the main thing, yeah. Even if you've got
nothing else, least you've got your health . . . at the moment.

MAGGIE: Yeah.

LOUISE: Talking of bad luck.

(SHE POINTS TO MAGGIE)

Did you hear about Barbara? Trevor's left her for a younger model. She is devastated, honestly, all alone, crying herself to sleep every night in that big house . . . She has got her own house, at least, which is something.

MAGGIE: Good for her.

LOUISE'S MOBILE BLEEPS.

LOUISE: Oh, that'll be Matty.

SHE FLIPS OPEN HER PHONE AND READS HIS MESSAGE.

LOUISE: Oh.

(SHUTTING PHONE)

No. Never mind.

MAGGIE REACTS.

SCENE 5. INT. SITCOM SET. DAY.

ANDY IS ON SET. SOME OF THE OTHER ACTORS ARE REHEARSING A SCENE FOR THE STUDIO CAMERAS. ANDY WATCHES THE MONITOR.

KIMBERLEY: Oh, he's late again. Alfie's going to be in so much trouble.

GOBBLER: Well, I'm not carrying the can for him again.

KIMBERLEY: Well, there's no excuses this time. Mr Stokes said if he's late one more time he's going to give him the brush off.

(KEITH CHEGWIN ENTERS, SMILING CHEERILY)

Oh, here he is. Alfie, not again. Why are you late?

KEITH: (happily) Because I buried me sister today!

ANDY LOOKS CONCERNED.

DIRECTOR: Yep. Great, let's move on. Next scene.

ANDY: Sorry, I don't want to interfere, is that how he's going to do it? Because it's meant to be a sad line. 'I buried my sister today.' He was smiling. It's got to be an emotional—

DIRECTOR: Hang on everyone...

ANDY: Sorry, Keith, can we try that again? You were smiling, mate. They all sort of think you're a joke because you're always late but today you've got a valid reason, you buried your sister. It's sort of like an emotional point in the show. Could we do it again?

KEITH: Yeah, no worries.

ANDY STANDS BEHIND THE MONITORS. KEITH COMES BACK IN, STILL SMILING.

ANDY: You're smiling again. You mustn't smile, you're sad. Okay? You've just been to a funeral.

KEITH EXITS AGAIN.

ANDY: Okay, in you come.

KEITH ENTERS, LOOKING SAD AND WALKS TO HIS MARK.

KIMBERLEY: Alfie, not again. Why are you late?

KEITH: Because I buried me sister today.

HE SAYS THE LINE PERFECTLY BUT THEN LOOKS STRAIGHT DOWN THE LENS OF THE CAMERA.

ANDY: Don't look at the camera. You mustn't look at the camera.

KEITH: Sorry.

ANDY: Okay?

KEITH: Yeah.

ANDY: It sort of breaks the illusion this is real life. Go again. Okay, in you come, action.

KEITH COMES IN AGAIN. HE IS SMILING.

ANDY: You're smiling. Sad!

(KEITH'S FACE DROPS BUT HE LOOKS STRAIGHT INTO THE CAMERA)

You looked straight at the lens again. Good, double whammy, and again.

(KEITH EXITS AGAIN)

Action.

KIMBERLEY: Alfie, not again. Why are you late?

KEITH: Because I—

KEITH HAS WALKED PAST HIS MARK AND IS BARELY VISIBLE IN THE SHOT. WE CAN ONLY SEE A LITTLE OF HIS SLEEVE.

ANDY: (exasperated) We can't see you, Keith, you've gone too far, okay. You got to stay on that mark, the blue mark down there, that's for you to stand on 'cause that's where the camera is pointing and then we can see your face. So, just to recap: come in, not smiling, because you're sad, because you just buried your sister, don't look at the camera and stand on that mark, so we can see you on the telly. Okay?

KEITH: There's a lot to remember, isn't there?

ANDY: There is a lot to remember, there is a lot to remember . . .

(ASIDE)

it's called acting. Okay, action!

KEITH ENTERS. HE SMILES.

ANDY: (angrily) Sad!

(KEITH WALKS OUT OF SHOT AGAIN)

Too far, left a bit . . .

(KEITH STARES UP AT ANDY)

Don't look at me! Okay, ask him the question.

KIMBERLEY: Why are you late?

KEITH: Because my sister buried me today.

ANDY: (bursting with anger) Oh for fuck's sake! Why would your sister bury you? That'd be mental!

KEITH: Oh, sorry, I get so confused. The thing is, my sister's not dead.

ANDY: What?

KEITH: I told them when I started: me sister, she's not dead.

ANDY: Do you mean in real life?

KEITH: Yeah.

ANDY: Presumably you don't work in a factory in real life?

KEITH: No.

ANDY: And your name's not Alfie?

KEITH: (serious) Yeah, you see, that's another thing. Sometimes, I don't know who's talking to who.

ANDY: Would you rather be called Keith in this?

KEITH: It would help.

ANDY: (frustrated, calling out) Okay, everyone, we're changing Keith's character-name from Alfie to Keith. Okay? Good.
(GOING BACK BEHIND THE MONITOR)
Let's go again.
(KEITH GOES BACK OUTSIDE)
This time then. Okay. In you come, Keith.

KEITH: (from behind the closed door) 'Keith' me or 'Keith' the character?

ANDY: (wits' end) It's the same person!

(HE GATHERS HIMSELF)

Okay, 'Keith' you and 'Keith' the character, all in one Keith, okay, in you come, action!

KEITH: The door's stuck.

ANDY: (snapping) That's lunch!

SCENE 6. INT. COURTROOM FILM SET. DAY.

LOUISE IS ON THE PHONE.

LOUISE: Okay, no, okay, bye, bye.

(SHE HANGS UP)

Yeah, just a call to do a small part in a film but I just had to let them down, I'm too busy.

MAGGIE: Oh.

LOUISE: Oh, I wonder if they'd want you.

MAGGIE: No, I wouldn't have thought so.

LOUISE: No, hang on, let me give them a call.

MAGGIE: No, no.

LOUISE: Try and help my bloody mates. You need the help.

MAGGIE: (whispers) But I'm not even a proper actress.

LOUISE: Hang on.

(INTO PHONE)

Hiya, Pauline. Listen, about that job, I've got a friend who's available . . . Does she have to be good-looking?

(MAGGIE REACTS)

Does she? Oh.

(SIZING MAGGIE UP)

Oh I don't know, late thirties, early forties. I'd say . . . mousy . . .

MAGGIE: Blonde.

LOUISE: But lovely girl, great personality, desperate for anything. No? All right, well, I tried, okay, cheers.

(SHE HANGS UP)

Oh, I'm sorry about that. It's not your lucky day.

MAGGIE: No.

AS A NEARBY CREW MEMBER COLLECTS A ROLL OF LIGHTING GEL, HE TURNS AND ACCIDENTALLY CLUNKS MAGGIE ROUND THE HEAD.

LOUISE: You okay?

MAGGIE: Yeah.

SCENE 7. INT. SITCOM SET. DAY.

DURING SOME DOWNTIME, KEITH AND ANDY FIND THEMSELVES NEXT TO EACH OTHER.

ANDY: All right?

KEITH: Yeah.
(LOOKING ROUND THE STUDIO)
I'm back again. Fourteen years I did here at the BBC. *Swap Shop*, *Cheggers Plays Pop*, all sorts.
(ANDY NODS WISTFULLY)
Still run by Jews and queers, is it?

ANDY: It's what?

KEITH: (deadpan) This place. Still run by your Jews and queers?

ANDY: I, I think there are some Jewish people and some gay people, yeah.

KEITH: 'Gay'. Yeah, I forgot, you're not meant to say queer, are you? Suggests something abnormal. What could be more normal than shoving your cock up a bloke's arse? I mean, put it this way: if God

had wanted a cock up an arse he wouldn't have given us minges.
(MIMING WITH HIS HANDS)
Men have knobs, women have fannies: pop knob in fanny . . .
not up the arse.

ANDY: Good. I should be making notes.

KEITH: You what?

ANDY: Nothing. It's, it's all good advice.

SCENE 8. INT. COURTROOM FILM SET. DAY.

MAGGIE IS READING A MAGAZINE. ORLANDO APPEARS, ACTING
NONCHALANTLY BUT CLEARLY WANTING TO SIT NEAR MAGGIE.
HE SITS DOWN BESIDE HER, CARRYING SOME MAGAZINES.

ORLANDO: Hi.

MAGGIE: Hello again.

ORLANDO: What you reading?

MAGGIE: Ah, just *Hello*.

ORLANDO: Oh, yeah.
(HOLDS UP A MAGAZINE)
Heat.
(MAGGIE NODS AND RETURNS TO HER READING. PAUSE. ORLANDO
GLANCES AT MAGGIE THEN PIPES UP, TRYING TO GET HER ATTENTION)
Oh no, I don't believe it.

MAGGIE: What is it?

ORLANDO: Just 'Top 5 Sexiest Film Stars'. For God's sake.

MAGGIE: Are you in it?

ORLANDO: Number one! Stupid. What do they mean, these lists?

MAGGIE: Nothing really.

ORLANDO: Well, don't slag them off. It's their opinion.
(ORLANDO HAS A COPY OF *WOMAN*)
Oh no. Look at this, *Woman* magazine.

HE HOLDS UP AN OPEN PAGE.

MAGGIE: (reading) 'I'm having an affair with my brother-in-law's ghost'?

ORLANDO: (tapping opposite page) No, that – 'Women's Top Ten Fantasy Snogs'. Number one again.

MAGGIE: What's that thing about the ghost?

ORLANDO: (reading) 'My, my husband's brother's ghost visits me at night and I think I'm falling in love with him.'

MAGGIE: Do they have sex?

HE SCANS THE ARTICLE.

ORLANDO: Well, it doesn't say, does it? But it doesn't matter, does it? Look, we were looking at the 'Number One Fantasy Snogs For Women'. Number one – Orlando Bloom. Oh, better not show this to Johnny Depp. He's only number four.

MAGGIE: Really? He'd be my number one.

ORLANDO: (snapping) Well, you'd be wrong, wouldn't you?
(HE THROWS HER THE MAGAZINE)
I'm number one, there's the proof. It was the same on the set of Pirates of the Caribbean. Me and Keira Knightley do a kissing scene, I do a brilliant take, everyone claps, the director goes, 'Oh, that was amazing.' Keira goes, 'Ooh, can we just do that kissing bit again?' Well, I know what she's up to. And I tease her, and I go, 'If you want to kiss somebody, why don't you kiss Johnny Depp?' She goes, 'Don't make me fucking sick, I'm going to vomit if you carry on like that.'

MAGGIE: Why do you keep talking about Johnny Depp?

ORLANDO: I don't keep talking about him, I never talk about him, he's boring. He's a prat. Where I'm from, he wouldn't last five minutes, he'd get a smack straight away.

MAGGIE: Where are you from?

ORLANDO: Haply on the Wold, near Royal Windsor.

MAGGIE: Ah. They're all subjective though, those lists, though, aren't they?

ORLANDO: Well, no. Obviously I am, objectively, really good-looking.

MAGGIE: But it's not objective, is it? Personally I think you're a, you're a wee bit . . .

SHE SUCKS HER FACE IN TO SUGGEST THIN.

ORLANDO: What's that? You winding me up? Come out for a drink later.

MAGGIE: I can't, I'm meeting my friend.

ORLANDO: Come out for a coffee, with me, you know. Come on. Just get to know me, get to know the normal me, take a better look and, you know, see the attractiveness.

MAGGIE: But I don't think you are.

ORLANDO: (incensed) Liar.

ORLANDO STORMS OFF, MAGGIE LOOKS BEMUSED.

SCENE 9. INT. COSTUME & MAKE-UP STORE ROOM. DAY.

DAMON AND A MAKE-UP WOMAN ARE HELPING KEITH AND ANDY FINALISE THEIR MAKE-UP. DAMON HANDS ANDY A PAIR OF OVERSIZED GLASSES.

DAMON: Try them on.

ANDY: Bit wacky, aren't they?

DAMON: Big glasses are funny.

ANDY: The real Ray didn't even wear glasses.

DAMON: Put 'em on.

EVERYONE LAUGHS.

DAMON: That's funny. Do the catchphrase.

ANDY: It's not a catchphrase. It's something he actually used to say.

DAMON: Do it.

ANDY: 'Are you having a laugh? Is he having a laugh?'

EVERYONE LAUGHS AGAIN.

DAMON: Now the wig.

MAKE-UP WOMAN: What about that one?

ANDY: It looks ridiculous.

MAKE-UP WOMAN: Go on.

DAMON: That looks funny.

ANDY: He didn't even have curly hair.

DAMON: Curly is funny.

ANDY: What do you mean 'curly is funny'?

DAMON: Curly hair is funny. Harpo Marx, Leo Sayer.

ANDY: I can name you loads of people with curly hair that aren't funny: Starsky from *Starsky and Hutch*, Jim Morrison.

KEITH: Blacks.

ANDY: Don't say blacks.

ANDY MILLMAN
CHARACTER WIG
'WHEN THE WHISTLE BLOWS'

KEITH: What shall I say?

ANDY: Say 'black people'.

KEITH: Okay, black people aren't funny.

ANDY: Black people are funny, Keith.

KEITH: Name one black person that's funny.

ANDY: (angrily) I can name you loads of black people that are funny: Dave Chappelle, Chris Rock, Eddie Murphy.

KEITH: English.

PAUSE. ANDY STARES AT KEITH.

ANDY: Don't change the rules halfway through. There are loads of funny English black people too.

KEITH: Who?

ANDY: Erm . . .

EVERYONE IN THE ROOM TRIES TO THINK OF SOMEBODY. ANDY, SEARCHING FOR A NAME, GLANCES UP AT A PICTURE OF LENNY HENRY HANGING ON THE WALL – BUT STILL ISN'T INSPIRED.

SCENE 10. INT. COURTROOM FILM SET. DAY.

MAGGIE IS WAITING AROUND. LOUISE APPROACHES.

LOUISE: Good news.

MAGGIE: (sarcastic) Oh, more good news, excellent.

LOUISE: Right, Eddie Osbourne, electrician . . .
(LOUISE POINTS IN THE DIRECTION OF A HUNKY ELECTRICIAN WIRING A PLUG)

series two

Extras

He split up with his wife a while ago and he's back on the market, lovely guy, just your type.

MAGGIE: Really?

LOUISE: Sweet guy. He's a lovely guy. Interested?

MAGGIE: (excitedly) Yeah.

LOUISE: Great. Eddie . . .

THE HUNK DOES NOT MOVE. INSTEAD, A SHORT FAT DUMPY ELECTRICIAN STOOD BEHIND THE HUNK TURNS AROUND.

ELECTRICIAN: Yo!

LOUISE: (pointing to MAGGIE) This is her.

(MAGGIE REACTS. THE ELECTRICIAN SIZES MAGGIE UP, SCREWS
UP HIS NOSE, SHAKES HIS HEAD AND GOES BACK TO WORK)
No? Oh, never mind.

MAGGIE: Not bothered.

LOUISE: (deeply patronising, stroking MAGGIE's hair) I just don't
know where you're going wrong.

ORLANDO BLOOM CHARGES OVER.

ORLANDO: (to MAGGIE) Right. Kiss me! One kiss, come on.

MAGGIE: No.

ORLANDO: Just one kiss, just let me show you how I do it. No tongues,
if you don't want.

MAGGIE: Right. If it's going to shut you up.

HE KISSES HER. LOUISE LOOKS ON, STUNNED. MAGGIE AND ORLANDO
PULL AWAY.

ORLANDO: Well?

MAGGIE: (nonplussed) Not really my cup of tea.

ORLANDO EXITS, EMBARRASSED.

MAGGIE: Sorry about that.

LOUISE IS STUNNED.

SCENE 11. INT.
SITCOM SET. DAY.

THE ACTORS ARE REHEARSING A BROAD SCENE.

KIMBERLEY: You're in this club, this vision walks up.
(HOLDING UP A MOP)
She says, 'Hiya handsome, want to buy me a drink?' What do you say?

GOBBLER: I say, 'I'm not made of money.'

KIMBERLEY: Oh you're never going to get a woman like that.

GOBBLER: (points to mop) No, I don't want a woman like that.

KIMBERLEY: Go on, be nice to her, caress her hair.
(HE PATS THE MOP)
No, don't pat her, she's not a dog.

ANDY: (as RAY) She must be a dog if she's going out with him! Oh!

KIMBERLEY: (laughing) Oh, Mr Stokes.

ANDY: (trailing off, out of character) I'm sorry, erm . . .

DAMON: Maybe waggle the glasses?

ANDY: I'm not sure about the glasses.

DAMON: Oh, you've got to have the glasses, it's hysterical.

ANDY: I don't think so.

DAMON: It's definitely funnier with the glasses.

IAIN: Yeah, oh yeah, it is, I agree.

ANDY: There's a surprise.

IAIN: (annoyed) Well, look, I'm sorry that my presence here as head of comedy irritates you but I've been in this business a lot longer than you and my opinion will be heard because I'm the man with the money.

ANDY: It's not your money though, is it?

IAIN: No, but I'm entrusted to make sure that it's spent correctly.

ANDY: Oh, well, we'll make sure it's spent correctly, which is apparently on funny glasses. I'll just take five, right?

IAIN: Yes.

ANDY WANDERS OVER TO THE BUFFET TABLE. SHAUN IS PUTTING SOME OF THE FREE SANDWICHES INTO A NAPKIN.

SHAUN: Do you mind if I take these for later on?

ANDY: No.

SHAUN: Can I just say that I know what you're going through. My character on *EastEnders*, he started out as an interesting three-dimensional person but then, over the years, the writers turned him into a joke and, and that's why I walked away, you know, it wasn't what I wanted to do. And I know some people look at me now and say I was a fool but I know that I walked away with my integrity and my pride intact. I just think you've got to do what you think is right.

ANDY MUSES ON THESE WISE WORDS. IT RESOLVES SOMETHING IN HIS OWN MIND AND HE DECIDES ON A COURSE OF ACTION. HE MARCHES OVER TO CENTRE STAGE AND CONFRONTS IAIN.

ANDY: Iain, can I have a word?

IAIN: Yeah, what is it?

ANDY: This isn't the comedy I set out to make, okay, in fact I think it's awful.

THE CAST AND CREW STOP WHAT THEY'RE DOING AND TURN TO LISTEN.

IAIN: Yeah, well, shall we not do this here, shall we go up to my office—

ANDY: No, I, I don't care who hears what I've got to say because I'm at that point now. Everyone's interfered, it's embarrassing. I don't want to get on television for the sake of it. I don't want to be famous for the sake of it, I want to do something that I'm proud of. And I won't be proud of shouting out catchphrases in a stupid wig and funny glasses. I want to do what I want to do, otherwise I'll hate myself for the rest of my life. And I tell you what, a case in point . . .
(HE CROSSES OVER TO SHAUN)
Shaun, on *EastEnders*, they started to turn his character into a joke and he walked away at the top of his game, that's called integrity. Okay, it doesn't matter what happens to him now 'cause he's got his dignity.

ANDY SLAPS SHAUN ON THE BACK. BUFFET SANDWICHES, CAKES AND SWEETS FALL OUT OF SHAUN'S JACKET AND POUR OUT ON TO THE FLOOR.

. . . AND KEEP POURING OUT, FLOODING INTO PILES AS EVERYONE STANDS AND STARES. EVENTUALLY THE STOLEN BOOTY DRIES UP. A FINAL LONE SANDWICH PLOPS OUT OF HIS COAT.

SHAUN: Shall I . . .

ANDY: Leave it.

ANDY WALKS BACK TOWARDS IAIN.

ANDY: So, basically, I'm not going to prostitute myself any more or my work. Okay? I'm just sick of people coming along, telling me how they think it should be done and me just having to bend over and take it up the arse.

AGENT: (interrupting quickly) Sorry, can we just say no disrespect to either of you, erm, as gays. Er, you know, we, we don't know if you're givers or receivers, very difficult to tell just from looking at you . . . although if I was putting money on it I'd probably go—

THE AGENT POINTS AT DAMON. ANDY SMACKS HIS ARM AWAY.

ANDY: We don't need to put money on it.

(THE AGENT SKULKS AWAY. ANDY STARES AT IAIN)

You've heard what I've got to say.

THERE IS A LONG PAUSE AS IAIN SOAKS THIS IN.

IAIN: Right, well, thank you for telling us how you feel. So here's how I see things going forward. You can either carry on and record this show as we've already planned or you can pull the plug, waste everyone's time and hard work, waste the thousands of pounds we've already spent so far, burn all your bridges with the BBC and you can go back to being an extra and then you can work your way back up again from nothing. What do you want to do?

(ANDY STARES DEFIANTLY AT IAIN . . . BUT A NOISE DISTRACTS HIM. HE LOOKS AROUND. SHAUN IS ON HIS HANDS AND KNEES PILING THE BUFFET FOOD FROM THE FLOOR BACK INTO HIS JACKET, STUFFING THE OCCASIONAL CAKE INTO HIS MOUTH AS HE GOES. ANDY LOOKS BACK AT IAIN)

What do you want to do?

ANDY: (quietly) Sitcom. This, this can be good. That's what I've been trying to say. This, finish this off, 'cause it can . . . I don't want to let people down. I want to get on with this, I want to get this on the telly and then in the future maybe look at doing it the way I wanted to do it.

IAIN: Yeah, or not.

ANDY: Or not, see how it goes. That's all I want to . . . yeah?

IAIN: Right, yeah, okay.

ANDY: Good.

ANDY WANDERS BACK TO THE SET.

IAIN: Andy?

ANDY: Yeah?

IAIN: (pointing to the discarded wig and glasses) Don't forget your—

ANDY: Glasses.

ANDY PICKS UP HIS WIG AND GLASSES.

SCENE 12. INT.
SITCOM SET – WINGS. NIGHT.

ANDY IS LOST IN THOUGHT, STARING INTO THE MIDDLE DISTANCE,
WAITING TO GO ON. HE IS HAVING HIS WIG ADJUSTED BY THE MAKE-UP
WOMAN. MAGGIE ARRIVES, BREATHLESS.

MAGGIE: Hi.

ANDY: You're cutting it fine, aren't you?

MAGGIE: (excitedly) Oh, sorry I'm late. Everything all right?

ANDY: Yeah.

MAGGIE: No first night nerves?

ANDY: No, no, no. I actually had to kick a bit of arse earlier 'cause
I was getting sick of all this 'Is it a good comedy? Is it a bad comedy?'
I just went, 'Look, it's a good comedy if it pleases people. Can we get
on with it?'
(MAGGIE LOOKS CONFUSED. THIS DOESN'T SOUND LIKE THE OLD ANDY)
Do you know what I mean? I think comedy should be as broad as
possible, so you take everyone in. I want the whole family to like
this, I want four-year-olds to like this.

MAGGIE: They will.

ANDY: Do you know what I mean? And if it doesn't stand the test of time, so what? Do something else but, you know, bring as much joy into the world as you can. That's all.

MAGGIE: (unconvinced) Yeah, well, as long as you're happy.

ANDY: I'm happy if people are happy.

THE AGENT APPEARS.

AGENT: Are you definitely going to do this?

ANDY: Yeah.

AGENT: Yeah. You're definitely going to go on and—

ANDY: Yes! Yeah.

THE AGENT WALKS AWAY. SHAUN IS WAITING NEARBY, DRESSED AS 'RAY' IN FULL WIG AND GLASSES.

AGENT: Forget it, Barry, he's doing it, mate.

SHAUN: Fuck!

AGENT: I know, I'm as annoyed as you are.

SHAUN WANDERS OFF, DESPONDENT.

TV CLIP: 'WHEN THE WHISTLE BLOWS'

THE STAFF ARE SAT ROUND. RITA ENTERS. JOKES ARE GREETED WITH LAUGHTER FROM THE LIVE STUDIO AUDIENCE.

KIMBERLEY: Bloody hell, Rita, you look terrible. Life as a single mum getting to you?

RITA: I was up till two a.m. doing my daughter's science homework. Did you know that Alexander Fleming discovered penicillin when he found mould on some old bread he'd left out?

BRAINS: Oh, he should look under Gobbler's bed – he'd find a new species.

RITA: He'd find a new species if he looked in Gobbler's bed.

GOBBLER: I don't get it.

RITA: You don't get it? I've been without a man so long I think I'd say 'Yes' if Ray asked me out.

ANDY AS 'RAY' ENTERS.

RAY: My ears are burning.

RITA: (looking at RAY) Maybe I can last a few more years.

RAY: Morning, campers. Well, congratulations are in order. You all successfully clocked in on time this morning – you just forgot to start bloody work!

KIMBERLEY: Steady on, Mr Stokes, we've been comforting Rita. She's been up all night trying to get her head round some fella called Alexander.

RAY: Oh, lucky beggar, no one who works here I hope.

KIMBERLEY: No, he's dead.

RAY: Why, she cooked for him as well?

KIMBERLEY: Oh, Mr Stokes, will you be nice to her?

RAY: (to RITA) Well, Rita, I know you've had your problems but I want you to know this: the door to my office is always open.

RITA: Thank you, Mr Stokes.

RAY: Yeah, I think it's the bloody hinges. Get off your arse and fix it, will you?

RITA: I haven't got any tools.

ANDY: You're joking, you've got two right here.
(HE POINTS TO GOBBLER AND BRAINS)
Gobbler's a complete spanner.

GOBBLER: I don't get it.

BRAINS: What Mr Stokes has cleverly done, with recourse to a pun, is take Rita's usage of the word 'tool' – a device that performs manual or mechanical work – and transpose its meaning into the vulgar, slang definition of 'tool', meaning the male reproductive appendage.

SILENCE.

RAY: Are you having a laugh? Is he having a laugh?

(THIS ELICITS BIG LAUGHS FROM THE STUDIO AUDIENCE. ANDY IS TAKEN ABACK BY THE RESPONSE BUT IS PLEASANTLY SURPRISED)

You're having a laugh!

(SUDDENLY HE CATCHES SIGHT OF A FAMILY IN THE AUDIENCE WHO ARE CACKLING AWAY. THEY EACH WEAR T-SHIRTS WITH DIFFERENT CATCHPHRASES ON THEM: 'WASSUP!', 'GARLIC BREAD?', 'I WANT THAT ONE', 'IT'S CHICO TIME!', 'I'M A LAYDEE', 'AM I BOVVERED?' ANDY SIGHS HEAVILY, SUDDENLY DEPRESSED BUT CONTINUES TO MUG MERCILESSLY)

He is having a laugh. Oh. You're having a laugh!

(HE EXITS THE SCENE TO RAPTUROUS APPLAUSE. ANDY COMES OFF THE SET, TAKING OFF HIS COMEDY WIG. HE LOOKS ACROSS AT MAGGIE WHO IS WATCHING FROM THE WINGS. SHE SMILES AT HIM POLITELY. ANDY REGISTERS HER SILENT DISAPPOINTMENT. HE TURNS TO AWAIT HIS NEXT CUE, LOST IN HIS OWN THOUGHTS)

EXTRAS
Episode 2

CAST LIST
Andy Millman RICKY GERVAIS
Maggie Jacobs ASHLEY JENSEN
Agent STEPHEN MERCHANT
Shaun SHAUN WILLIAMSON

Guest Starring DAVID BOWIE

Rita LIZA TARBUCK
Kimberley SARAH MOYLE
Gobbler ANDREW BUCKLEY
Brains JAMIE CHAPMAN
Greg SHAUN PYE
Cathy CLAIRE ADAMS
Mr Yamaguchi RYOZO KOHIRA
Homeless Man RICHARD MORRIS

Obsessive Fan DAVID EARL
Receptionist NICOLA SANDERSON
Mark PASCAL LANGDALE
Girl in Nightclub KATY WIX
Nightclub Punter BOB MERCER
Bouncer CHAD SHEPHERD
Linda NAOMI BENTLEY
Count Fuckula JAMES DOWDESWELL

Written & Directed by
RICKY GERVAIS &
STEPHEN MERCHANT

AUDIENCE LAUGHTER. RAY (PLAYED BY ANDY) IS TALKING TO THE TEAM.

RAY: Right, Mr Yamaguchi's on his way up now with his lovely wife. As you know, he's thinking of investing in us and if he does it'll be the best thing that happened to this company since old Gladys the cook burnt down the canteen.

RITA: She wasn't a bad cook.

RAY: Are you having a laugh? Is she having a laugh?

RAY MUGS MERCILESSLY AS THE AUDIENCE LAUGH.

RITA: Oh, be fair, Ray, she wasn't that bad. We all loved her milky puddings.

RAY: Not when they dragged in the mash we didn't. Now, I don't want you and your team mucking things up for me. You've prepared the traditional Japanese cuisine, have you?

RITA: Yes, it's here.

RAY: Right.

RITA: But I'm still not sure you should have let Gobbler organise the traditional Japanese entertainment.

RAY: Why, what's he planning?

RITA: Well—

RAY: No time, here they come.

A JAPANESE BUSINESSMAN AND HIS WIFE ENTER. RAY AND THE TEAM BOW.

RAY: Mr Yamaguchi, hello, hello. This is Rita and my team. We've prepared some traditional Japanese cuisine.

RITA: (offering a plate of food) Welcome, I hope you like it.

THE COUPLE TASTE THE FOOD. EVERYONE WAITS ANXIOUSLY FOR THE VERDICT. MR AND MRS YAMAGUCHI'S FACES LIGHT UP.

MR YAMAGUCHI: Lovely.

RAY: (aside) Well done, Rita.
(TO MR YAMAGUCHI)
And now for your delectation, may I present Gobbler and Kimberley with some traditional Japanese entertainment.
(GOBBLER AND KIMBERLEY COME OUT OF RAY'S OFFICE. THEY BOTH HAVE THEIR EYES TAPED UP AND ARE WEARING YELLOW MAKE-UP. KIMBERLEY IS WEARING A 'SUZIE WONG' CHINESE DRESS. GOBBLER IS IN A JUDO SUIT WITH HIS HANDS INSIDE THE SLEEVES. THEY START TO SING)
What the f—. Ohh!

GOBBLER/KIMBERLEY: (singing) 'Ching chang chinaman milked a cow
Ching chang chinaman didn't know how
Ching chang chinaman pulled the wrong tit
Ching chang chinaman covered in shit!'

ON THIS FINAL LINE, KIMBERLEY SPLATS A CHOCOLATE CAKE INTO GOBBLER'S FACE.

GOBBLER: (deep baritone) 'Oh, I'm all done covered in shittttt!'

THERE IS SILENCE (ACCEPT FOR THE STUDIO AUDIENCE, WHO ARE IN HYSTERICS).

RAY: What do you think?

MR YAMAGUCHI: (in a sitcom Japanese accent) Is he 'avin' a raugh?

AUDIENCE LAUGHTER AND APPLAUSE.

RAY: Ohhhhh!

MUSIC STARTS, CREDITS ROLL. IT'S RITA SINGING THE THEME TUNE.

RITA: 'Tick tock, alarm clock
I'm gonna be late
Porridge, toast, kids, car
Bloody school gate.
Factory floor, what a chore
Another week's graft
And fifty times a day I hear . . .'

RAY: 'Are you having a laugh?'

RITA: 'Whatever happened to my dreams?
Is this the life I chose?
The highlight of my ruddy day
Is when the whistle blows.
When the whistle blows
When the whistle blows'

PULL OUT TO REVEAL:

SCENE 1. INT.
AGENT'S OFFICE. DAY.

ANDY AND HIS AGENT ARE WATCHING THE SITCOM ON A TV.
THE AGENT YAWNS. ANDY REACTS.

ANDY: It's bad.

AGENT: It's not bad, is it?

ANDY: It is.

AGENT: No, no, 'bad' suggests that, you know, it's evil or something, you know, it's not, it's . . . it's poor, it's rubbish, you know it's, it's shit . . . it's a shit sitcom.

ANDY: It's a 'shitcom'. Oh, we've sorted that out. Thanks very much. That's the career over.

AGENT: That's what one of the reviews said.

THE AGENT LAUGHS. ANDY GLOWERS AT HIM.

AGENT: (off his look) Shouldn't really, no, shouldn't really joke about it, it's not . . .

ANDY: What are the reviews like?

AGENT: If I was being kind I'd say it was a mixed bag.

ANDY: Let me have a look.

AGENT: Really?

ANDY: Yeah, let me see them.

AGENT: (buzzing intercom) Bar?

SHAUN: (on the intercom) Yo.

AGENT: Can you bring some of the reviews in?

ANDY: Why has he got them?

AGENT: He's got to do something with his mornings, hasn't he?

SHAUN ENTERS WITH AN ARMFUL OF NEWSPAPERS.

SHAUN: Found another one.

AGENT: Oh, have you?

SHAUN: (reading from a newspaper) 'Perhaps it's unfair to judge a sitcom on its first episode but when a TV programme makes you want to gouge out your own eyes rather than watch one more minute, you know it's probably not your cup of tea.'

AGENT: Ouch. God, pop it in the scrap book.

ANDY: No, don't pop it in the scrap book, put good ones in the scrap book.

SHAUN: What good ones?

ANDY: What, there's no good ones?

AGENT: Best one was the *Telegraph*.

ANDY: What did they say?

AGENT: They didn't review it.

SHAUN EXITS.

AGENT: See you later, B.

ANDY: Career's over.

AGENT: Well, no, because despite what they say, the viewing figures were really good, six point two million.

ANDY: Six million people watched it last night and yet none of these liked it?

AGENT: (pointing to the reviews) Well, these people know about comedy, don't they? They know what they're talking about, but the general public . . .

ANDY: You said if you get your own show, the offers would come flooding in. You said the phone would never stop ringing. Have you had any phone calls at all?

AGENT: No.

ANDY: No.

AGENT: Oh no, what am I talking about? Sky called.

ANDY: And?

AGENT: They say they can put your dish up Thursday.

SCENE 2. INT. ANDY'S FLAT/MAGGIE'S FLAT. DAY.

ANDY IS RE-READING THE REVIEWS, STILL AGONISING OVER WHAT'S BEEN WRITTEN. HE PICKS UP THE PHONE.

MAGGIE: Hello.

ANDY: What you doing?

MAGGIE: I'm actually flicking through the phone book and I'm pointing my finger on a random page to see what my name could be if I wanted to change it.

ANDY: What have you got?

MAGGIE: P. B. Grout.

ANDY: Good, as long as you're filling your days.

MAGGIE: C. T. Punchaganowno.
(LAUGHS)
But I don't look like a Punchaganowno.

ANDY: You hungry?

MAGGIE: Yeah.

ANDY: Greasy spoon?

MAGGIE: Yeah. Where am I meeting you?

ANDY: Garage, in ten minutes?

MAGGIE: Yep. Do you want to hear one more?

ANDY: Oh, go on.

MAGGIE: T. P. Bronze—

ANDY HANGS UP AND LEAVES.

SCENE 3. EXT.
ANDY'S FLAT. DAY.

ANDY IS LEAVING HIS BUILDING. AN ATTRACTIVE WOMAN (CATHY)
IS CARRYING A PORTABLE TV TOWARDS THE FRONT DOOR.

ANDY: Hi.

CATHY: Hi.

ANDY: You moving in here?

CATHY: Yeah.

ANDY: Oh, good . . . I mean, do you want a hand?

CATHY: No, I'm fine.

ANDY: (flirting) Phew! I'm Andy, by the way. I live here, obviously.
I live on the, the second floor: 21.

CATHY: Okay. I'm Cathy.

ANDY: Oh. Nice to meet you.

CATHY: Nice to meet you.

ANDY: Nice to meet you. Oh, welcome to the building.

CATHY: Thanks. It's nice to see someone under forty.

ANDY CLEARS HIS THROAT LOUDLY.

CATHY: I thought I'd moved into an old people's home.

ANDY: No, there are some oldies in there, some over-forties but they're quiet.
(POINTING TO THE PORTABLE TV)
The old telly there. Watch a lot of telly?

CATHY: I don't, no, no.

ANDY: No? Last night, BBC1? No? Some good stuff on.

CATHY: Okay.

ANDY: Okay, well, if you need someone to show you around at all, just come and . . .

CATHY: Thanks, that'd be nice.

ANDY: Oh, good. All right.

CATHY: Okay.

ANDY: See you later.

CATHY: See you later, bye.

ANDY LEAVES, PLEASED WITH HIMSELF.

SCENE 4. EXT. STREET. DAY.

MAGGIE AND ANDY WALKING ALONG.

MAGGIE: Oh, saw it last night.

ANDY: And?

MAGGIE: Yeah . . . It was good.

ANDY: Are you just saying that?

LONG PAUSE.

MAGGIE: No.

ANDY: Too long a pause! If you're going to lie, lie well.

MAGGIE: Bits of it were funny.

ANDY: It doesn't count, you laugh at anything.

MAGGIE: What?

ANDY: I found you laughing to yourself once and I said, 'What you laughing at?' and you said, 'My toes.'

MAGGIE: Oh yeah, ha! Well, they are funny though, the way they waggle.

ANDY: It's you that's making them waggle.

THEY PASS A HOMELESS GUY.

HOMELESS GUY: Spare any change?

ANDY: Sorry, mate.

HOMELESS GUY: Okay, have a nice day.

ANDY: Cheers.

HOMELESS GUY: And good luck with the show, Andy!

ANDY'S FACE DROPS. HE KEEPS ON WALKING.

ANDY: Cheers.
(TO MAGGIE)
How does he know who I am? Where does he watch the show, through Dixons' window?

MAGGIE: Well, you've been in all the magazines.

ANDY: Oh, he reads *Heat*, does he?

MAGGIE: Everybody reads *Heat*.

ANDY: 'Everybody reads *Heat*.' Now I'll have to start giving money to the homeless.

MAGGIE: Why?

ANDY: Because I don't want people to say Andy Millman hates the poor.

MAGGIE: You don't just hate the poor, you hate everyone.

ANDY: That's why it's so unfair.

ANDY WANDERS BACK TO THE HOMELESS GUY, PUTTING HIS HANDS
INTO HIS POCKETS. HE PULLS OUT A TWENTY-POUND NOTE WITH ONE
HAND AND A FEW COPPERS WITH THE OTHER.

ANDY: Sorry, but I've only got like 8p in change or, or a twenty . . .

MAGGIE: Just give him the twenty.

ANDY: No, he said change.
(TO HOMELESS GUY)
You said change, didn't you . . .

HOMELESS GUY: (polite) Yeah, whatever.

ANDY: Cheers.

HOMELESS GUY: Yeah. Your TV show's doing all right though, is it?

ANDY: Yeah, yeah.

HOMELESS GUY: Good, good. Pay well?

ANDY: (guiltily) Yeah. Erm . . .

HE LOOKS AT THE TWENTY-POUND NOTE.

ANDY: (to MAGGIE) Haven't you got anything else, like, a quid?
(MAGGIE SHAKES HER HEAD. ANDY CONSIDERS THE TWENTY AGAIN.
TO HOMELESS GUY)
You haven't got a ten and five, have you?

HOMELESS GUY: I haven't.

MAGGIE: 'Course he doesn't, he's homeless.

ANDY: (to MAGGIE, annoyed) I know he's homeless, I'm not blind.
(GRUDGINGLY, ANDY HANDS THE HOMELESS GUY THE TWENTY
AND SIGHS)
Twenty . . . for nothing. Is that the most you've ever been given?

HOMELESS GUY: One bloke gave me fifty once.

ANDY: That is mental! He must have been a pervert. Twenty quid
though. Considering your average is probably what, 20p or something.
I do come past here quite a lot so we'll count that as a few goes. Can't
do that every day. Let's say it's, three months of leaving me alone.

HOMELESS GUY: Leaving you alone?

ANDY: No . . .

HOMELESS GUY: Now, look, if you're going to have this attitude I don't
want it.

ANDY: No, no, no—

HOMELESS GUY: No, seriously, take it back, don't want it.

THE HOMELESS GUY GIVES THE MONEY BACK.

ANDY: I'm just saying I couldn't do that every . . . what will you say to
people about this?

HOMELESS GUY: I'll probably say, 'Don't ask Andy Millman for money
because he'd only give it to you begrudgingly.'

ANDY: Well, no, say that I offered you twenty – the second most you've
ever been given – and then I insulted you and you made me take it back.
But mention the twenty in any anecdote slagging me off.
(GUILTY)
Oh, just take it, just take it, it's fine.

HOMELESS GUY: Fine. Nice aftershave, by the way.

ANDY: Cheers.

HOMELESS GUY: What is it?

ANDY: Calvin Klein.

HOMELESS GUY: Apparently Vernon Kay uses that.

ANDY: (a little taken aback) Okay, cheers.

ANDY AND MAGGIE WALK OFF IN THE SAME DIRECTION THEY CAME FROM.

ANDY: Why are we walking back this way? This is the way we came. Now I've got to walk past him again.

ANDY AND MAGGIE WALK BACK PAST THE HOMELESS GUY AND HEAD TOWARDS THE CAFE.

HOMELESS GUY: See you later.

ANDY GRUNTS AND SCURRIES PAST.

SCENE 5. EXT.
ANDY'S FLAT. DAY.

MAGGIE AND ANDY ARE ABOUT TO ENTER ANDY'S BLOCK. ANDY SPOTS CATHY, THE ATTRACTIVE WOMAN FROM BEFORE. SHE'S UNPACKING SOME BOXES FROM HER CAR.

ANDY: Oh, she's moving into my block, I spoke to her earlier, I think there's a bit of a vibe. Right, I'm going to go and talk to her, you come over, okay, just ask for an autograph—

MAGGIE: (unenthusiastic) Oh.

ANDY: Yeah, and just say something like, 'Oh I think you're the most amazing actor on TV'.

MAGGIE: You're already using your new powers for evil.

ANDY: You've got to use what you can.

MAGGIE: Fair enough.

ANDY APPROACHES CATHY.

ANDY: Hello. Need any help yet?

CATHY: Thank you. A big strong man's just what I need.

ANDY: (flirting) Will I do?

CATHY: (flirting back) Yeah!

THEY LAUGH. MAGGIE APPROACHES.

MAGGIE: Excuse me? Are you Andy Millman?

ANDY: Yeah.

MAGGIE: Star of the new sitcom *When The Whistle Blows*?

ANDY: (showing off to CATHY) Yeah.

MAGGIE: Can I get your autograph, please?

ANDY: No worries. Who's it to?

MAGGIE: Me.

ANDY: Yeah, but I don't know your name, do I?

MAGGIE: Oh. Maggie.

ANDY: (writing) Maggie.

MAGGIE: Can I just say that I think you're the most amazing comedy actor on television.

ANDY: (rolling eyes, faux modest) Oh! Not 'amazing'!

MAGGIE: (confused) But that's what you told me to say.

CATHY REACTS. ANDY IS CAUGHT OUT.

ANDY: Okay?
(TO CATHY, LOOKING AT HER PACKING BOX)
How many you got?

CATHY: (to MAGGIE) Er, did he ask you to come over and say that?

MAGGIE IS CAUGHT IN THE HEADLIGHTS. SHE LOOKS AT ANDY, THEN BACK AT CATHY. ANDY LAUGHS.

MAGGIE: I don't know.

CATHY: You don't know if he asked you to say it?

MAGGIE: No, I don't know.

CATHY: Are you friends?

ANDY: Are we friends?

CATHY: Yeah.

ANDY: Unlikely.

MAGGIE: Well, we . . . we have met.

ANDY: (looking closely at MAGGIE, beginning to mumble) Have we? Oh yeah . . . I didn't . . . changed your . . . hello . . . you all right? I didn't realise, are you, erm, are you still, erm . . . ?
(TO CATHY, LOOKING TOWARDS HER BOXES)
Those aren't going to move themselves.
(CATHY STARES WITHERINGLY AT ANDY)
See you later.

HE WALKS OFF TOWARDS THE BUILDING.

MAGGIE: (calling after) Andy, am I coming with you?

ANDY: (not looking back) Yeah.

SCENE 6. INT.
ANDY'S FLAT. DAY.

ANDY AND MAGGIE SAT IN SILENCE. ANDY IS LOST IN THOUGHT.

MAGGIE: Are you still thinking about the reviews?

ANDY: Yes, the terrible, terrible reviews.

MAGGIE: Think about the good ones.

ANDY REACTS.

ANDY: What am I going to do now? I'll never get over this, I'll just spend years and years trying to claw back credibility by doing anything, just popping up in bad films and charity events, just begging forgiveness.

MAGGIE: They'd forgive you if you did *Celebrity Fit Club*.

ANDY: (sarcastic) Brilliant, what else? What else could I do?

MAGGIE: There's *Celebrity Love Island*.

ANDY: Why would I do a show that, when I watched it, I was praying for a tsunami?

MAGGIE: Ahh. Do you want to just go to the pub?

ANDY: Yeah. That's the beginning. 'Depressed TV star drinks himself to death.'

MAGGIE: Oh, don't be daft. You're not a star. And being fat will kill you before the drink does.

ANDY: Are you sure you can come to the pub? You're not manning the phones at The Samaritans tonight?

MAGGIE: (missing the sarcasm) No.

ANDY: No? Okay, pub it is then.

SCENE 7. INT.
PUB TABLE. NIGHT.

MAGGIE AND ANDY ARE SAT IN THE PUB, NURSING DRINKS.

MAGGIE: Right, here's one: who would you rather fight and have a decent chance of winning – a big, fat, hairy silver-backed gorilla or a Thomson's gazelle?

ANDY: Well, the gazelle.

MAGGIE: I know, but you'd have to catch it first 'cause they're like . . .

MAGGIE WHISTLES.

ANDY: Well, I wouldn't catch it. I turned up for the fight, it ran away, I win. Not my problem.

ANDY'S AGENT APPROACHES THE TABLE. SHAUN WILLIAMSON IS IN TOW.

AGENT: Oy, oy.

ANDY: (visibly annoyed) Oh . . .

AGENT: Now, don't be like that. Little bit of good news here.

ANDY: All right, Shaun.

SHAUN: All right.

AGENT: Barry and I were scouring the Internet and we found a glowing review of your sitcom.

ANDY: Really?

AGENT: Listen to this:
(READING FROM A PRINT-OUT)
'This charming story of lovable, larger-than-life characters will please all the family.
(ANDY LOOKS PLEASED)
This is a delightful woodland romp with many of the best scenes featuring a roly-poly toad.'

HE POINTS TO ANDY.

ANDY: Give me that.
(THE AGENT HANDS HIM THE PRINT-OUT)
This is a review of *The Wind In The Willows*.

AGENT: What's yours called then?
(REMEMBERING)
Oh, *When The Wind Blows* is his.

ANDY: Whistle!

AGENT: Whistle. Yeah.
(TO SHAUN, STUDYING THE PRINT-OUT)
I said that was a picture of a frog, didn't I? And not—

SHAUN: But it's got the same throat.

AGENT: Yeah, I know, yeah. Well, you can see where we went wrong, yeah.

THEY BOTH LOOK AT THE PICTURE AND THEN AT ANDY, NODDING
AT THE SIMILARITY.

ANDY: I'm going to get a drink.

AGENT: (to MAGGIE) Have a look.

SHAUN: He's a ringer.

MAGGIE: Oh yeah, except he's green.

AGENT: Who Andy or—

MAGGIE: The frog.

AGENT: Oh, the frog.

SCENE 8. INT. PUB BAR. NIGHT.

ANDY APPROACHES THE BAR. A *WHEN THE WHISTLE BLOWS* FAN
IS STOOD NEARBY WITH HIS GIRLFRIEND. HE RECOGNISES ANDY.

FAN: God, it's you.

ANDY: Hi.

FAN: Love it. What you doing here?

ANDY: Just having a drink.

FAN: Oh, so are we. 'Mazing. Do you live near here or . . . ?

ANDY: Yeah.

FAN: (standing too close) Where?

ANDY: Just round—

FAN: What street?

ANDY: Well, it doesn't matter, does it? Just locally. Just . . .

FAN: I love your show.

ANDY: Oh good, cheers.

FAN: The wig, the glasses, the catchphrase. Brilliant.

ANDY: Thanks.

FAN: Everything about it.

ANDY: Oh.

FAN: The wig. The glasses. The catchphrase. Brilliant.

ANDY: That's becoming quite a catchphrase itself.

FAN: Yeah. Oh, the wig.

ANDY/FAN: The glasses.

FAN: And the catchphrase.

ANDY: Brilliant?

FAN: Yeah. Can I take a picture?

ANDY: Yeah.

FAN: You got a wig with you?

ANDY: No.

FAN: (holding up a cameraphone) No. Do the face then. Do the face.

ANDY: Erm.

FAN: Do the face.
(ANDY DOES THE FACE)

Oh, ha ha ha ha, look at that! It works even without the wig or the glasses. Can you do the catchphrase?

ANDY: I'd rather not.

FAN: Do the catchphrase.

ANDY: No, it's just a bit—

FAN: Do the catchphrase. Just do the catchphrase!

ANDY: Okay, okay. 'Are you having a laugh?'

FAN: Do it properly.

ANDY: 'Are you having a laugh? Is he having laugh?'

FAN: Oh, ha ha ha, I love everything about it.

ANDY: Cheers.

FAN: The wig, the glasses, the catchphrase.
(ANDY ROLLS HIS EYES)
Can I call my mate Pete?

ANDY: Why not.

FAN: (dialling) Oh, he'll love this.

ANDY: You can't call the barman as well, can you?

FAN: I haven't got his number.
(INTO PHONE)
Pete, what's your favourite catchphrase? He's only here. Yeahhh, ha ha, speak to him. Speak to him.

ANDY: I can't.

FAN: Speak to him. Just speak to him.

ANDY: All right, Pete, how you been, mate? Yeah, yeah? He likes that as well. Yeah, no, I haven't got the wig on me, no, no. Oh, Pete, I've got to go mate because . . . life's too short. Okay? Yeah, see you.

FAN: (into phone) Uh? Yeah. That was actually him, yeah. Come down.

ANDY: (walking away) Ah, that's me.

FAN: Bring Ralph and Walnut. And tell Count Fuckula. Oh yeah. He loves him. All right. I've got to go.
(HE HANGS UP AND FOLLOWS ANDY)
Quick, quick, quick, Jilly.

SCENE 9. INT.
PUB TABLE. NIGHT.

ANDY GOES BACK TO THE TABLE.

ANDY: Forget it, drink up. We're going.

MAGGIE: Why?

ANDY: 'Cause I've just been spotted by something from *The Hills Have Eyes*.

THE FAN WANDERS OVER WITH HIS GIRLFRIEND.

FAN: Hello!

ANDY: Oh.

AGENT: Hello, mate, all right? How's it going? Darren Lamb, agent. Nice to meet you.

FAN: This is my girlfriend Jilly.

AGENT: Hello.

SHAUN: Hello, Jilly.

FAN: (looking at SHAUN) Oh, I recognise you.

SHAUN: (proudly) Yes, possibly.

FAN: You did my mum's guttering, didn't you?

SHAUN: (deflated) Maybe, yeah, where does she live?

FAN: Arundall Court, opposite the BP garage.

SHAUN: Yeah, yeah.

AGENT: (angrily) What's this? You didn't tell me anything about this. What's going on here? How much did you get paid for that?

SHAUN: Not much.

FAN: It was two hundred quid. Mum said he did such a good job she gave him a twenty-pound tip.

AGENT: Two hundred and twenty quid?

SHAUN: I don't have to tell you everything.

AGENT: Oh no, no, you don't have to tell me everything, no. Although I notice you're happy to tell me when you're sleeping in your car and you need somewhere to have a bath – then you can't keep your mouth shut – but this you're keeping shtum about?

SHAUN: You're supposed to be my agent for acting, not bloody Artexing or whatever.

AGENT: Rumbled! Rumbled! He said guttering. Now it's Artexing! What else are you keeping from me? I can't . . . I'm appalled, I can't . . . this is scandalous, Barry, you're . . . such a slap in the face.

FAN: Do you do roofing?

AGENT: Do you need some roofing done? He'll do roofing.

SHAUN: No, it's too dangerous, I'm not, I'm not . . .

AGENT: (sarcastic) Oh, I'm sorry, you're turning down work now, are you? I'm sorry, it seems that beggars can be choosers! My mistake, unbelievable.
(THE AGENT GETS OUT A CALCULATOR)
Right, how much was it? Two twenty? Right, you owe me £27.50.

SHAUN: Can I give you a cheque?

AGENT: Yeah, if you must, yeah. Unbelievable.
(TO FAN, INDICATING ANDY)
Here, I tell you this, if you like his show, you'll love this.

Extras   series two

(HE TYPES SOMETHING INTO THE CALCULATOR, THEN HANDS IT TO THE FAN)

Right, have a look at that, just regular, turn it up the other way.

THE FAN TURNS THE CALCULATOR UPSIDE DOWN.

FAN: (laughing) Boobs!

AGENT: It's good, isn't it?

FAN: How do you do that?

AGENT: It's just numbers.

FAN: What numbers?

AGENT: 58008. Have a look.

FAN: Boobs.
(SHOWING HIS GIRLFRIEND)
Jilly, look. 58008.

AGENT: Turn it up the other way.

FAN: (turning the calculator upside down) Boobs.

MAGGIE: Let me have a wee look.

MAGGIE /FAN: Boobs.

ANDY ROLLS HIS EYES. HE MEETS SHAUN'S GAZE.

SHAUN: You want to get used to this, mate.

ANDY: It's doing my head in.

SHAUN: I know, they see you on telly and they all want to be your best mate. When I was on *EastEnders* we used to go to a place called Castro's, it's quiet and they treat you well if they recognise you.

ANDY: Let's go there.

SHAUN: Yeah, all right.

SHAUN HAS BEEN WRITING A CHEQUE. HE GIVES IT TO THE AGENT.

AGENT: Cheers, mate.
(TO THE FAN)
Oi, oi, oi! Boing!

HE MIMES THE CHEQUE BOUNCING.

SHAUN: Yeah, if it does whose fault's that?

AGENT: All right, Barry, let's not start talking about business, mate, in front of a couple of nobodies like this, no disrespect. Unbelievable. I'm already annoyed with you, giving it backchat.

ANDY: (to FAN) Anyway, give me your number, we'll meet up again.
(THE FAN PATS ANDY ON THE SHOULDER)
Don't touch me.

SCENE 10. INT. CASTRO'S RECEPTION AREA. NIGHT.

CASTRO'S IS AN UPMARKET, MEMBERS-ONLY-TYPE CLUB. ANDY, MAGGIE, SHAUN AND THE AGENT ENTER. SHAUN APPROACHES THE RECEPTION.

SHAUN: Er, excuse me.

RECEPTIONIST: Yeah, hi.

SHAUN: Erm, I used to come here a lot a few years ago, I don't know if you remember me, when I was in *EastEnders*?

RECEPTIONIST: Oh yes, hi, hi, how you doing? Yes.

SHAUN: I'm out with three friends . . .

ANDY PEERS INSIDE. HE SEES GREG, HIS OLD RIVAL, STOOD NEAR THE BAR PONTIFICATING.

ANDY: Oh, Greg's in here.

MAGGIE: Well? You don't have to speak to him.

ANDY: Yeah, like he's not going to come over and gloat. Big, fat, smug face.

MAGGIE: We're here now. Shh.

SHAUN: It's fine, you just got to sign in.

ANDY: Okay.

RECEPTIONIST: (recognising ANDY) Oh, hello, look who it is. Hi. Welcome.

ANDY: Oh.

RECEPTIONIST: Enjoyed the show last night.

ANDY: Really?

RECEPTIONIST: (to colleague) Yeah. Mark, can you get Mr Millman to the VIP area, please?

ANDY: Oh, thanks very much.

RECEPTIONIST: No need to sign in, that's fine.

ANDY: Cheers. Thanks.

MARK: If you'd like to follow me, thanks.

RECEPTIONIST: Okay, enjoy, good.

SHAUN: Thank you.

RECEPTIONIST: Okay.

SCENE 11. INT. CASTRO'S BAR AREA. NIGHT.

MARK LEADS THE GANG THROUGH THE BAR AND THEY PASS GREG.

GREG: (spotting ANDY) Ah, Andy Millman—

ANDY: I can't stop, mate. I'm going to the VIP area.

THEY HURRY PAST. HEADS TURN AS ANDY AND HIS POSSE ARE LEAD TO A ROPED-OFF AREA MINDED BY A BURLY BOUNCER.

SCENE 12. INT. CASTRO'S VIP AREA, NIGHT.

THEY SIT DOWN. ANDY AND MAGGIE SMILE AT EACH OTHER.

ANDY: More like it. Thanks very much.

MARK: Can I get you anything to drink?

ANDY: Erm, some champagne?

MAGGIE: Yeah!

ANDY: Can we get a bottle of champagne please?

MARK: No problem.

ANDY SMILES, CONTENT AT LAST.

ANDY: Finally, a little bit of respect.

(HE NOTICES SOMETHING OFF-CAMERA)

Oh God, David Bowie. Oh my God. Unbelievable. Don't look.

DAVID BOWIE HAS ENTERED WITH A SUPER-COOL-LOOKING ENTOURAGE.
MARK REAPPEARS.

MARK: Sir, I'm going to have to ask you to leave.

ANDY: You just put us here.

MARK: David Bowie's here.

ANDY: I know, but it's just, it's really embarrassing. Oh.

SCENE 13. INT. CASTRO'S BAR AREA. NIGHT.

MARK MAKES THEM MOVE AS BOWIE AND HIS FRIENDS TAKE THEIR SEATS. ANDY AND CO. WANDER BACK THROUGH THE VIP ROPE AND INTO THE REGULAR BAR AREA. GREG IS WAITING FOR HIM, LOOKING SMUG.

GREG: Quick sit down.

ANDY: Yeah, at least I had a sit down. Quick little sit down, energy, back into it.

GREG: How's it going?

ANDY: Brilliant, you?

GREG: Excellent. Doing Chekhov at the Wyndham, just been nominated for an Olivier award, so . . .

MAGGIE: (impressed) Ohh!

ANDY: (to MAGGIE) No.

GREG: How's your sitcom going?

ANDY: Brilliant, ratings are brilliant.

GREG: Yeah, the reviews – very harsh, very harsh.

ANDY: Don't read reviews. Don't bother.

GREG: No?
(TAKING A CLIPPING FROM HIS WALLET)
I think I've got one here actually. Sorry, can you just hold that?

GREG PASSES HIS DRINK TO MAGGIE.

ANDY: Don't hold—

GREG: Been meaning to throw it away.

ANDY: Throw it away then.

GREG: (reading) '*When The Whistle Blows* – as I watched this abysmal time-warp comedy, I found myself expecting someone to shout "I'm free" and for Andy Millman to exclaim, "Hmm, Betty, the cat's just shat out the worst sitcom of all time."'

MAGGIE LAUGHS. ANDY REACTS.

ANDY: Don't really care about his opinion. If I want an opinion, it won't be a snotty little reviewer, it'll be the people that count, the man on the street.

MAGGIE: Yeah, he gave him twenty quid earlier.

ANDY: (to MAGGIE) Not that specific man on the street.

GREG: If you want to chase ratings, that's great.

ANDY: Not chase 'em.

GREG: I'd rather win the respect of my peers than get big ratings and everything . . .

ANDY: Both, get both. Anyway, always nice to see you, mate.

BEHIND GREG, A PUNTER LEANS IN.

PUNTER: 'You having a laugh?'

ANDY LAUGHS.

ANDY: All right, mate.

PUNTER: Sitcom's shit, mate.

ANDY: Oh, he's changed his tune . . .

GREG: The man on the street – so fickle.

MAGGIE: No, he didn't have a bald head.

ANDY: No, not that specific man.

GREG: Does that happen a lot?

ANDY: No, never. It's all good usually. So I don't—

PUNTER: (turning to ANDY again) I tell you who's not having a laugh – the public.

THE PUNTER GOES BACK TO HIS FRIENDS, LAUGHING.

ANDY: Well, they are.

GREG: It's just rude . . .

ANDY: It's not rude, it's stupid, it's ignorant.

GREG: . . . To say that.

ANDY: He's a little ant to me.

GREG: I feel it's just social rudeness.

ANDY: Well . . .

SCENE 14. INT. CASTRO'S BAR AREA. NIGHT.

THE AGENT AND SHAUN ARE STOOD AT THE BAR. THE AGENT IS EYEING UP THE LADIES.

AGENT: Bar, don't look round, right, there's a couple of birds over there without drinks. I think you know what to do.

SHAUN: Oh, yes.
(TO BARMAN)
Excuse me. There's a couple of girls over there not drinking. So I think you should probably tell them to either buy something or get out.

AGENT: No, sorry, no . . . sorry, that's a mistake, no, no, no. I didn't mean that, sorry, what I meant was we could buy them some drinks, that's an 'in', isn't it? To start a conversation.

SHAUN: Well, I thought you were worried that they're taking up valuable space and costing him money.

AGENT: Why would that concern me? It's not my concern.

SHAUN: Well, the man's running a business. The overheads are probably extortionate.

AGENT: But he probably makes a lot of money on food, if you're worried about—

SHAUN: No, no, don't give me that. There's twenty pubs a day closing down in this country and it's due to people like that. All right?

AGENT: What and you're suddenly an expert, are you, on that? I don't know why it's your concern is what I'm—

SHAUN: Leave it.

CUT TO: TWO WOMEN CHATTING. THE AGENT AND SHAUN APPROACH THEM.

AGENT: Ladies, pardon us, can I just introduce myself? Darren Lamb - agent to the TV actor Andy Millman, star of the sitcom *When The Wind Blows*.

SHAUN: (correcting) Whistle.

AGENT: Whistle, thank you. And, er, do you remember this guy? It's only Barry off *EastEnders*.

SHAUN: Hello.

GIRL ONE: Oh, yeah, how's it going?

SHAUN: Not so good, actually. Things aren't quite panning out as I'd hoped.

AGENT: Let's not talk about that now, Barry. Let's not bring the mood down now, couple of sorts like this are up for it.

GIRL ONE: What do you mean, 'Up for it'?

AGENT: What, you're out and about, you know, no guys with you, you meet a couple of players like us, ships in the night. Let's get down to business: who wants Barry off *EastEnders*?

GIRL ONE: Neither of us.

AGENT: All right, Bar, you're out in the cold, mate.

SHAUN: That's the story of my life, you know. My house was repossessed last—

AGENT: Again, let's not bring the mood down, you're ruining it again. I'm still in the frame.
(TO THE GIRLS)
Who wants Barry to walk 'em home, while the other one comes home with me?

GIRL ONE: Neither of us.

AGENT: Okay, final scenario, listen to this, right: neither of you are interested in Barry so obviously I choose the fit one, no disrespect to you.
(HE POINTS TO GIRL TWO)
We all go back to mine, Barry keeps you talking . . .
(HE POINTS TO GIRL ONE)
 . . . whilst you and I get down to it . . .
(HE POINTS TO GIRL TWO)
It will take, I swear to God, ten minutes max, I can get everything done in that time. Then you get a cab fare home, anywhere you want to go, up to say a maximum value of fifteen pounds. Or, you could walk home, pocket the cash, you've made a sweet, sweet profit. So it's up to you.

GIRL ONE: No.

AGENT: No? All right, Bar, forget it mate. Always know when to cut your losses, let's go.

THEY WALK AWAY.

SCENE 15. INT. CASTRO'S VIP AREA. NIGHT.

DAVID BOWIE AND LINDA, HIS FRIEND, ARE TALKING.

BOWIE: I mean, he was actually a qualified surgeon, if I'm not wrong.

LINDA: (laughing) Really?

BOWIE: And he used to sing in the operating theatre.

LINDA: No.

BOWIE: That's where he got his first start, because one of the patients he was operating on was an A & R man from Decca Records. You won't know Decca.

ANDY APPROACHES THE BOUNCER WITH MAGGIE IN TOW.

ANDY: Sorry. I'm getting a bit of hassle out here, can I just pop myself down there?

HE POINTS TO A FREE SEAT INSIDE THE VIP AREA.

BOUNCER: Well, not really, this is the VIP section. Can you just step away from the rope, please, sir.

ANDY: No, I know, I was in there a minute ago. I was a VIP a minute ago, what happened?

BOUNCER: There's nothing I can do, sir, sorry. Look, can you just step away from the rope?

THE BOUNCER STEPS ASIDE AND LIFTS THE ROPE TO LET SOME OF BOWIE'S ENTOURAGE THROUGH.

ANDY: (gesturing to the rest of the club) Come on. I've got more in common with David Bowie than this rabble.

BOUNCER: How do you work that out?

ANDY: Well, we're both entertainers. We've both done something with our lives.

BOUNCER: I don't think you can equate yourself to David Bowie. He's one of the seminal artists of the last thirty-five years, doing work tantamount to genius – whereas you've just made a camp, catchphrase-based comedy.

ANDY: (aside, to MAGGIE) Just got a bad review off a bouncer.

BOUNCER: No, I just know what I like.

ANDY: Yeah? Do you like money?

BOUNCER: Sorry?

ANDY: Do you like money? Twenty quid.

BOUNCER: Sorry, you're trying to bribe me to sit next to David Bowie now?

ANDY: I'm giving you twenty quid to sit there in those spare seats.

BOUNCER: No.

ANDY: Fifty?

BOUNCER: Fifty quid?

ANDY: Yeah.

PAUSE.

BOUNCER: Let's see it.

ANDY LOOKS IN HIS WALLET.

ANDY: Have you got a ten? I've only got twenties.

BOUNCER: No.

ANDY: Well, it's either forty or sixty then.

BOUNCER: Well, sixty then.

ANDY: 'Sixty then!' That's for both of us.
(THE BOUNCER LIFTS THE ROPE. ANDY AND MAGGIE PASS THROUGH AND SIT DOWN. TO MAGGIE)
Go and get a drink. I haven't got any money now.

THE AGENT AND SHAUN APPEAR.

AGENT: Hey, what are you doing in there?

ANDY: It's the VIP area, isn't it?

AGENT: Well, can we come in? Because we're getting no action out here.

SHAUN: It's a wasteland.

ANDY: You're on your own, not made of money.

THE SEAT THAT ANDY HAS JUST PAID SIXTY POUNDS FOR IS PART OF
ONE LONG BENCH-SEAT DIVIDED IN HALF BY THE ROPE – WHICH MEANS
WHEN THE AGENT SITS DOWN HE AND ANDY ARE SAT NEXT TO EACH
OTHER, SAVE FOR A ROPE BETWEEN THEM.

ANDY: It's the same seat! It's actually the same seat for sixty quid!

AGENT: (laughing) You paid sixty quid to go in here? You should've let me negotiate.

PUNTER: (heckling from off-screen) Show's shit, mate.

ANDY: And they can still see me! There should be an actual barrier or something.

MAGGIE: Look, let's go and sit next to David Bowie. He's not getting any hassle.

ANDY: You just can't go and just sit next to him.

MAGGIE: Oh, come on, we'll just go and speak to him.

ANDY: I don't know him, do I?

MAGGIE: (calling to BOWIE) Excuse me.

ANDY: What are you doing?

MAGGIE: It's all right. Excuse me, Mr Bowie, can I just say that we're both very big fans.

BOWIE: I can't hear you, love, come over here.

MAGGIE: Go on, go on, go on.

BOWIE: Budge up a bit, Linda. Thank you.

ANDY AND MAGGIE SIT DOWN NEXT TO BOWIE.

ANDY: Hi.

BOWIE: Hi, hi.

ANDY: I was just saying that, erm, I'm an entertainer too.

BOWIE: Oh yeah, what do you do?

ANDY: I'm in a sitcom.

MAGGIE: It's called *When The Whistle Blows*, have you seen it?

BOWIE: I haven't, no. Is it any good?

PUNTER: (heckling as before) No, it's shit.

ANDY: Oh, riff-raff everywhere.

BOWIE: Not going down too well, eh?

ANDY: It's getting six million viewers. I mean it's not exactly how I meant it to be because the BBC have interfered and sort of chased ratings and made it lowest common denominator sort of comedy, sort of catchphrases and wigs and . . . I think I've sold out to be honest . . .

BOWIE: Yeah?

ANDY: It's difficult, isn't it? To keep your integrity when you're going for that first . . .

BOWIE: (suddenly gripped with inspiration, ad-libbing a few lines of song) 'Little fat man who sold his soul.'

ANDY: The little—?

BOWIE: 'Little fat man who sold his dream . . . chubby little loser.'
(BOWIE TURNS TO A NEARBY PIANO. HE BEGINS TO PLAY A FEW NOTES AND SING A FEW IMPROVISED LINES)
'Chubby little loser, national joke.' No, not, not chubby little loser.

ANDY: No.

BOWIE, SUDDENLY INSPIRED, TOYS WITH NOTES AND CHORDS.

BOWIE: No.

(PLAYING AND SINGING)

'Pathetic little fat man, no one's bloody laughing.

The clown that no one laughs at.

They all just wish he'd die.

He's so depressed at being useless,

The fat man takes his own life.' No, no . . . 'He's so depressed at being hated,

Fatty takes his own life.'

(TO MAGGIE)

Fatty, fatso?

MAGGIE: Fatso. I like fatso.

BOWIE: Yeah, let's go with fatso.

(ANDY REACTS)

'Fatso takes his own life,

He blows his bloated face off.' No . . . 'He blows his stupid brains out.'

LINDA: (chipping in) But the twat'd probably miss!

BOWIE: Yes, Linda, I like that.

ANDY: (sarcastic) Yes, so do I, it's brilliant, Linda.

BOWIE IS IN THE SWING OF IT NOW.

BOWIE: (singing and playing, increasingly anthemic) 'He sold his soul
for a shot at fame.
Catchphrase and wig and the jokes are lame.
He's got no style, he's got no grace.
He's banal and facile, he's a fat waste of space.'
(TO THE CROWD THAT HAS GATHERED)
Yeah, yeah, everybody sing that last line. One, two, three.

CROWD: (singing along) 'He's banal and facile, he's a fat waste of space.'

BOWIE: 'See his pug-nosed face . . .'

MAGGIE LOOKS AT ANDY'S NOSE AND NODS TO THE CROWD AS IF TO SAY,
'IT IS PUG-NOSED.' ANDY REACTS.

BOWIE/CROWD: 'See his pug-nosed face . . . Pug, pug, pug, pug.'

BOWIE: Again.

BOWIE/CROWD: 'See his pug-nosed face . . . pug, pug, pug, pug.'

ANDY HAS NO CHOICE BUT TO SIT AND LISTEN AS THE CROWD'S
SINGING GETS LOUDER. THE AGENT AND SHAUN JOIN IN.
SHAUN BEGINS TO HARMONISE.

BOWIE: 'The little fat man with the pug-nosed face'

BOWIE/CROWD: 'Pug, pug, pug, pug.'

GREG JOINS A CROWD WHO HAVE GATHERED AROUND THE PIANO. HE POINTS OUT ANDY'S 'PUG-NOSED FACE' TO THE PEOPLE NEARBY. ANDY COVERS HIS NOSE WITH HIS HAND.

BOWIE: 'Little fat man, pug-nosed face, hey.'

BOWIE/CROWD: 'Pug, pug, pug, pug.'

BOWIE: 'He's a little fat man, pug-nosed face.'

BOWIE/CROWD: 'Pug, pug, pug, pug.'

CLOSE-UP ON ANDY AS DAVID BOWIE AND A CROWD OF STRANGERS DECRY HIS VERY EXISTENCE.

SCENE 16. INT. PUB BAR. NIGHT.

THE SAME PUB AS BEFORE. THE OBSESSIVE FAN AND HIS GIRLFRIEND HAVE BEEN JOINED BY SOME EQUALLY NERDY MATES.

FAN: What did you have for tea?

MATE: Turkey.

FAN: Turkey. What else?

MATE: Turkey, just turkey.

FAN: (giggling) Just turkey, you can't have just turkey.

ANDY AND MAGGIE RE-ENTER.

ANDY: Pint of Fosters.

MAGGIE: (to the barman) Hi, a pint of Fosters and a dry white wine, please.

BARMAN: That's five eighty thanks.

ANDY: (spotting the FAN and his friends) Five eighty?
(LOUDLY)
'Are you having a laugh?'

THE FAN HEARS THIS AND SPINS ROUND, HIS FACE LIGHTING UP. HE POINTS OUT ANDY TO HIS MATES. THEY'RE OVERWHELMED WITH EXCITEMENT, EAGER FOR PHOTOS AND AUTOGRAPHS.

FAN: It's him! It's him! It's Andy Millman.

EXTRAS
Episode 3

CAST LIST
Andy Millman RICKY GERVAIS
Maggie Jacobs ASHLEY JENSEN
Agent STEPHEN MERCHANT
Shaun SHAUN WILLIAMSON

Guest Starring DANIEL RADCLIFFE
with DIANA RIGG

Warwick WARWICK DAVIS
Claire ELEANOR TREMAIN
Kimberley SARAH MOYLE
Gobbler ANDREW BUCKLEY
Brains JAMIE CHAPMAN
Dougie's Mum WENDY NOTTINGHAM
Dougie RUSSELL RAMSEY
Daniel's Mum HELEN ANDERSON
Journalist RUFUS JONES
Waitress LUCIA GIANNECCHINI
A.D. MATT GREEN

With JUDY FINNIGAN, RICHARD
MADELEY, NICK FERRARI, PHILLIP
SCHOFIELD, FERN BRITTON,
MATTHEW WRIGHT, LOWRI TURNER

Written & Directed by
RICKY GERVAIS &
STEPHEN MERCHANT

TV CLIP:
'WHEN THE WHISTLE BLOWS'

AN ANIMATED OPENING SEQUENCE BEGINS THE SHOW. DISSOLVE THROUGH TO RAY, BRAINS, GOBBLER AND KIMBERLEY ARE AROUND THE TABLE. GOBBLER IS READING THE PAPER.

GOBBLER: Oh, I don't like the sound of that.

RAY: What's up with you?

GOBBLER: There's a story here about the Brazilian rowing team. They were practising on t'Amazon, and it's full of piranha fish, and they capsized. Says in t'paper they were in danger of having their cox eaten. Why would piranhas go for the cox first?

RAY: It doesn't mean what you think it . . . the cox is the little fella who sits at back of boat shouting 'stroke'. Oh.

GOBBLER: If I were a piranha, I'd draw the line at eating cox.

RAY: It doesn't mean their c— . . . oh, you don't get it, do you?

GOBBLER: I don't get it.

RAY: I know you don't get it. Why, what would you go for first if you were a piranha?

GOBBLER: I'd probably just have a bag of crisps.

RAY: Are you having a laugh? Is he having a laugh?

AUDIENCE LAUGHTER AS WE CUT TO:

SCENE 1. INT.
SITCOM SET (WINGS). NIGHT.

ANDY'S AGENT IS TALKING ON HIS MOBILE PHONE IN THE WINGS AS THE SHOW IS BEING TAPED.

AGENT: He'd definitely be interested in a film, yeah. Who, who else is in it? . . . The fella who played who? Harry Potter? I've never heard of him. What . . . little magical kid with glasses? You know Andy's in his forties, do you? . . . Oh, they've got someone for him, okay. And how much would you be paying him?
(HE GIGGLES)

You've got more money than sense, mate.

(PAUSE)

No, I am his agent, yeah.

WE CUT BACK TO:

TV CLIP:
'WHEN THE WHISTLE BLOWS'

ON SET, THE CONVERSATION CONTINUES.

KIMBERLEY: Do you know, I met a bloke once who said he'd love to take me up the Amazon.

RAY: (splurting out his tea) What did *you* say?

KIMBERLEY: Oh, I said all right, as long as you're paying.

RAY: (splurting out more tea) What did *he* say?

KIMBERLEY: Well, he was a bit shocked to be honest.

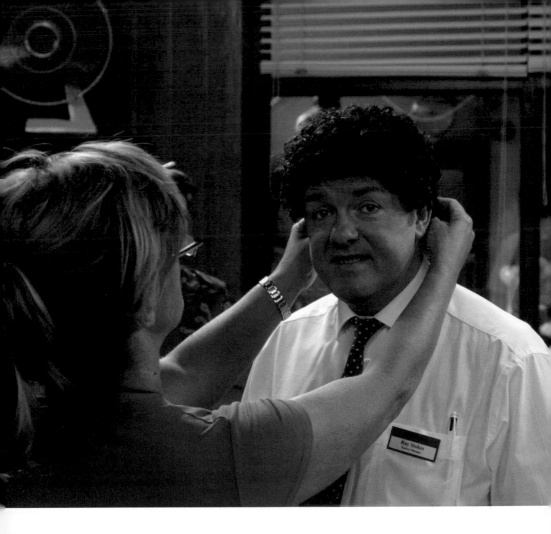

RAY: Not surprised.

KIMBERLEY: Not as shocked as when I told him I'd only do it if we could take lots of photos to show me mum.

RAY IS ABOUT TO SPLURT OUT MORE TEA BUT HIS MUG IS NOW EMPTY.

RAY: Oh, I've finished.

SCENE 2. INT.
ANDY'S DRESSING ROOM. NIGHT.

ANDY SITS IN AN ARMCHAIR, IN FULL 'RAY' COSTUME. HE SLOWLY
REMOVES HIS GLASSES AND WIG, LOOKING DESPONDENT.

AGENT: Knockety, knock, knock. Hello. All right? Great show, brilliant
show tonight, very, very funny.

ANDY: Yeah, what was your favourite bit?

AGENT: Uh . . .

ANDY: You didn't watch it, did you?

AGENT: It's not my cup of tea to be honest, if I'm being truthful.
It's not my thing, I can't get with it. I'd like to talk some business.
How do you fancy three days with Billie Piper?

ANDY: Three days with Billie Piper?

AGENT: Yeah, good money, you'd be in and out.

ANDY: What are you talking about?

AGENT: Billie Piper, little magical kid with glasses.

ANDY: Do you mean Harry Potter?

AGENT: Yes. Who did I say?

ANDY: Billie Piper.

AGENT: Now, I've heard of him, who's he?

ANDY: She. She's an actress. She's in *Doctor Who*, she was a pop—
Do you watch television?

AGENT: Do I watch television? I have just bought myself a brand-new 52-inch plasma TV set.

ANDY: 52 – that's way too big for your flat.

AGENT: It is too big, I don't know what I was thinking. It's too bright. I was wiring it up and David Dickinson came on and his tan nearly took me eyeballs out. I'm all over the place, I've got headaches. I've got it in the box now, I'm just watching a little portable. You don't want to buy a TV, do you?

ANDY: How much did you pay for it?

AGENT: Three and half grand.

ANDY: What would you sell it to me for?

AGENT: Three and half grand, face value.

ANDY: Obviously not, I'd just go buy a new one. No, you've got to give me a discount, it's second-hand. Fifteen hundred quid.

AGENT: That's an insult. I would rather smash it up than give it to you for fifteen hundred quid, that is pathetic.

ANDY: All right, this project, go on.

AGENT: Well, yeah, big British movie, lots of stars, Dame Diana Rigg's in it, all sorts of people. I know you want to get into movies so this could be a good 'in' – plus I checked with them straight away, I said, 'Will he still get paid even if his performance is crap?' They said yes, so it's win-win for us.

ANDY: You didn't ask them that?

AGENT: Well, yeah, because obviously I was worried that if you got the gig and then they saw the sitcom they might fire you, you know. But they've already seen the show so . . .

ANDY: (sarcastic) Oh, they've seen the show? Oh, because they're in the business and they watch television? They're, yeah.

AGENT: I wonder if they want to buy a TV.

ANDY: Don't ask them if they want to buy your telly. Right, call them and say yes, I'm interested. And get Maggie some extra work on it, I don't want to spend three days with loads of actors I don't know. Nightmare. Call them now.

AGENT: Well, I'll call them later.

ANDY: No, no, call them now.

AGENT: (getting up and walking towards the door) Well, I'll call them outside.

ANDY: Call them in here.

AGENT: No, yeah, I just don't want, I don't want to call them in front of you and everything, you know . . .

ANDY: Don't ask them if they want to buy your telly.

AGENT: (turning round) Oh, I might as well do it in here then.

ANDY: Ridiculous.

SCENE 3. INT. DANIEL RADCLIFFE FILM SET. DAY.

ESTABLISHING SHOTS: THE SET OF A BIG-BUDGET FANTASY FILM. LIGHTS, CAMERAS, TECHNICIANS, ETC. ANDY IS SAT ON THE FILM SET. AN A.D. IS WALKING ACROSS WITH WARWICK DAVIS, WHO IS HOLDING HANDS WITH HIS FIANCÉE, AN ATTRACTIVE WOMAN CALLED CLAIRE.

WARWICK: So, what scene are we starting with?

A.D.: We're starting with 1/41. I'll just introduce you to . . . to Andy, this is Warwick.

ANDY: Oh, hi.

WARWICK: Hi.

ANDY: Nice to meet you.

WARWICK: Good to meet you. This is my fiancée Claire.

CLAIRE: Hi.

ANDY: Hi.

AS ANDY IS SAT DOWN, HE HAS TO LOOK RIGHT UP TO SAY 'HELLO'
TO CLAIRE AND BACK DOWN AGAIN TO SPEAK TO WARWICK.
THE JUXTAPOSITION IN THEIR HEIGHT IS VERY PRONOUNCED.

WARWICK: So, do you know your lines?

ANDY: Well, I've only got two but er . . .

THE AGENT WANDERS ACROSS CARRYING A PLATE STACKED UP
WITH BREAKFAST TREATS.

AGENT: Are you sure all this food's definitely free?

ANDY: Yes.
(TO WARWICK)
This is my agent.

THE AGENT NOTICES CLAIRE BUT NOT WARWICK.

AGENT: (to CLAIRE) Darren Lamb, nice to meet you.

CLAIRE: Hi.

ANDY: This is Warwick.

AGENT: Where?

ANDY: (pointing down) There.

AGENT: Ooh. Midget. Hello.

CLAIRE: (to WARWICK) Babe, I'm going to get some coffees.

WARWICK: All right.

SHE WANDERS OFF.

AGENT: (to WARWICK) What was your name, sorry?

WARWICK: It's Warwick.

AGENT: Warwick, mm, funny little name, as well, to match.

ANDY REACTS. THE AGENT STARES AT WARWICK, INTRIGUED THE
A.D. APPROACHES ANDY.

A.D.: Sorry, Andy, can I just show you where you're going to be
standing?

ANDY: Yes.

A.D.: It won't take a second.

ANDY: (worried about leaving the AGENT) Don't . . . yeah.

THE AGENT IS LEFT ALONE WITH WARWICK, WHO IS READING HIS
SCRIPT. THE AGENT LOOKS DOWN AT WARWICK AND PATRONISINGLY

TAPS HIM ON THE HEAD.

AGENT: Are those your own clothes?

WARWICK: Er . . . no.

AGENT: No, no. Where'd you get your normal clothes from? I mean, what are they? Are they children's clothes? Or are they toy clothes? How does it work, you know, I mean, like, your shoes for instance, would they be like a little toy bear's booties? You know what I mean, like you sometimes see like a toy monkey or something that has little trainers on, would you have a pair of those for yourself?

WARWICK: No.

AGENT: No?

WARWICK: There are specialist shops. And I do a lot of Internet shopping.

AGENT: Internet. That makes sense, that's clever, yeah.
(PAUSE)
Could I fit in your house? Would that . . . , how would it work?

ANDY REJOINS THEM.

ANDY: What have you been talking about?

AGENT: Yeah, we've been talking about the Internet and stuff.

ANDY: Right, yeah.

AGENT: Yeah, this would be a laugh: imagine if I followed him home to his tiny little house right, and as he goes up to bed, right, I just put my face up against the window just like Godzilla, just going aarrggh, freaking him out or whatever or reaching in through the window like King Kong, trying to—

THE AGENT GRABS AT WARWICK'S NECK.

ANDY: (shocked) What are you doing?

AGENT: I'm just having a chat with him.

ANDY: Why are you still here?

AGENT: I'm having a . . .

ANDY: Well, we've got to learn our lines.
AGENT: ALL RIGHT.
(PATRONISINGLY, TO WARWICK)
Bye.

THE AGENT LEAVES THE SET.

WARWICK: Agent?

ANDY: Idiot.

FILM CLIP: 'THE GRIFFIN'S LAIR'

WE SEE FEET CRUNCHING THROUGH A WOODLAND CLEARING. WARWICK, DRESSED AS AN ELF, IS SAT IN TOP OF A GIANT TOADSTOOL QUIETLY SOBBING. A HAND TAPS HIM ON THE SHOULDER. IT IS DANIEL RADCLIFFE IN A SCOUT'S UNIFORM.

DANIEL: Wood elf, why do you cry?

WARWICK: Blow as I might, my flute makes no sound. Without my music, the birds cannot sing their morning song.

DANIEL: May I take a look?

WARWICK: Certainly, but I don't know what a boy can do – especially one dressed so strangely.

DANIEL GETS OUT A PENKNIFE AND FIDDLES WITH THE FLUTE.

DANIEL: Try it now . . .

THE FLUTE PLAYS ITS WONDERFUL MAGICAL SOUND. THE BIRDS BEGIN TO SING.

WARWICK: Oh! Sweet music is born again. But I am curious, how did you know you'd need such an implement?

DANIEL LAUGHS WRYLY.

DANIEL: Always be prepared!

FIRST A.D.: Okay, cut there, thank you, check the gate.

SCENE 4. INT. FILM SET. DAY

WE SNAP BEHIND THE SCENES OF THE FILM CLIP WE HAVE JUST SEEN.

WARWICK: (to FIRST A.D.) Can I get a drink of water, please?

A COSTUME LADY APPROACHES DANIEL AND BEGINS TO ADJUST HIS UNIFORM.

DANIEL: You married?

COSTUME: Yes.

DANIEL: That don't stop me . . . a ring don't mean a thing.

SCENE 5. INT. FILM SET. DAY.

MAGGIE IS SAT READING A MAGAZINE. IN FULL COSTUME DANIEL RADCLIFFE NOICES HER AND POINTS TO AN EMPTY CHAIR.

DANIEL: (trying to be cool) This chair free?

MAGGIE: Er, yeah.

DANIEL MOVES THE CHAIR SO THAT HE IS SAT DIRECTLY IN FRONT OF MAGGIE. MAGGIE SMILES POLITELY. DANIEL SITS, STARING AT HER, TRYING TO LOOK BROODING.

DANIEL: How you doing?

MAGGIE: Okay.

HE SUDDENLY REALISES HE IS WEARING HIS GLASSES.

DANIEL: Oh God, have I still got these on? I don't need these. They're just for the character. Even if I did need glasses in real life, you know, I, I never read.

MAGGIE: Right.

HE SNAPS BACK INTO HIS BROODING 'JAMES DEAN' MANNER. WITHOUT WARNING, HE SUDDENLY HOLDS UP AN UNOPENED PACKET OF CIGARETTES.

DANIEL: Oh, hey.

MAGGIE: What?

DANIEL: Fags.

MAGGIE: Yeah. Do you smoke, do you?

DANIEL: Me, oh yeah, just a little bit yeah. You?

MAGGIE: No.

DANIEL: No, no, no. Good girl, good girl, very wise. I've got to cut down, really.

DANIEL FAKES A CHESTY SMOKE'S COUGH. MAGGIE GOES BACK TO HER MAGAZINE. PAUSE.

DANIEL: I've done it with a girl.

MAGGIE: What?

DANIEL: I've done it with a girl. Intercourse-wise. So if you're looking for—

FEMALE VOICE: (off-screen) Daniel?

DANIEL NOTICES SOMEONE APPROACHING AND HIS COOL FACADE DISAPPEARS.

DANIEL: Here's my mum, say they're your fags.

HE THROWS THE CIGARETTES TO MAGGIE, WHO CATCHES THEM INSTINCTIVELY. SHE TRIES TO HAND THEM BACK AS DANIEL'S MUM APPEARS.

DANIEL'S MUM: What you doing?

DANIEL: Nothing. She's trying to give me fags.

MAGGIE: What? No, I'm not!

DANIEL'S MUM: (reprimanding MAGGIE) You should know better, you're old enough to be his mother.

DANIEL: Yeah, and she was trying to have it off with me.

MAGGIE PUTS HER HAND UP TO TRY AND INTERRUPT.

DANIEL'S MUM: Oh, well, course she was, you're bloody gorgeous. Come on you.

SHE LEADS HIM AWAY, GLOWERING AT MAGGIE.

SCENE 6. INT. DANIEL RADCLIFFE FILM SET. DAY.

ANDY AND MAGGIE ARE WATCHING WARWICK CHATTING WITH HIS FIANCÉE CLAIRE.

ANDY: Makes me sick.

MAGGIE: What?

ANDY: These showbiz dwarfs who use their powers to get women out of their league.

MAGGIE: Who, Warwick?

ANDY: No, Paul Daniels.

MAGGIE LAUGHS.

MAGGIE: Here, if she's into short men, you could be in with a chance.

ANDY: I'm not short.

MAGGIE: Yeah, you are.

ANDY: No, I'm not, no, no, five-foot-eight, average height.

MAGGIE: Well, average in your day.

ANDY: My day? I was born in the sixties.

MAGGIE: Early sixties.

ANDY: Quite early, yeah.

MAGGIE: 1960?

ANDY: No.

MAGGIE: 1961?
(ANDY NODS RELUCTANTLY)
Ah, that'll be why you didn't grow.

ANDY: I did grow.

MAGGIE: All the powdered egg and the rationing and everything.

ANDY: That was the war.

MAGGIE: Yeah, well, whatever. Do you know what, you've got a 'small man' complex.

ANDY: What's that?

MAGGIE: You're bad-tempered, you're grumpy, you want power and people to respect you. Oh like that little famous person what's his name? Begins with an 'n'.

ANDY: Napoleon.

MAGGIE: Noel Edmonds.

ANDY: I'm not short, I'm average height, and that's the . . .

MAGGIE: I can see how it is upsetting for you . . .

ANDY: It's not upsetting.

MAGGIE: (gesturing to WARWICK) There's him, he's even smaller than you are and . . .

ANDY: 'Cause I'm not small.

MAGGIE: . . . He is getting all these attractive and beautiful women and . . .

ANDY: We all are, we all are.

MAGGIE: But you're getting nothing.

ANDY: Well, no way, I'm getting, I'm getting them.

MAGGIE: Well, there was the one that looked like Ronnie Corbett – and we know why you went for her.

ANDY: (sighs) Why?

MAGGIE: (laughing) Because she could look you in the eye.

ANDY: It's not a competition.
(HE POINTS TO WARWICK'S FIANCÉE)
It's not like she saw us both and went, 'Oh, I'll have the short one.'

MAGGIE: Is that you or him?

ANDY: Him!

MAGGIE: See, there's the temper.

ANDY: I'm saying, if she'd have met us both at the same time, we don't know who she'd have chosen but, well, I think I know who she'd have chosen . . .

MAGGIE: Who?

ANDY: Eh? No, I'm not going to say because it will sound arrogant. I don't want to . . . but if she was single and she'd have met us both—

MAGGIE: Yeah.

ANDY: Yeah.

MAGGIE: (not understanding) Tell me.

ANDY: Oh for . . . just think your own thoughts, stay out of mine.

SCENE 7. INT. DINING BUS. DAY.

MAGGIE AND ANDY ARE EATING.

MAGGIE: It's really stodgy, isn't it?

ANDY: Honestly, I'm sick of this. Can we go somewhere nice tonight? My treat, but a proper restaurant.

MAGGIE: Yeah?

ANDY: Yeah.

MAGGIE: All right then.

DANIEL RADCLIFFE SITS DOWN AT THE TABLE.

DANIEL: Hey gang, what we doing?

MAGGIE: Just been eating.

DANIEL: Yeah, yeah, sweet. Look, thanks for covering my arse earlier, the offer still stands.

MAGGIE: What offer?

DANIEL: You know . . .

HE MAKES SOME KIND OF SEX GESTURE WITH HIS FINGERS.

MAGGIE: (making excuses) I'm just going to go and get a drink, does anyone want anything?

ANDY: I'll have a cup of tea.

DANIEL: Yeah, get me a bourbon, would you, babe?

MAGGIE: Well, I think it's mostly just teas and coffees and things . . .

DANIEL: Oh, yeah, then get me a cup of joe, would you? And make it strong. I don't like the weak shit. Ooh.

HE CATCHES HIMSELF SWEARING AND LOOKS AROUND, WORRIED HIS
MUM MAY HAVE HEARD. MAGGIE HEADS OFF.

DANIEL: (conspiratorial) Look, when she comes back, right, make some excuse and leave us alone, will you?

ANDY: What you got planned?

DANIEL PULLS OUT A CONDOM FROM HIS TOP POCKET, ALREADY
UNWRAPPED. HE HOLDS IT UP.

ANDY: You've unravelled it.

DANIEL: Ready for action.
(HE STRETCHES IT LIKE A RUBBER BAND)
Just hope it's big enough.

(THE CONDOM PINGS OFF INTO THE AIR. DANIEL LOOKS ROUND THE BUS, PANICKED, SEARCHING FOR IT. IT HAS LANDED ON THE FOREHEAD OF DAME DIANA RIGG. LIKE A KID ASKING FOR HIS BALL:)

Erm, can I have my Johnny back?

DAME DIANA: (correcting him) *May* I have my Johnny back.

DANIEL: May I have my Johnny back?

DAME DIANA: Please.

DANIEL: Yeah.

DAME DIANA: It's not called a Johnny though, is it?

DANIEL: Durex.

DAME DIANA: No, that's a brand name. May I have back my prophylactic or sheath?

DANIEL: May I have my prophaleck . . .

DAME DIANA: (correcting his pronunciation) . . . Tic.

DANIEL: Tic, prophylactic. Can I have it please?

DAME DIANA: Yes.
(DANIEL TAKES THE CONDOM BACK AND TURNS AWAY)
Excuse me. Haven't you forgotten something?

DANIEL: Oh, thank you, Dame Diana.

DANIEL BEGINS TO PUT THE CONDOM BACK IN HIS POCKET.

ANDY: Still going to use it, yeah?

DANIEL: Yeah, that'll be fine.

ANDY: Lucky girl.

SCENE 8. INT. FILM SET. DAY.

WARWICK IS TALKING WITH CLAIRE, HIS FIANCÉE. HE GIVES HER A QUICK KISS AND WANDERS OFF. MAGGIE IS SAT NEARBY. SHE OBSERVES THIS.

MAGGIE: (pointing after WARWICK) You're getting married to . . .

CLAIRE: Yeah, yeah.

MAGGIE: Yeah. That's really nice of you.

CLAIRE: It's 'really nice' of me?

MAGGIE: Yeah, well, me and my friend Andy – Andy Millman – were talking and he was surprised that, that you'd chosen someone like Warwick over, well, you . . . someone, someone like him who's . . . do you only like small people?

CLAIRE: I don't like him because he's small, I like him because he has a nice personality.

MAGGIE: Oh, well, that's good then because Andy was just saying that if you didn't mind someone who's a little bit taller, then he's up for it.

CLAIRE: Sorry, so your friend is so arrogant he thinks he just has to give the word and I would immediately leave my fiancé for him, because he's taller? Do you understand how offensive that is?

MAGGIE: Yeah, it's a bit out of order, isn't it?

CLAIRE: It is out of order.

MAGGIE: He shouldn't really have said that, should he?

CLAIRE: No, he shouldn't have said that.

SCENE 9. INT. POSH RESTAURANT. NIGHT.

ANDY AND MAGGIE ARE EATING. NEARBY, A BOY IS DINING WITH HIS MOTHER. THE BOY IS PLAYING ON A PSP GAMES CONSOLE, WHICH IS VERY NOISY AND MAKES LOTS OF BEEPS AND SQUEALS. THE BOY GETS EXCITED EVERY TIME HE DOES WELL.

KID: Yes!

MAGGIE: This is all right, isn't it?

ANDY: Share the wealth.

KID: Yes!

ANDY: (distracted by the child) That kid's doing my head in, though.

MAGGIE: (not hearing him, sidetracked by the posh surroundings) It's lovely place though. Hey, bit depressing though.

ANDY: Why?

MAGGIE: Well, here I am with you in a nice place, instead of a proper man.

ANDY: None taken.

MAGGIE: No, I mean, like, on a date. The only person with money that finds me attractive is a teenage boy.

ANDY: Could be worse, he's a film star, he's got his own condom . . .

MAGGIE: What?

ANDY: Nothing.

A WAITRESS APPEARS.

WAITRESS: Excuse me, hi, erm, I know this isn't really . . . could I please get your autograph?

ANDY: Yeah. Sure.

WAITRESS: Thanks.

ANDY: Who's it to?

WAITRESS: Er, to Emma.

ANDY: No worries.

KID: (off-screen) Yes!

ANDY: You can do me a favour actually.
(HE SIGNS THE AUTOGRAPH)
Can you tell that woman to shut her kid up? It's doing my head in, cheers.

WAITRESS: Thanks.

THE WAITRESS WALKS OVER TO THE MOTHER AND SON.

ANDY: I'll never get used to that. Why does someone want your name on a piece of paper?

MAGGIE: I know, wee bit weird.
(MAGGIE WATCHES THE WAITRESS TALKING TO THE MOTHER. SHE CAN'T HEAR WHAT'S BEING SAID BUT WE SEE THE WAITRESS POINT OUT ANDY)
Oh, she's told them it's you! She's coming over!

THE MOTHER IS CLEARLY ANNOYED. SHE GETS UP AND MARCHES ACROSS.

MOTHER: Excuse me, I understand you have a problem with me bringing my son into a restaurant?

MAGGIE LOOKS ACROSS AT THE CHILD. SHE (AND WE) SEE THAT HER SON IS A BOY WITH DOWN'S SYNDROME.

ANDY: If he's like that, yes.

MAGGIE: Andy.

MOTHER: What do you mean, 'like that'?

ANDY: Well, why should we be burdened?

MAGGIE: (trying to interrupt) Andy, don't . . .

MOTHER: Sorry, you think that just because you're on TV you can order the rest of the world around?

ANDY: It's nothing to do with that, but if he's going to make that sort of noise . . . I mean it's a restaurant, for God's sake.

MOTHER: Well, that's not my fault is it?

ANDY: Well, it is your fault. You decided to have him.

MOTHER: (shocked) Of course I decided to have him.

MAGGIE: Andy . . .

MOTHER: You'll be pleased to know we're about to leave anyway so . . .
(GETTING UPSET)
. . . I hope you have a wonderful evening and that you realise you're a horrible little man.

SHE SHAKES HER HEAD IN DISBELIEF AND WALKS BACK ACROSS TO HER CHILD, CLEARLY UPSET. ANDY GLANCES BEHIND HIM – AND FOR THE FIRST TIME SEES HER SON.

ANDY: Oh, no, I didn't realise. I didn't realise.

MAGGIE: I was trying to tell you.

ANDY: Oh, why didn't you say something?

MAGGIE: I was trying to tell you . . .

ANDY: Well . . .

SCENE 10. EXT. ANDY'S FLAT. DAY.

ANDY IS COMING OUT OF HIS FRONT DOOR. A MAN IS SEARCHING THROUGH ANDY'S BINS. HE SEES ANDY AND SIDLES UP TO HIM. ANDY LOOKS PERPLEXED.

JOURNO: Hello, Andy, how's it going, mate? Paul, mate . . . I was just passing, want to clear up all this nonsense about you having a go at Down's syndrome people.

ANDY: About what?

JOURNO: We've had this woman come to us, saying that you were having a go at her kid who's all Down's and that.

ANDY: Sorry, are you a journalist?

JOURNO: Uh?

ANDY: Are you a journalist?

JOURNO: Sort of, mate, yeah, just freelance, just trying turn this round for you, get the truth out there for you, mate.

ANDY: Right. Yeah.

JOURNO: So what happened? The Down's syndrome's making a racket, you tell him to shut up, suddenly his mum's up in arms. You can't say anything nowadays, can you?

ANDY: I didn't tell him to shut up, I didn't tell anyone to shut up.

JOURNO: It's political correctness gone mad, isn't it? You can't say what you think any more . . .

ANDY: Well—

JOURNO: Is that yes?

ANDY: No . . .

JOURNO: (writing) Yeah.

ANDY: I didn't know he was Down's syndrome for a start.

JOURNO: So you're in a restaurant with your girlfriend—

ANDY: She's not my girlfriend.

JOURNO: Yeah, but she's a girl who's your friend.

ANDY: Yeah.

JOURNO: Well, I'll put girlfriend for the sake of ease . . .

ANDY: She's not my girlfriend.

JOURNO: Girlfriend, I'll put, for sake of shorthand.

ANDY: (correcting) Well, why put girlfriend if she's not my girlfriend?

JOURNO: And you're in there and you heard a noise and it was driving you mad? You can't say 'mad' nowadays, can you?

ANDY: Well, he was making a noise and I got a little . . .

JOURNO: Mad? You got mad? The mad kid was driving you mad?

ANDY: No, I wouldn't say that.

JOURNO: You can't say he's mad nowadays, can you? Or 'mental'.

ANDY: Well, I wouldn't, well I wouldn't say he was – can you make it clear I didn't know he was Down's syndrome?

JOURNO: I will, I will.

ANDY: Write that down.

(THE JOURNO PRETENDS TO WRITE SOMETHING)

Are you actually writing anything down?

JOURNO: Yeah, yeah. So, you complained, the mum came over, she went nuts?

ANDY: Well, she was agitated because . . .

JOURNO: So she went mad?

ANDY: Well—

JOURNO: So, you could say she was going 'madder than her son'?

ANDY: Well, I wouldn't say that, no.

JOURNO: So, would you say, 'She was going mental'?

ANDY: No, I wouldn't say that.

JOURNO: So, you might say mental?

ANDY: Well, no, I wouldn't say mental.

JOURNO: You can't say anything nowadays, can you?

ANDY: Well, I wouldn't say—

JOURNO: If you want to say mental, you can't.

ANDY: I wouldn't . . . I've got to go.

JOURNO: Cheers, mate, cheers.

ANDY: (walking away) See you later.

JOURNO: Got everything I need.

SCENE 11. INT.
AGENT'S OFFICE. DAY.

SHAUN IS STOOD NEXT TO THE AGENT, READING FROM A TABLOID
NEWSPAPER. ANDY AND THE AGENT ARE LISTENING.

SHAUN: (reading) 'In a shocking outburst that will stun comedy fans
everywhere, so-called TV funny-man Andy Millman lost his temper and
blasted a Down's syndrome child for supposedly ruining his dinner at
a one-hundred-pounds-a-head restaurant.'

AGENT: Hundred-pounds-a-head?

ANDY: Well, it was about eighty quid between us but . . .

AGENT: (not listening) Two hundred quid for a meal for two people!
How the other half live.

SHAUN: Sorry, that makes me sick.

AGENT: Yeah.

SHAUN: (reading) 'Millman had been glugging red wine with his
girlfriend . . .'

AGENT: Ooh, pissed.

ANDY: No, I'd had one drink.

SHAUN: Did you glug it though?

ANDY: Did I what?

SHAUN: It says here you glugged it.

ANDY: I don't know what glugging is.

SHAUN DEMONSTRATES GUZZLING A DRINK DOWN.

AGENT: (pointing at ANDY) Never glug. Always sip a lovely wine.
Never glug it.

ANDY: Can we stop saying 'glug'? And I wasn't even drinking red wine.
Maggie was drinking red wine, I had a beer.

SHAUN: (reading) 'Millman had been glugging red wine and let off a tirade of abuse at the innocent child and his stunned mother, who he claimed was as "mad as her son".'

ANDY: I didn't say that.

AGENT: Well, someone did.

SHAUN: 'Says mum Maureen Wilson, "I used to be a fan of Andy's but after his torrent of hate, if he thinks I'll ever watch his programme again,"' here, '"he's having a laugh."'

AGENT: (laughs) Ooh, she's used the old catchphrase against you. Stitched you up there, it's clever, it's witty.

ANDY: Yeah, as if she ever said that, as if she's making little jokes if she's that angry. She didn't say that.
(ANDY GIVES UP)
Sorry, what can we do about this? Can we sue?

AGENT: I don't think it's worth it, to be . . . I mean, this sort of thing is tomorrow's fish and chip paper, isn't it?
(ASIDE, TO SHAUN)
Not that he's having fish and chips any more, eh? Two hundred quid for a meal!

SHAUN: You'd have trouble doing two hundred quid in a chippie, wouldn't you?

AGENT: You certainly would.

ANDY: I didn't spend two hundred quid.

SHAUN: It says two hundred and thirty in this one.

ANDY: Lies.

SHAUN: No, it does.

ANDY: No, I don't mean you're lying, I mean they're lying. They make stuff up, don't they?

AGENT: I don't know about that.

ANDY: You've never heard of a paper making stuff up? Well, of course they do, they made stuff up about you two, when they said you went into the *EastEnders* bosses to beg for his job back, and you're on your knees and then you burst into tears. They made that up.

SHAUN AND THE AGENT LOOK AT EACH OTHER SHEEPISHLY, THEN AT ANDY.

AGENT: Yep.

ANDY: Didn't they?

AGENT: Yeah. Bullshit.

TV CLIP: 'THE WRIGHT STUFF'

MATTHEW WRIGHT AND LOWRI TURNER ARE DISSECTING THE MORNING'S PAPERS.

WRIGHT: . . . I guess only time will tell. Anything else?

LOWRI: (looking through paper) Well, let's move to this story about the actor Andy Millman . . .

WRIGHT: Who's he?

LOWRI: He's that guy, you know who does the 'is he having a laugh?'.

WRIGHT: Yeah, yeah, yeah, yeah, I'm with you, I'm with you, yeah, go on.

LOWRI: Okay, well, he's in a restaurant and he's insulted a Down's syndrome boy. Both mother and son are completely devastated because it was an unprovoked attack.

WRIGHT: Did he hit him?

LOWRI: Well it, it doesn't say. If he did strike the boy then he deserves to be banned from television.

THE STUDIO AUDIENCE APPLAUDS. CUT TO:

A PHONE-IN IS IN PROGRESS.

NICK FERRARI: So, have you heard about this: TV actor Andy Millman has hit a Down's syndrome child. Today we're asking: are celebrities out of control? Is it one rule for us and another for the rich and famous? Tony's on the line – what do you make of this Millman character?

CALLER: What can you say, Nick? It's disgusting, it's absolutely disgusting. I mean, excuse my French, but I think he's a shit.

NICK FERRARI: No, you're excused in this case because I think you're right. You know I don't normally tolerate foul language on the air but what else can you say about this piece of work?

CALLER: Well, the thing is, I heard he also hit the mother, he punched her in the face.

NICK FERRARI: He punched the mother? Oh my God. Tony, thank you, that gives a whole fresh new life to the story.

CUT TO:

TV CLIP: 'THIS MORNING'

PHIL AND FERN ARE TRAILING WHAT'S COMING UP ON THE SHOW.

PHILLIP: Coming up today: what made rising star Andy Millman punch a defenceless Down's syndrome child and his elderly, wheelchair-bound mother in the face? Denise Robertson will be here to speculate.

FERN: Plus, Rwanda revisited. Twelve years after the genocide, a harrowing report from *Big Brother 2* winner, Brian Dowling.

SCENE 13. INT. ANDY'S FLAT. DAY.

MAGGIE IS SAT ON THE COUCH, FLICKING THROUGH THE TV CHANNELS.

MAGGIE: Andy, quick, come here, come here, look, look!

ANDY RACES IN. ON HIS TV SCREEN HE SEES THE *RICHARD AND JUDY SHOW*. SAT ON THEIR SOFA, BEING INTERVIEWED, IS ANDY'S AGENT. INTERCUT BETWEEN ANDY AND THE TV SHOW.

ANDY: Oh! What the—

AGENT: (on TV) Thank you so much indeed for having me on, it's great just be able to – well, it's great to be able to clear the air, you know, because I know there's been a lot of press speculation and so on.

JUDY: Yes, yeah.

ANDY: What's he doing?

AGENT: Well, I spoke to Andy and he's explained everything to me and the truth is this: he is successful now and he wanted to go to a classy restaurant, as I'm sure you sometimes want to yourselves. As he said to me, he's got some cash now, he does not want to have to associate with riff-raff. And why should he? So, he's gone in this posh restaurant with his friend and there is a mother in there with her kid, and her kid's making a load of noise, load of racket, you know and it's ruining it for everyone. And he's obviously furious, Andy, because he's paying through the nose for this grub, I mean, it's silly money, and so he complains to the mother and they get into this ruck. And the thing is, he didn't realise that the kid was, erm, you know, erm, mentally deranged, or whatever, because he could only see him from behind. And I defy anyone to be able to identify, from behind, you know, one of these mongoloids.

ANDY ROLLS HIS EYES IN DESPAIR.

JUDY: I'm sorry, a mongoloid?

AGENT: Yeah, no, I mean if you had a bunch of people lined up over there and one of them was a mongoloid and they had their backs to you, I defy anyone to be able to tell which one it was.

RICHARD: I think I could.

AGENT: Well, big words, Richard, but I don't think you could.

RICHARD: No, I'm sorry, I think I could, erm, look . . .
(LOOKING OFF-CAMERA)
Can we try and sort that out for tomorrow, you know, just get a few in?

JUDY: I don't, I don't think we can do that, Richard.

RICHARD: Oh, come on, Judy, let's see, it'll be interesting. Let's try it out.

AGENT: It would be interesting.

JUDY: Darren, thank you very much.

AGENT: Thank you. Oh, before I go actually, do you remember Barry off *EastEnders*?

JUDY/RICHARD: Yes.

AGENT: (holding up a CD) Well, he's recorded a, a CD. Did it in his garage, and it's only available on the Internet, it's Barry singing songs from the shows . . .

RICHARD: Oh, okay.

AGENT: He's got a lovely voice, Richard, really.

RICHARD: Yeah, yeah.

AGENT: And, er, the great thing about it . . .

CUT BACK TO: ANDY AT HOME, DUMBSTRUCK.

ANDY: Good, well, that's sorted that out, at least I've got my best man on it.

ANDY DIALS A NUMBER ON HIS PHONE.

AGENT: (on TV) Because I said to him, I said, 'You know, you say something's for charity, doesn't matter if it's a load of old tat, it'll go straight to the top of the charts.' And then of course . . .

ANDY: Yeah, erm can I have the *Sun* newspaper please?

SCENE 14. INT. SITCOM SET. DAY.

ANDY AND THE MOTHER AND SON ARE HAVING THEIR PICTURE TAKEN
BY A PHOTOGRAPHER. ANDY IS IN FULL 'RAY' COSTUME AND MAKE-UP.
THE JOURNO IS PRESENT. THE AGENT AND A FEW OTHERS ARE
LURKING NEARBY.

ANDY: Erm, okay, thanks, thanks everyone. Now Dougie, I asked your mum what's the one thing you'd most like in the whole world. And she said an Xbox. Is that right?

KID: Yes.

ANDY: Okay, so what have we got here then?

ANDY HANDS THE BOY A BRAND-NEW XBOX.

KID: Good. Thank you.

JOURNO: Do you apologise then, Andy?

ANDY: It wasn't a case of an apology, it was a misunderstanding so, no apology necessary.

MOTHER: The Xbox is apology enough.

ANDY: Well, it's not an apology, but you know—

JOURNO: (cutting in) And you're happy with that, then?

KID: I am, thank you.

MOTHER: Very happy.

AGENT: And can I just say as well, as a further apology—

ANDY: It's not an apology . . .

AGENT: Well, I've been talking to Maureen and we both agree it would be appropriate for Andy to donate – to a charity of Maureen's choosing – his entire fee for the film that he's currently working on, after agency deductions.

JOURNO: Well, that's very generous, it's a lovely surprise.

ANDY: It is a surprise, big surprise.

THE AGENT PUTS HIS ARMS ROUND EVERYONE AND THE
PHOTOGRAPHER SNAPS AWAY. ANDY LOOKS WEARY.

SCENE 15. INT. FILM SET. DAY.

WARWICK'S FIANCÉE CLAIRE IS READING A MAGAZINE, MINDING HER
OWN BUISNESS. DANIEL RADCLIFFE SAUNTERS PAST. HE NOTICES HER
AND DECIDES TO WORK HIS MAGIC.

DANIEL: Hi.

CLAIRE: Oh, hiya, hi.

DANIEL: Well, you know who I am. What's your name?

CLAIRE: Erm, my name's Claire.

DANIEL: Claire. You've got a lovely necklace on, Claire.

CLAIRE: Thank you, that's very nice, thanks.

DANIEL: Would you, do you fancy dinner, are you free tonight?

CLAIRE: I'm not actually, no, no, I'm engaged.

DANIEL: What about lunch tomorrow?

CLAIRE: No, thank you, no, I won't, I won't go out for any meal with you.

DANIEL: No?

CLAIRE: Yeah.

DANIEL: Not even brunch?

CLAIRE: No, not even brunch.

SCENE 16. INT. DANIEL RADCLIFFE FILM SET. DAY.

MAGGIE IS READING A MAGAZINE. ANDY IS STANDING NEARBY. DANIEL APPROACHES.

DANIEL: Hey, Maggie, listen. I'm going to cut to the chase because I respect you too much to bullshit you. It's over, yeah?

MAGGIE: Sorry?

DANIEL: It's over between us. I don't want tears, that's the kind of guy I am, you knew that going in. I just think it's better we end things now, before you fall in love with me any deeper. You knew it wasn't for ever, I said it was playtime, we had some laughs but I cannot be tied down to one chick.

MAGGIE: Okay.

DANIEL: (holding condom) And I don't want to waste this on you, I've got a better bird now.

MAGGIE: Well, thanks for your honesty.

DANIEL LUNGES IN AND KISSES HER FULL ON THE LIPS. HE PULLS AWAY, CONVINCED HE'S QUITE THE HEART-THROB.

DANIEL: Something to remember me by.

MAGGIE: You brushed your teeth today?

DANIEL: (like a kid) Yes!

WE HEAR A VOICE FROM OFF-SCREEN.

WARWICK: Oy, Radcliffe.

DANIEL: What?

WARWICK APPROACHES DANIEL.

WARWICK: What have you been up to?

DANIEL: Nothing.

WARWICK: Don't lie, you've been chatting up my fiancée. She's just told me.

DANIEL: (calling out) Mum . . .

WARWICK: Don't call for your mum, you were chatting up my bird so act like a man and deal with the consequences.

DANIEL: I was just—

WARWICK: 'I was just nih nih nih nih.' You speccy little git.

DANIEL: These aren't real glasses.

WARWICK: You're a speccy git.

MAGGIE: Here, leave him alone, he's just a boy.

DANIEL: I'm 17.

WARWICK: Oh, and what's this got to do with you?

MAGGIE: Well, what's he . . . he's doing nothing is he?

WARWICK: Oh, don't stick your big nose in, love.

ANDY: All right, calm down.

ANDY HAS BEEN TALKING WITH AN A.D. NEARBY. HE CHIPS IN.

WARWICK: (turning to ANDY) Oh, you! I'm glad you're here 'cause you had the same idea.

ANDY: What?

WARWICK: Well, I know you sent your little mate in here to do your dirty work for you, trying to undermine me.

ANDY: (to MAGGIE) What have you done?

MAGGIE: Nothing.

ANDY: What have you done?

WARWICK: You think it's okay, do you, trying to steal my fiancée?

ANDY: Right, okay, I don't know what you think but—

WARWICK: You shit.

HE HITS ANDY.

ANDY: What are you doing?
(WARWICK HITS HIM AGAIN)
What are you doing?

WARWICK: What do you think I've got this ring for?

ANDY: I don't know, you're a hobbit? Just stop—

WARWICK: You fat shit!

ANDY: Look, I don't know what the rules are for fighting a midg—
(ANDY PUTS HIS HAND ON WARWICK'S HEAD, HOLDING HIM AT ARM'S
LENGTH. WARWICK KNOCKS HIS ARM AWAY AND PUNCHES HIM IN
THE STOMACH)
That usually works in cartoons. What are you doing? Mate . . . I just don't—
(ANDY KICKS HIS FEET UP TO DEFEND HIMSELF. A KNEE MAKES
CONTACT WITH WARWICK'S CHIN AND WARWICK FLIES BACKWARDS
AND CRASHES TO THE FLOOR, UNCONSCIOUS. THE SET FALLS SILENT.
EVERYONE STARES AT ANDY LIKE HE IS PURE EVIL)
Oh, ah, no, no, no, no, no, no, no, no, no, no, no, no. Accidental knee.

CLAIRE: Oi, oi, oi, what are you doing?

ANDY: A lucky shot.

CLAIRE: What have you done?

ANDY: He was going mad at me.

CLAIRE: Warwick!

ANDY: And so the face . . .

CLAIRE: (trying to revive WARWICK) Babe, babe, babe, babe, sweetheart, Warwick, Warwick.

ANDY: Is he not . . . ?

CLAIRE: Sweetheart, Warwick.

ANDY: He's breathing. Oh, it's all right, he's breathing.

CLAIRE: I can see he's breathing, Warwick, are you all right? Sweetheart, sweetheart.

CUT TO: DAME DIANA RIGG LOOKING ON, APPALLED. DANIEL RADCLIFFE IS NEXT TO HER.

DANIEL: Have you still got that catsuit from *The Avengers*?

DAME DIANA: Go away, Daniel.

SCENE 17. INT. AGENT'S OFFICE. DAY.

ANDY AND HIS AGENT ARE SAT AT THE DESK.

AGENT: Remember that charity that you promised to give half of your film fee to . . . ?

ANDY: You mean, the charity you promised to give half my film fee to?

AGENT: Well, that *we* agreed to give some money to, well, it, they're basically quite keen to get hold of the cash because . . .

ANDY: Well, yeah, but I was kicked off the film, there is no fee.

AGENT: Yeah, but they're expecting the money aren't they? We've got to give it to them.

ANDY: Well, they don't know what the fee was for the film, do they?

AGENT: They do, they do because, erm, I mentioned it to them.

ANDY: I've got to give them wages I haven't even earned?

AGENT: Well, it's okay because we can just pay them the money we owe them from the money we get for the sitcom.

ANDY: How much is it?

AGENT: Oh, it's about half—

ANDY: Half an episode?

AGENT: Well, half the whole series.

ANDY: (angrily) I've got to give them half my wages for the entire series?

AGENT: It's not my fault, you're the one who insulted the kid with the—

ANDY: I didn't insult him, I didn't know he was . . . did I?

AGENT: Well, you must have upset him in some way 'cause you made it into the papers.

ANDY: (frustrated) Oh.

AGENT: Actually, talking of the papers, you've made quite a splash again but annoyingly they, they didn't sort of go with the 'Giving the kid an Xbox' angle.

ANDY: What did they go with?

AGENT: (holding up the *Sun*) 'TV Bully Kicks Dwarf In Face'.

ANDY: Accurate. But as you say, there's no such thing as bad publicity.

AGENT: (holding up the *Mirror*) 'Pick On Someone Your Own Size, Fatty.'

ANDY: Oh, maybe there is.

AGENT: This is the worst one. 'Suicide Bombers Get Lotto Funding.' Look at that.

ANDY: What's that got to do with me?

AGENT: Well, nothing, it's just shocking, isn't it? What they're up to. (WE HOLD ON ANDY'S REACTION) Oh, no, actually, what am I talking about? This is the worst one, in the *Mail*: 'Gypsies Are Eating Our Pets.'

FILM CLIP: 'THE RICHARD AND JUDY SHOW'

RICHARD IS CONCENTRATING ON A LINE-UP OF MEN WITH THEIR BACKS TO HIM.

RICHARD: Oh, mmm, yep, yeah, I know, it's number three. (NUMBER THREE TURNS ROUND) Ahh, damn.

EXTRAS

SCENE 4/03pt   SLATE 668

DIRECTOR: RICKY GERVAIS & STE

CAMERA: MARTIN HAWKINS

DATE: 27/07/05   ROLL# 1

COLDPLAY

GREATEST HITS

EXTRAS
Episode 4

CAST LIST
Andy Millman RICKY GERVAIS
Maggie Jacobs ASHLEY JENSEN
Agent STEPHEN MERCHANT
Shaun SHAUN WILLIAMSON
Damon Beesley MARTIN SAVAGE
Greg SHAUN PYE

Guest Starring CHRIS MARTIN
RONNIE CORBETT

Kimberley SARAH MOYLE
Brains JAMIE CHAPMAN
Gobbler ANDREW BUCKLEY
Andy's Old Flame PATRICIA POTTER
Boutique Saleswoman
GERALDINE ALEXANDER
Sales Assistant LEE WHITE
Telethon Producer JULIA RAYNER
BAFTA Executive TOBY LONGWORTH
'Holby' Producer JOHN PETERS
Security Guard PERRY BLANKS
Reporter DONNA BERLIN
Autograph Hunter MAREK LARWOOD

With RICHARD BRIERS,
MOIRA STUART, STEPHEN FRY

Written & Directed by
RICKY GERVAIS & STEPHEN MERCHANT

The British Academy Award is based on a design by Mitzi Cunliffe

TV CLIP: CHARITY APPEAL

ANDY MILLMAN ADDRESSES THE CAMERA, LOOKING EARNEST.

ANDY: Hi, I'm Andy Millman. What would you rather do: have your child die of thirst or dysentery? That's not a choice that you or I have to make, is it? But one in five people don't have access to clean drinking water. Every day, millions of people have to drink the only water available to them and they run the risk of dying. You can help put an end to that terrible risk by pledging just five pounds. Please help.

SCENE 1. INT. TV STUDIO. DAY.

PULL OUT TO REVEAL ANDY BEING FILMED BY A SMALL CREW. DAMON BEESLEY IS PRESENT. THE DIRECTOR THANKS ANDY AS CHRIS MARTIN ENTERS.

DIRECTOR: Chris! Hi!

CHRIS MARTIN: Hi.

DIRECTOR: Hello, how are you?

CHRIS MARTIN: What's this for today?

DIRECTOR: It's for people in the Third World . . .

CHRIS MARTIN: Yeah.

DIRECTOR: . . . Who don't have clean drinking . . .

CHRIS MARTIN: (pointing to white backcloth) This screen, are you going to project anything on there?

DIRECTOR: We don't know yet, I'm not quite sure . . .

CHRIS MARTIN: Okay, 'cause we have an album coming out, *Greatest Hits* . . . ?

DIRECTOR: Oh.

CHRIS MARTIN: Maybe just put the picture of the album cover on it.

DIRECTOR: Oh, ah.

CHRIS MARTIN: Just simple.

DIRECTOR: I think probably, if we're going to project anything, we'll show pictures of people dying because of a lack of clean water.

CHRIS MARTIN: Could they be holding the album?

DIRECTOR: Not really, no, erm. I think that might be a bit inappropriate, perhaps?

CHRIS MARTIN: I presume at some point you're going to have some footage of these people walking around, looking sad, miserable. What about some music? Check this out.

CHRIS MARTIN SINGS A FEW BARS.

DIRECTOR: Is that one of yours?

CHRIS MARTIN: Yeah, yeah, 'Trouble'. Just say, at the bottom, this is available, *Coldplay: Greatest Hits*.

DIRECTOR: Yeah, I'm just not quite sure . . .

CHRIS MARTIN: Easy, easy.

DIRECTOR: . . . What's going to happen yet, so . . .

CHRIS MARTIN: . . . So easy. All right, all right. Okay . . . now, where do you want me to stand?

DIRECTOR: Just there, that's great.

CHRIS MARTIN: Okay.
(CHRIS POSITIONS HIMSELF IN FRONT OF THE CAMERA. HE UNBUTTONS HIS JACKET TO REVEAL HE IS WEARING A *COLDPLAY: GREATEST HITS* T-SHIRT. HE NOTICES ANDY)
Hey, I know you.

ANDY: All right?

CHRIS MARTIN: (doing a poor 'RAY' impression) 'Are we having a laugh!'

ANDY: 'Are you having a laugh?' Yeah.

CHRIS MARTIN: Yeah, I could come on your show.

DAMON: Oh!

CHRIS MARTIN: What's your audience, five or six million?

DAMON: That'd be fab.

ANDY: Well, I don't know. I just think it's a bit weird, just celebrities just popping up in a sitcom, you know what I mean?

DAMON: No, no, no, we'll get him in.

CHRIS MARTIN: No, it'd be good. I could play myself.

ANDY: Right. What would Chris Martin be doing visiting a factory in Wigan?

CHRIS MARTIN: I don't know, you work it out.

DAMON: We will.

ANDY: Well, we won't.

DAMON: We will.

CHRIS MARTIN: Erm, when do you shoot?

ANDY: Thursdays, but it's just—

CHRIS MARTIN: I can't do Thursdays.

ANDY: (fake disappointment) Oh, never mind . . . okay.

CHRIS MARTIN: I can do Wednesdays.

DAMON: We can move it.

ANDY: We can't move it, can we?

DAMON: No, we can.

ANDY: Well.

CHRIS MARTIN: Move it.
(to DIRECTOR)
Can we crack on with this? I've got to do AIDS and Alzheimer's and land mines this afternoon and I want to get back for Deal or No Deal. Plus, Gwyneth's making drumsticks.

TV CLIP:
'WHEN THE WHISTLE BLOWS'

ANDY AS 'RAY' IS POTTERING AROUND.

RAY: Do some bloody work, what's up with you lot?

KIMBERLEY: We're depressed Mr Stokes.

RAY: Why?

GOBBLER: Radio's broken, Mr Stokes.

BRAINS: Statistics prove that workers are much more productive with musical accompaniment.

RAY: Are you having a laugh? Is he having a laugh?

KIMBERLEY: Oh, we can't work without music.

RAY: 'Can't work without music'? Who are you, seven bloody dwarfs?

BRAINS: You'll just have to buy us another one.

RAY: Hrrumph! I'm not made of money and we've spent budget for t'year so . . . I don't know what we're going to do.

INEXPLICABLY, CHRIS MARTIN ENTERS. APPLAUSE.

CHRIS MARTIN: Maybe I can help?

RAY: I don't believe it. It's only Chris Martin from Coldplay.

HE WAITS FOR THE APPLAUSE TO SUBSIDE. THOUGH ANDY IS IN CHARACTER DURING THE SCENE HIS 'RAY' FACADE SOMETIMES DROPS AND WE GLIMPSE ANDY'S REAL FEELINGS ON THE ABSURDITY OF CHRIS MARTIN BEING IN THE SHOW.

CHRIS MARTIN: Hey. Hi.

RAY: Chris, what are you doing here . . . in a factory in Wigan? It's mental.

CHRIS MARTIN: Well, Ray, I'm just in the area to promote our new album, *Coldplay: Greatest Hits* and I thought I'd pop on over, say hello.

A FEW CHEERS FROM FANS IN THE AUDIENCE. CHRIS MARTIN WAVES AT THEM.

RAY: Right. When's that due out?

CHRIS MARTIN: It's coming out on the seventeenth of this month, and it's going to be really great.

RAY: Oh, fantastic. Well, this is going to sound absolutely ridiculous but do you mind performing a song for us?

CHRIS MARTIN: 'Are you having a laugh?'

RAY: Oh!

CUT TO: CHRIS MARTIN, SAT AT A PIANO ON THE SITCOM SET, WEARING SHADES AND PLAYING 'FIX YOU'.

SCENE 2. INT.
AGENT'S OFFICE. DAY.

ANDY, FURIOUS, IS READING FROM A NEWSPAPER.

ANDY: 'This week *When The Whistle Blows* sunk ever lower in its desperate attempts to appeal to as many of the great unwashed as possible by roping in the services of rock star Chris Martin, whose inexplicable appearance was the latest attempt by Andy Millman to shamelessly prop up his lame duck of a sitcom.' I told you, I told everyone. Why did I let people convince me?

ANDY'S AGENT HOLDS UP A MUFFIN.

AGENT: Calm down. Muffin?

ANDY: No.

AGENT: Have a lovely bit of muffin.

ANDY: I don't want any.

AGENT: Do you mind if I have a little bit of muffin?

ANDY: No.

AGENT: Thank you.
(INTO INTERCOM)
Bar?

SHAUN: (on intercom) Yo.

AGENT: I'm having the muffin.

SHAUN: I'll come through.

ANDY: Why is this an event?

AGENT: He's excited.

ANDY REACTS. SHAUN ENTERS.

SHAUN: All right? All right, Andy?

ANDY: All right, Shaun.

SHAUN AND ANDY SHAKE HANDS.

AGENT: Lovely bit of muffin.

SHAUN: (to the muffin) Hello you.

AGENT: Oh, lovely.

HE OFFERS THE MUFFIN TO SHAUN, WHO LEANS DOWN AND BITES
INTO IT WITHOUT USING HIS HANDS.

ANDY: Why's he eating it like that?

AGENT: Yeah, why are you eating like that?

SHAUN: (holding up his hands) Me hands. I've been cleaning out the
toilets. I've got no gloves.

ANDY: You shook my hand when you came in.

SHAUN: Well, it's politeness isn't it, it's . . .

AGENT: Just being polite. We are celebrating with that lovely bit
of muffin. What would be the best news you could get today?

ANDY: You're going full time at the Carphone Warehouse.

AGENT: I don't work at the Carphone Warehouse any more.
Well, I do Saturday mornings while Nirinda's pregnant.

ANDY: All right.

AGENT: No, what news could you get that would mean you've finally
got the critical respect you've been looking for?

ANDY: I don't know, BBC1 comedy with catchphrases and stupid
wigs filmed in front of a live studio audience of morons is suddenly
considered cool?

AGENT: Ha ha ha. That's never going happen, is it? No, you've been
nominated for a BAFTA. Best Comedy Performance.

ANDY: Really?

AGENT: Yeah.

ANDY: Not going to win though, something classier than this'll win.

AGENT: No, no, 'cause I was thinking the same and then I was looking
down the list of nominees and . . . it's all crap this year, so you've got
as good a chance as anyone.

ANDY: (disheartened) Cheers.

AGENT: More good news as well, had a call from a toy manufacturer and they're quite keen to put out a 'Ray' doll for Christmas. You know, and you sort of press a button and it goes, 'Are you having a laugh?'

ANDY: Oh, who's going to buy that?

AGENT: Same people who watch your show, you know, thick kids. And their thick parents. And thick—

ANDY: Yeah, thick people, I get it. The thick demographic, that's what I'm going for.

AGENT: Don't slag them off, 'cause those people spend a fortune on this sort of tat. And ringtones as well. Ah, that Crazy Frog made millions.

ANDY: (facetious) Yeah, where is he now?

AGENT: Probably working on a follow-up album, I'd have thought, or trying to crack Japan.

SHAUN: It's not bad for a frog, though, is it?

AGENT: It's very good for a frog, Bar, if you don't mind me saying. I'd have thought he's probably the second richest frog in the world. After Kermit.

SHAUN NODS IN AGREEMENT.

SHAUN: Kermit, yeah. There was his nephew, Robin.

AGENT: Ah, Robin was good.

SHAUN: Looked set to take over the empire for a while, didn't he?

AGENT: Ah, yeah, he was a very good actor and singer.

SHAUN: 'Halfway Up The Stairs'.

AGENT: Good song.

ANDY SOAKS IN THE INSANITY OF THE CONVERSATION AND THEN JUST GETS UP AND LEAVES.

SCENE 3. EXT. BOUTIQUE. DAY.

THE CAMERA IS FOCUSED ON THE SHOP WINDOW. MAGGIE AND ANDY
APPEAR, LOOKING IN THE WINDOW.

MAGGIE: Do you know, I've never been to an awards ceremony before.

ANDY: Nor have I.

MAGGIE: Do you think there will be photographers there?

ANDY: Probably.

MAGGIE: Oh, what if I fall or dribble something down my front?

ANDY: What are you, a toddler?

MAGGIE LOOKS IN THE WINDOW.

MAGGIE: Oh, there're some nice frocks in here. Come on in and have
a look, help me choose something.

ANDY: No, I'll wait out here.

HE WANDERS OFF.

SCENE 4. INT. BOUTIQUE. DAY.

MAGGIE ENTERS THE PONCY FASHION BOUTIQUE – THE SORT OF PLACE
WHERE THERE ARE THREE OR FOUR INCREDIBLY EXPENSIVE ITEMS AND
A PAIR OF SHOES ON A PEDESTAL. SHE ENTERS NERVOUSLY AND SMILES
AT THE SALESWOMAN. THE SALESWOMAN SMILES A SHORT, INSINCERE
SMILE. MAGGIE ADMIRES ONE OF THE DRESSES.

MAGGIE: How much is this one?

SALESWOMAN: That's two thousand five hundred pounds.

MAGGIE: Oh. That's a bit much.

SALESWOMAN: Yes.

MAGGIE: Are there any of these that are . . . ?

SALESWOMAN: It's all very expensive. I don't think you can afford anything.

MAGGIE: How do you know what I can afford?

THE SALESWOMAN LOOKS HER UP AND DOWN.

SALESWOMAN: Oh, just a hunch.

MAGGIE: (muttering) Hunch. You're a hunch.

SALESWOMAN: Hmm?

MAGGIE: Nothing.

SHE LEAVES.

SCENE 5. EXT. BOUTIQUE. DAY.

MAGGIE FINDS ANDY OUTSIDE THE BOUTIQUE.

ANDY: Nothing in there?

MAGGIE: No, nothing, come on, let's go.

SHE STARTS WALKING OFF.

ANDY: Oh, where we going now?

MAGGIE: Somewhere, just anywhere else.

ANDY: Oh, what exactly are you looking for?

MAGGIE: I'm looking for a place where people aren't quite as rude.

ANDY: Who was rude?

MAGGIE: Her, in there.

ANDY: What happened?

MAGGIE: She just looked at me like I shouldn't be there, like I was a piece of dirt.

ANDY GLANCES BACK AT THE SHOP.

ANDY: Come on.

MAGGIE: Oh, no, no.

ANDY: Come on.

THEY WALK BACK TOWARDS THE SHOP. ROY ORBISON'S 'PRETTY WOMAN' PLAYS.

SCENE 6. INT. BOUTIQUE. DAY.

MAGGIE AND ANDY ENTER THE BOUTIQUE.

ANDY: (pointing to SALESWOMAN) That one?

MAGGIE: Yeah.

ANDY STRIDES UP TO THE SALESWOMAN.

ANDY: Good day.
(ACTING LIKE A BIG SPENDER)

My friend here was looking for a dress.

(HE TWIDDLES HIS GOLD CREDIT CARD BETWEEN HIS FINGERS)
I wondered if we could help her with that. Gold card, there.

SALESWOMAN: (smelling money) Well, I'm sure we can.

ANDY: Mmm, good.

SALESWOMAN: Yes, I think she was looking at this one.

ANDY: Oh, wonderful. How much is that?

SALESWOMAN: Two thousand five hundred pounds.

ANDY: (flustered) Two thousand five hundred pounds?
(RECOVERING HIMSELF, TO MAGGIE)
Oh, do you want that?

MAGGIE: Yeah.

ANDY: If you don't want it, don't have it.

MAGGIE: No, I, I want it.

ANDY: Definitely afford it, it's just a matter of, is it 'the right dress?'

MAGGIE: Yes.

ANDY: (to SALESWOMAN) Could we, could we bring it back if
there's something wrong with it, say after this coming Sunday?

SALESWOMAN: No, we don't do refunds.

ANDY: No, no, no, no, no, no, no, but if it didn't fit?

SALESWOMAN: Oh, she should try it on.

ANDY: I know but what if she got . . . fat?

SALESWOMAN: By Sunday?

ANDY: No, what if the, oh, the stitching there was to be pulled
apart slightly?

SALESWOMAN: Pulled apart?

ANDY: Just came apart? Just normal wear and tear, the sweat rot under the old armpit, cuts through the old stitches.
(MAGGIE REACTS. THE SALESWOMAN LOOKS AT MAGGIE)
Let's make absolutely sure, okay, always good to be sure. Sorry about this.
(TO MAGGIE)
You're not thinking . . .

MAGGIE: What?

ANDY: I'm going to ask you a question now, consider the answer, okay? Do you really want me to spend two thousand five hundred pounds on that dress?

MAGGIE: Yes.

ANDY: She does! Ah! Go on!
(MAGGIE PICKS UP THE DRESS AND HEADS INTO THE CHANGING ROOM. TO SALESWOMAN)
We've all learnt a lesson today. There's a chance it won't fit. It's not even tax deductible.

(A THOUGHT STRIKES HIM)
Do you do celebrity discount?

SALESWOMAN: Well, I don't know who she is.

ANDY: She's nobody.
(MILD 'RAY')
'Are you having a laugh?'

SALESWOMAN: No, we don't do discount.

ANDY: No, not are *you* having a laugh. Watch this and comprehend.
(AS 'RAY')
'Are you having a laugh?'
(THE SALESWOMAN LOOKS BLANK)
Does no one here know . . .
(TO TEENAGE ASSISTANT)
'Is she having a laugh?' Do you know . . . ?

TEENAGE ASSISTANT: Oh, yeah, you're from that sitcom.

ANDY: Correct.

SALESWOMAN: Any good?

TEENAGE ASSISTANT: Not really, it's a bit broad, relies on catchphrases and funny wigs.

ANDY: Sorry, did I ask for a critique? Shall I come down to the storeroom and say you haven't swept up right, mate? Unbelievable.
(TO SALESWOMAN)
So, you don't do celebrity discount?

SALESWOMAN: No.

ANDY: No, not one per cent? Couldn't give me one per cent?

SALESWOMAN: Oh, okay, I'll do you a one per cent discount.

ANDY: What's that?

SALESWOMAN: On two thousand five hundred? Twenty-five pounds.

ANDY: Not worth it. I'd rather you stuck it on if anything.

SALESWOMAN: Well, shall we just leave it as it is?

ANDY: (to MAGGIE) That's your Christmas and birthday.

MAGGIE: (from inside the changing room) Yeah, okay.

ANDY: Never'd spent that much.

ANDY WANDERS OVER TO A RACK OF EXPENSIVE GENTLEMAN'S SHOES.
HE PICKS ONE UP.

SALESWOMAN: Those are six hundred pounds.
(ANDY THROWS THE SHOE BACK ON THE SHELF, LIKE IT'S JUST BURNT
HIS HAND, CHUCKLING NERVOUSLY)
They're very expensive.

ANDY: That's not why I was laughing. I was laughing, they weren't expensive enough, in a way. That's what tickled me when I first saw the six hundred.

AT THIS MOMENT, MAGGIE APPEARS FROM THE CHANGING ROOM.
IT'S A TRANSFORMATION AND THE DRESS MAKES ANDY'S HEAD TURN.

MAGGIE: What do you think? Do you think it's all right?

ANDY: (looking away) Yeah.

MAGGIE: Can I get it?

ANDY: Yep.

HOLD ON ANDY, GLANCING BACK ACROSS AT MAGGIE.

SCENE 7. EXT.
BAFTA CEREMONY. NIGHT.

THE GROVESNOR HOTEL. CELEBRITIES ARE ARRIVING TO THE GLARE OF
PAPARAZZI FLASHBULBS. ANDY AND MAGGIE MAKE THEIR WAY UP THE
RED CARPET. A REPORTER STICKS A MICROPHONE UNDER ANDY'S NOSE.

REPORTER: Andy, Andy . . . will you win tonight?

ANDY: Oh, it's just, er, you know, flattering to have been nominated. So . . .

REPORTER: (of MAGGIE) Is that your girlfriend?

ANDY: No, no, no, no, no, no, no, no.

MAGGIE: (affronted) All right.

ANDY: Well, always tell journalists the truth, and let them change the
facts later.

REPORTER: (to MAGGIE) And who are you wearing?

MAGGIE IS PERPLEXED.

MAGGIE: Maggie.

ANDY: No.

REPORTER: Who are you wearing?

MAGGIE: Maggie Jacobs.

ANDY: No, whose dress is that?

MAGGIE: It's mine.

ANDY: Oh, okay, thank you . . .
(TO REPORTER)
She won a competition.
(HE LEADS MAGGIE AWAY)
Don't speak to anyone else tonight.

MAGGIE: What did I . . .

ANDY: Not even to me.

REPORTER: (noticing a new arrival) Dale! Dale! Darling, Dale.

SCENE 8. INT. BAFTA RECEPTION. NIGHT.

PEOPLE ARE MILLING AROUND, SIPPING CHAMPAGNE. ANDY AND MAGGIE ARE CHITCHATTING.

ANDY: (looking off-screen) Toby Anstis.

MAGGIE: Have you ever eaten a worm?

ANDY: (mocking her Scottish accent) I don't even know what a 'wuhrum' is.

MAGGIE: There's an 'r' in it, you should pronounce it – worm.

ANDY: (suddenly spotting someone off-camera) Old girlfriend, ah, God.

MAGGIE: What?

ANDY: Shall we—

A WOMAN APPROACHES THEM.

OLD FLAME: Andy.

ANDY: Hi!

OLD FLAME: Hi!

ANDY: You all right?

OLD FLAME: Yeah, I'm really good thanks, yeah. God, you've done well.

ANDY: Yeah. All downhill from here. Who are you . . . erm . . . what was I going to . . . what are you, BAFTA tonight, are you . . . first time?

OLD FLAME: Well, yeah, as part of the *Holby* team.

ANDY: Oh, good luck with . . . erm.

OLD FLAME: Yeah, thanks, thanks and good luck to you as well.

ANDY: Absolutely. Yeah, it's a pity, erm . . . no, we should ask . . .

AWKWARD PAUSE.

OLD FLAME: Yeah, I'll see you later.

ANDY: I'll see you there. Okay, good luck with the, erm . . .

OLD FLAME: Thanks.

ANDY: Good to . . .

OLD FLAME: Good luck.

ANDY: See you later. Cheers.

THE OLD FLAMES LEAVES.

MAGGIE: Who was that?

ANDY: The most boring woman in the world.

MAGGIE: Really?

ANDY: Yeah.

MAGGIE: How do you know her?

ANDY: I went out with her for a while, when I was an extra on *Holby City*.

MAGGIE: Oh, and then she dumped you?

ANDY: No, I dumped her.

MAGGIE: (incredulous) You dumped her?

ANDY: Yes.

MAGGIE: Really?

ANDY: Yes, it does happen.

MAGGIE: When was this?

ANDY: Couple of years ago.

MAGGIE: Was that before or after you lost your virginity to the one who looked like Ronnie Corbett?

ANDY: After, obviously. It was two years ago.

MAGGIE: What, so you lost your virginity a long time ago then, did you?

ANDY: Yes, I'm in my forties.

MAGGIE: I know, but when?

ANDY: A long time ago.

MAGGIE: Exactly, like, what age were you?

ANDY: Oh, I don't know.

MAGGIE: What, sixteen? Seventeen?
(ANDY SAYS NOTHING)
Were you older than that?

ANDY: Oh, what are all these questions? I lost my virginity, full stop.

MAGGIE: Why were you attracted to Ronnie Corbett?

ANDY: I wasn't attracted to Ronnie Corbett, she just happened to look like Ronnie Corbett, it was the bank's Christmas do, I was drunk, all right?

MAGGIE: Oh, the bank's Christmas do?

ANDY: Yeah.

MAGGIE: But you didn't start working there till you were twenty-eight.

ANDY: Who are you? Columbo? Leave it.

SCENE 9. INT.
BAFTA CEREMONY – TABLE. NIGHT.

HOST DAVINA MCCALL INTRODUCES THE SHOW. WE HOLD ON MAGGIE
AND ANDY AS VARIOUS NOMINATIONS AND WINNERS ARE ANNOUNCED.
THROUGH A SERIES OF DISSOLVES WE SEE ANDY AND MAGGIE MOVE
FROM EXCITEMENT TO OVERWHELMING BOREDOM. GREG APPROACHES
ANDY'S TABLE.

ANDY: Oh.

GREG: Well, hello.

ANDY: All right.

GREG: Everything all right here?

ANDY: We could do with some more wine please, waiter.

GREG: Comedy gold, absolute comedy gold.

ANDY: Thank you.

GREG: I love it, no, actually here in an official capacity.

ANDY: Oh, yeah.

GREG: One of the Best Drama nominations, for Paul Abbott's *Cock Of The North*. I imagine you saw it.

ANDY: I didn't.

GREG: I had quite a large part. Best Drama, the Holy Grail, as it were, of BAFTAs. But you're, of course, you're here with your sitcom, aren't you?

ANDY: Yeah.

GREG: Yeah, well good luck, good luck.

ANDY: Yeah, and you mate.

GREG: I understand it's very popular.

ANDY: Yeah, yeah, good luck, mate.

GREG: Well, I'd better get back.

ANDY: See you later.

GREG: To the 'Drama crowd', as it were.

ANDY: Yeah.

GREG: But, erm, yeah. Catch you later. Cheers, mate.

ANDY: Yeah.

SCENE 10. INT. BAFTA CEREMONY STAGE. NIGHT.

RICHARD BRIERS IS GIVING A MOVING EULOGY IN HONOUR OF VETERAN PRODUCER LEN SHEARMAN, RIP.

RICHARD: Many of you at home – and in this room – probably don't recognise Len Shearman, but you'd certainly recognise his work. Len was one of the most influential and passionate drama producers in the history of television and, in an industry famous for backbiting and bitchiness, he was a gentleman of unquestionable integrity. In fact, the only thing I didn't like about Len was the way he'd dip into the second layer of biscuits before we'd finished the first.

ANGLE ON: THE AGENT ARRIVING, SQUEEZING PAST PEOPLE WITH A RUSTLING CARRIER BAG, APOLOGISING AS HE GOES.

AGENT: Excuse me, excuse me.

ANDY ROLLS HIS EYES. THE AGENT SITS DOWN CLUMSILY AT ANDY'S TABLE, RATTLING THE SILVERWARE AS HE GOES.

ANDY: Oh, for . . .

AGENT: Sorry I'm a bit late, I erm—

ANDY: Shut up!

AGENT: (looking at the stage) Richard Briers. I was a bit late because I was just waiting for this, it's the prototype of the 'Ray' doll.

HE RUSTLES INSIDE THE BAG NOISILY AS THE EULOGY CONTINUES.

ANDY: I don't care.

THE AGENT PRODUCES A PROTOTYPE OF THE 'RAY' DOLL.

AGENT: There he is.

ANDY: Oh, who's going to buy that?

AGENT: Like I said before, stupid people.

ANDY: Yeah, who are these stupid people?

MAGGIE: (noticing it) That is brilliant. Can you buy them?

AGENT: It's good, isn't it? You will be able to buy them.

ANDY REACTS. SUDDENLY THE DOLL BURSTS INTO LIFE, SQUAWKING ITS CATCHPHRASE.

'RAY' DOLL: 'Are you having a laugh? Is he having a laugh?'

ANDY: What are you doing?

'RAY' DOLL: 'Are you having a laugh? Is he having a laugh? Are you having a laugh? Is he having a laugh?'

THE 'RAY' DOLL WON'T STOP JABBERING. PEOPLE ARE STARTING TO LOOK OVER WITH ANGRY FROWNS. RICHARD BRIERS, THOUGH DISTRACTED, FIGHTS ON WITH HIS SPEECH

RICHARD: . . . I was with Len only a few days before the end . . .

'RAY' DOLL: 'Are you having a laugh? Is he having a laugh?'

RICHARD: . . . And he didn't have long . . .

'RAY' DOLL: 'Are you having a laugh? Is he having a laugh?'

ANDY: Just turn it off, just take the batteries out or something.

RICHARD: (increasingly distracted) . . . But he would never hide the truth . . .

'RAY' DOLL: 'Are you having a laugh? Is he having a laugh?'

AGENT: Have you got one of those very, very tiny screwdrivers?

RICHARD: (angry now) . . . His wife . . . he leaves his loving wife . . .

'RAY' DOLL: 'Is he having a laugh? Are you having a laugh? Is he having a laugh?'

RICHARD BRIERS CAN TOLERATE THE INTERRUPTIONS NO LONGER
AND STORMS OFF THE STAGE, CHARGING DOWN TOWARDS ANDY AND
THE AGENT.

ANDY: Take the batteries out.

AGENT: I don't think—

RICHARD BRIERS GRABS THE 'RAY' DOLL AND SMASHES IT FURIOUSLY
AGAINST THE TABLE HE THROWS IT ONTO THE FLOOR AND BEGINS TO
STAMP IN IT. THIS GOES ON FAR LONGER THAN IS NECESSARY TO SHUT
THE TOY UP – NOW HE IS JUST EXORCISING SOME PENT-UP RAGE.
FINALLY HE STOPS AND CATCHES HIS BREATH

RICHARD: Tacky shit.

RICHARD MAKES HIS WAY BACK TO THE STAGE AS THE ENTIRE BAFTA
AUDIENCE RISE TO THEIR FEET TO GIVE HIM A STANDING OVATION.
GREG APPEARS.

GREG: Oh dear, I think it's broken.

AGENT: Yeah, I think you're right.

THE AGENT HAS PICKED UP THE DOLL. ANDY NOTICES ITS TROUSERS
ARE FALLING OFF.

ANDY: Pull my trousers up.

SCENE 11. INT.
WOMEN'S BATHROOM. NIGHT.

ANDY'S OLD FLAME IS TOUCHING UP HER MAKE-UP. MAGGIE ENTERS
AND SPOTS HER.

MAGGIE: Oh, hello. Andy's friend. Maggie.

OLD FLAME: Yes, hi. Yeah.

MAGGIE: Didn't introduce us, so, hello, pleased to meet you.

OLD FLAME: Hi.

MAGGIE: God, you two used to go out?

OLD FLAME: Oh, for about ten minutes.

MAGGIE: Why did he let you go? Look at you, all lovely.

OLD FLAME: Oh, thanks.

MAGGIE: Bit of a catch for him. A man that didn't lose his virginity till
he was twenty-eight and that was to a woman who looked like Ronnie
Corbett so . . .
(THE OLD FLAME CHUCKLES AT THE REVELATION)
God, what did you say to him when he said he couldn't
go out with you any more because he thought you were boring?

PAUSE.

OLD FLAME: He said it was because I was boring?

IT DAWNS ON MAGGIE THAT SHE'S PUT HER FOOT IN IT.

MAGGIE: Mmm?

OLD FLAME: He told me it was because he'd just come out of a long-term
relationship and he wasn't ready for something else.

MAGGIE: Not the boring . . . not boring, not, not boring, he didn't say
that you were boring. He said, I think he said that the BAFTA thing,
kind of the ceremony, the, all the clapping was probably going to be
boring 'cause, erm . . .

MAGGIE BACKTRACKS DESPERATELY BUT ITS TOO LATE – THE OLD
FLAME HAS GONE INTO SILENT SHOCK.

SCENE 12. INT.
BAFTA CEREMONY STAGE. NIGHT.

DAVINA ANNOUNCES THAT THE NEXT AWARD IS THE BEST COMEDY PERFORMANCE. ANDY AND MAGGIE LOOK EXPECTANT.

DAVINA: Coming up we have the prestigious BAFTA fellowship, but first the award for comedy performance. So please, will you all welcome Harry Hill.

SCENE 13. INT.
MEN'S BATHROOM. NIGHT.

ANDY IS WASHING HIS HANDS, LOOKING INTO THE BATHROOM MIRROR. A BAFTA AWARD IS PERCHED NEXT TO HIM ON THE SIDE OF THE SINK. A HAND APPEARS AND PICKS UP THE BAFTA. WE SEE THE HAND BELONGS TO STEPHEN FRY.

STEPHEN FRY: Commiserations again, Andy.

ANDY: I knew I wouldn't win. No, I'm not in it for the awards anyway, well done, though.

STEPHEN FRY: Still, it's nice to have some recognition from one's peers, isn't it? Listen, it's not really my business but have you considered doing something without a laughter track? I think they're considered rather old-fashioned these days, you know . . . if you want to pick up one of these old gongs.

ANDY: Not bothered, as I say, not in it for the awards but . . .

STEPHEN FRY: Also, I don't know, wigs and silly glasses, bit undignified for men of our age, don't you think?

ANDY: Well, I don't think we're the same age, but cheers.

STEPHEN FRY: Looks desperate, is all I'm saying.

ANDY: I don't feel desperate. As I say, it's a knock-about comedy, I'm not into high art, so . . .

STEPHEN FRY: Ah, yes, but as Oscar Wilde so wonderfully put it, 'We are all in the gutter, but some of us are looking at the stars.'

HE WALKS OUT OF SHOT.

ANDY: (under his breath) He was probably looking up men's trousers, the old poof.

STEPHEN FRY: (reappearing in shot) Sorry?

ANDY: He was looking up at the, erm, stars, yeah . . .

STEPHEN FRY: Yes, that's right. I'm off to look at some stars myself, right now.

HE LEAVES THE SHOT AGAIN.

ANDY: You'll be seeing stars in a minute.

STEPHEN FRY: (reappearing again) What?

ANDY: Nothing. Why'd you keep coming back in?

FRY FINALLY EXITS. ANDY DRIES HIS HANDS WITH A TOWEL.

AGENT: Andy.

ANDY LOOKS ROUND. THE AGENT IS PEERING OVER THE TOP OF ONE OF THE TOILET CUBICLES.

ANDY: What are you doing?

AGENT: Come in here, it's all kicking off in here.

ANDY: I'm not coming in there, no.

AGENT: Come in here.

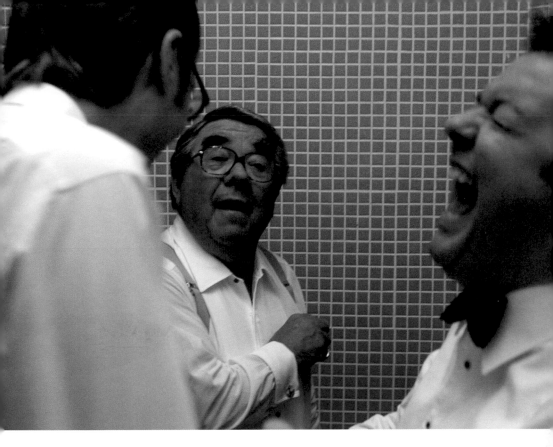

ANDY: What are you doing?

AGENT: Just come in.

THE AGENT OPENS THE DOOR OF THE CUBICLE.

ANDY: Who's that?

A FIGURE IS CROUCHED OVER THE TOILET SEAT. HE LOOKS ROUND: IT'S RONNIE CORBETT.

RONNIE: Oh, hi, how you doing, all right?

ANDY: Yeah.

AGENT: (to RONNIE) He's one of us, don't worry.

ANDY: I'm not into this . . .

AGENT: No, it's all right, just have a little bit, eh? It'll cheer you up a bit.

THERE IS A KNOCK ON THE CUBICLE DOOR. IT'S A SECURITY GUY.

SECURITY GUY: What's going on in there?

AGENT: (doing a high-pitched lady's voice) I'm just finishing up, excuse me for five minutes.

ANDY: (whispering) Why are you doing a woman's voice?

SECURITY GUY: How many people are in there?

AGENT: (normal voice) One.

ANDY: That's a different voice.

AGENT: Two . . . including the woman that you just heard.

SECURITY GUY: Open the door.

ANDY: Oh, for . . .
(THEY SHEEPISHLY OPEN THE DOOR)
Right, let me explain, okay. I was just in here and I was leaving,
and he put his – that's my agent.

AGENT: Darren Lamb, nice to meet you.
(REALISING HIS MISTAKE)
You shouldn't say your name, never tell them your name.

SCENE 14. INT. HOTEL BACKROOM. NIGHT.

ANDY, RONNIE AND THE AGENT ARE STOOD IN A LINE.

RONNIE: It was your fault.

AGENT: Why was it my fault?

RONNIE: Well, because they saw your head over the cubicle door.

ANDY: They saw your head under the cubicle door, but there's no point
in arguing amongst ourselves, we're—

AN OFFICIOUS-LOOKING BAFTA EXEC ENTERS WITH THE SECURITY GUY.

BAFTA EXEC: Well, well, well, The Three Stooges.
(ANDY LAUGHS, CRAWLING)
Sorry, is something funny?

ANDY: Your joke was excellent.

BAFTA EXEC: Shut up.
(TO RONNIE)
Corbett. It's always bloody Corbett.
(TURNING TO ANDY)

You see, I expect it of him but you, you're the new kid on the block, aren't you? I mean, how'd you fall in with his crowd?

(ANDY SHRUGS. THE BAFTA EXEC HOLDS UP A SMALL PLASTIC BAG. TO RONNIE)

Is this it or is there any more?

RONNIE GINGERLY REACHES INTO HIS POCKET.

RONNIE: Just a bit of whizz, you know, to blow away the cobwebs.

BAFTA EXEC: Yeah, hand it over then, come on. And where'd you get it?

RONNIE: (lying like a hardened con) I don't remember.

BAFTA EXEC: Now, don't piss me about. Where'd you get it?

RONNIE: I don't remember.

BAFTA EXEC: Was it Moira Stuart?

ANDY REACTS.

RONNIE: I can't say.

BAFTA EXEC: Look, we don't want you. Just give us a name, you can walk free.

RONNIE: You don't get it, mate, do you? I don't remember.

BAFTA EXEC: All right, here's something you will remember. You're banned from BAFTA, you can never win a BAFTA now.

ANDY: What, me as well?

BAFTA EXEC: Yeah, all of you.

ANDY: Oh.

BAFTA EXEC: You can never attend any of our varied events, you can't come to the film BAFTAs, you can't come to the TV BAFTAs, you can't even come to the children's BAFTAs.

RONNIE: What about the Welsh BAFTAs?

BAFTA EXEC: Well, would you attend the Welsh BAFTAs if you were asked?

RONNIE: Probably.

BAFTA EXEC: Okay, expect a call.

AGENT: (pointing to ANDY) He'll, he'll come to the Welsh BAFTAs, if you want him.

ANDY: Yeah.

BAFTA EXEC: Yeah, we're after, you know, more respected comedians.

AGENT: Makes sense.

ANDY ROLLS HIS EYES.

BAFTA EXEC: Get out of my sight, that's all of you.

ANDY: 'Makes sense.'

AGENT: Well . . . I reckon I could have had him in a fight.

ANDY: Yeah, you . . . idiot.

ON STAGE, ANOTHER WINNER IS BEING ANNOUNCED.

BAFTA ANNOUNCER: And the winner is . . . *Holby City.*

THE *HOLBY* TEAM MAKE THIER WAY TO THE STAGE.

HOLBY PRODUCER: Thank you all very, very much indeed. I'd like to thank . . .

ANDY AND THE AGENT ARRIVE BACK AT THE TABLE.

MAGGIE: (seeing someone off-screen) Is that the girl you lost your virginity to?

ANDY: Who?

MAGGIE: The one that looks like Ronnie Corbett.

ANDY: That is Ronnie Corbett! Why would she be wearing a tuxedo?

MAGGIE: She might be a lesbian.

ANDY: And why would I lose my virginity to a lesbian?

MAGGIE: I don't know, she might have turned lesbian after you slept with her.

ANDY REACTS.

ANDY: Well, I can never win a BAFTA as long as I live.

MAGGIE: Why?

ANDY: I don't want to go into it. This is a shitty night. Can't get any worse, though.

ANDY'S OLD FLAME, CLEARLY DRUNK, IS AT THE MICROPHONE.

OLD FLAME: I'd just like to say to Andy Millman, right, I may be boring but at least I didn't lose my virginity when I was twenty eight . . . to a woman who looks like Ronnie fucking Corbett.

CUT TO: RONNIE CORBETT IN THE AUDIENCE, NATURALLY CONFUSED. Prick.

ANDY STARES AT THE STAGE. MAGGIE OPENS HER MOUTH TO SPEAK.

ANDY: No explanations needed.

(CONSULTING PROGRAMME)

What's up next? Huw Weldon award for Specialist Factual, brilliant.

SCENE 16. INT. BAFTA AWARDS FOYER. NIGHT.

ANDY AND MAGGIE ARE LEAVING.

MAGGIE: Oh, can we get a cab?

ANDY: No, we'll walk . . . I'm joking, if we sell the dress we can get a limo.

MAGGIE: Oh.

AN AUTOGRAPH HUNTER APPEARS.

AUTOGRAPH HUNTER: Sorry, can I get your autograph, please?

ANDY: Sure. What's your name?

AUTOGRAPH HUNTER: It's Paul.

ANDY BEGINS TO SIGN AN AUTOGRAPH BUT HE'S DISTRACTED BY A KERUFFLE. AMAZINGLY, IT IS A POLICEWOMAN FRISKING MOIRA STUART. MOIRA LOOKS ACROSS AT ANDY WITH A POISONOUS STARE. SHE MAKES A THROAT-SLITTING GESTURE. ANDY REACTS.

EXTRAS
Episode 5

CAST LIST
Andy Millman RICKY GERVAIS
Maggie Jacobs ASHLEY JENSEN
Agent STEPHEN MERCHANT
Shaun SHAUN WILLIAMSON
Iain Morris GUY HENRY
Damon Beesley MARTIN SAVAGE
Greg SHAUN PYE

Guest Starring IAN MCKELLEN

Rita LIZA TARBUCK
Kimberley SARAH MOYLE
Gobbler ANDREW BUCKLEY
Brains JAMIE CHAPMAN
Bunny GERARD KELLY
Steve Sherwood JONATHAN CAKE
Make-up Woman SARAH PRESTON
Fran RUFUS WRIGHT
Third A.D. NADIA WILLIAMS
Woman ANNA CRILLY
George PRIYANGA BURFORD

With GERMAINE GREER, MARK
KERMODE, MARK LAWSON

Written & Directed by
RICKY GERVAIS &
STEPHEN MERCHANT

TV CLIP:
'WHEN THE WHISTLE BLOWS'

RITA: Oh, it says here I'm going to meet a handsome man with bags of personality.

RAY ENTERS.

RAY: I told you, I'm married.

RITA: I still can't believe you got somebody to marry you.

RAY: Don't be too amazed, you haven't seen her. Ohh.

RAY BERATES DITZY KIMBERLEY.

RAY: Bloody hell, Kimberley, are you still doing that time sheet? Hurry up.

KIMBERLEY: It's complicated, Mr Stokes.

RAY: Are you having a laugh? Is she having a laugh?

KIMBERLEY: You know it gives me a headache if it's too hard.

RAY: Funny, that's what the wife said to me yesterday. I said, 'Don't flatter yourself, love, that's not hard, it died years ago, that's rigor mortis.'

TV CLIP: 'NEWSNIGHT REVIEW'

WE REALISE WE HAVE JUST BEEN WATCHING A CLIP WITHIN
NEWSNIGHT REVIEW.

MARK LAWSON: Andy Millman as Ray Stokes in a scene from BBC1's
new sitcom *When The Whistle Blows*. The catchphrase is 'Are you having
a laugh?' Did you, Germaine Greer?

GERMAINE GREER: Oh, for goodness' sake, why me? Why do you
make me watch this stuff? This was sexist, misogynistic, Neanderthal
garbage. It was nothing but really nasty sub-*Carry On* innuendo.
And it seems that this talentless Millman individual also wrote
the script. Wrote? It's supposed to have had a writer?

MARK LAWSON: I think he needs a defender: Mark Kermode.

MARK KERMODE: I think Germaine's being flattering about it.

CUT TO:

SCENE 1. INT.
AGENT'S OFFICE. DAY.

ANDY AND THE AGENT ARE WATCHING THIS ON THE TV IN THE AGENT'S
OFFICE. SHAUN IS PRESENT.

MARK KERMODE: (on television) I thought it was absolutely horrible . . .

ANDY: Oh, I get the idea. They all seemed to like it.

AGENT: No, I don't think so, I think they're slagging you off.

ANDY: I'm being sarcastic.

AGENT: Oh, okay.

MARK KERMODE: You know, everyone involved should be thoroughly
ashamed of themselves.

THE AGENT SWITCHES OFF THE TV.

AGENT: Why did Germaine Greer and all those feminists burn their
bras? What was going on there?

SHAUN: Well, it was a symbolic gesture to suggest emancipation from
a patriarchal society.

ANDY REACTS TO SHAUN'S UNEXPECTED ERUDITION.

AGENT: But I thought a bra was supposed to help a lady, you know, stop her getting backache or whatever.

SHAUN: You couldn't tell them at the time, they were furious.

AGENT: I bet they're kicking themselves now, aren't they, Bar? I bet their boobs are all saggy round their ankles.

ANDY: Sorry, can we concentrate on the matter at hand?

AGENT: Yeah, well, I was going to say, the weird thing is the worse the reviews are, the better the ratings. And it's strange, I was thinking about all those people that are making really great programmes, but not getting half the audience that you're getting, and thinking, 'Oh wouldn't it be great to work with them?' You know, because they get a load of critical respect and everything, and then I thought no, I much prefer working with you because you've . . . er . . . you've sold out. Do you know what I mean? We're all making a fast buck now, which is great, 'cause I don't want to be doing this for the rest of my life.

ANDY: I do want to be doing this for the rest of my life, actually. Do you know how exhausting it is getting panned by the critics every week? I've got no respect and why should I have? I'm not an actor. I shout a catchphrase. Do you know why I got into acting in the first place? Robert De Niro. Do you think he'd be impressed with wigs and shouting the same thing every week?

AGENT: No.

ANDY: No, he's got a body of work he can look back on and be proud of. That's what I want. Get me something I can be proud of. Has anything classy come in?

THE AGENT LOOKS THROUGH HIS NOTES.

AGENT: Well, funny you should say that. BBC are doing more of those modern adaptations of Shakespeare.

ANDY: Right.

AGENT: Doing *King Lear* . . .

ANDY: Okay. Who's playing Lear?

AGENT: Robson Green.

ANDY: No. Get me some real Shakespeare. Get me any play. A play always sorts out an actor whose career's struggling or they always pretend it was their first love and they do a bit of theatre and it gives them a bit of cred. Get me a play, the play's the thing.

AGENT: I'm going to write down 'play', Bar, all right? I'm going to put this in an email so you remember as well.

SCENE 2. INT.
MAKE-UP ROOM. DAY.

ANDY IS CHATTING WITH MAGGIE. A MAKE-UP WOMAN IS WORKING ON LIZA TARBUCK.

ANDY: I've got the worst management in the world. Do you know what I mean?

MAGGIE: Yeah.

ANDY: I'm successful now. I'm still surrounded by the D team. I want the A Team.

MAGGIE: Yeah, it's hard though, isn't it? I mean, they're hiding in the Los Angeles underground, so . . .

ANDY: Not *The A Team*.

MAGGIE: That's what you said.

ANDY: No, they're fictional characters.

MAGGIE: Oh, I thought it was a bit weird you mentioned them.

ANDY: I didn't, I meant the phrase.

MAGGIE: What phrase?

ANDY: 'The A team', it means the best possible people for the job, doesn't it?

MAGGIE: What about *The Six Million Dollar Man*? Was that a phrase?

ANDY: No.

MAGGIE: Oh.

ANDY: That was very specific to him because he cost six million dollars.

MAGGIE: No, no, no. That could have been a phrase: 'Oh, look at him, he's a right old six-million-dollar man, isn't he?'

ANDY: When would you ever say that?

MAGGIE: If you saw a man that could run fast and see really well out of one eye.

ANDY: What are the chances of that? What are the chances of that ever happening?

MAGGIE: I don't know, I didn't make up the phrase, did I?

ANDY: It's not a phrase, it's . . .

LIZA TARBUCK IS FINISHED AND HEADS OUT OF THE DOOR.

LIZA: See you down there.

ANDY: See you later.

MAKE-UP WOMAN: Oh Liza, before you go, could you sign a picture for me?

SHE HANDS HER A PUBLICITY PHOTO AND A BIRO.

LIZA: Yeah. What's your name again, love?

THE MAKE-UP LADY GOES QUIET.

MAKE-UP WOMAN: Don't worry about it, you know, if you can't remember my name it really doesn't matter.

LIZA: No, I've just forgotten because there's so many people.

MAKE-UP WOMAN: Right.
(NODDING AT ANDY)
So, have you forgotten his name then? Or do you remember the actors but not the little people? I've been doing your hair and make-up for five weeks!

LIZA: I'm very sorry, I just—

MAKE-UP WOMAN: It's fine, it's fine, doesn't matter.

LIZA: I've got a terrible memory.

MAKE-UP WOMAN: Don't worry about it. Don't worry.

LIZA: (embarrassed) Okay. Sorry.

LIZA ROLLS HER EYES TO ANDY AND LEAVES.

MAKE-UP WOMAN: God. What a bitch. Do you know, it's always the same with some of these people: 'Oh I'm on the telly, so I'm more important than the fucking crew.' Makes me sick.

ANDY: I know. What can you do?

ANDY TURNS TO MAGGIE AND MOUTHS, 'I DON'T KNOW HER NAME EITHER.' THEY GIGGLE.

MAKE-UP WOMAN: Oh, Andy, by the way . . .

ANDY: Yep?

MAKE-UP WOMAN: Can you sign me a picture?

(ANDY LOOKS PANICKED. THE MAKE-UP WOMAN HANDS HIM ONE OF HIS PUBLICITY SHOTS AND A BIRO)

Can you sign that?

HE TAKES THE PHOTO AND THE BIRO.

ANDY: This one?

MAKE-UP WOMAN: Yeah.

ANDY: Who's it to?

MAKE-UP WOMAN: Oh, it's just to me.

ANDY: Ahh. What shall I put though? To . . . ?

MAKE-UP WOMAN: Erm, to me and I don't know, 'best wishes' or whatever.

ANDY STALLS FOR TIME.

ANDY: Erm . . .

MAKE-UP WOMAN: What? Do you not want to sign that?

ANDY: No, no, with pleasure. I was just thinking, I don't want to spell your name wrong. How are you spelling it?

MAKE-UP WOMAN: Oh, it's just the usual.

ANDY REACTS.

ANDY: Okay, let's go for it.

(BUT HE DOESN'T GO FOR IT. HE STARES AT THE PHOTO. A THOUGHT
STRIKES HIM. HE HOLDS UP THE BIRO)

Oh, can't do it with that though, let me go to my dressing room, I've got
a magic marker.

MAGGIE: Oh, I've got a magic marker.

ANDY: Have you?

MAGGIE: In my bag.

ANDY: Thanks.

MAGGIE GETS A MAGIC MARKER OUT OF HER BAG AND HANDS IT
TO ANDY. HE SNATCHES IT FROM HER AND GIVES HER A DIRTY LOOK.
SHE LOOKS AT HIM, CONFUSED BY HIS ANNOYANCE.

ANDY: Right. Let's start with me first.

(HE SIGNS HIS NAME)

'Andy Millman'. Work backwards.

(WRITING)

'Best wishes'. I mean that, 'To . . .' and then your name. Oh, right, sorry,
before we do that.

(HE GRABS HIS MOBILE PHONE AND SENDS A TEXT)

Sorry about this . . . must . . . no, hold on, let me do this and we can get
on with it. Good.

MAKE-UP WOMAN: Do you want to get this done . . .

ANDY: Yep.

MAKE-UP WOMAN: Because I'm really conscious of time, I've got to get
back down to set . . .

ANDY: Right, yeah, no, no, I know.

MAGGIE'S MOBILE PHONE BLEEPS, ANNOUNCING THE ARRIVAL OF A
TEXT. THE MAKE-UP WOMAN LOOKS ACROSS SUSPICIOUSLY. MAGGIE
READS THE MESSAGE.

MAGGIE: (bluntly, to the MAKE-UP WOMAN) What's your name?

THE MAKE-UP WOMAN REACTS.

MAKE-UP WOMAN: Well, you'll see what it is now because Andy is about to write it down.
(ANDY LAUGHS AND STARTS BLOWING DRY THE INK OF THE SIGNATURE)
Oh, stop blowing.

ANDY: Well, don't . . .

MAKE-UP WOMAN: You don't know my name, do you?

ANDY: It's not that I don't know it.

MAKE-UP WOMAN: Yeah? What is it then?

PAUSE.

ANDY: What, in this context?

MAKE-UP WOMAN: Oh, forget it.

ANDY: Well . . .

MAKE-UP WOMAN: Honestly, forget it. It doesn't matter, I've got to get down to set. Just unbelievable. Un-fucking-believable.

SHE EXITS.

MAGGIE: She was upset.

ANDY: Yes, she was. You knew I didn't know her name. I said to you, 'I don't know her name,' so why did you give me the magic marker?

MAGGIE: Just 'cause you needed one.

ANDY: No, no, that was an excuse to leave and ask someone her name, wasn't it?

MAGGIE: That's clever, I'd never had thought to do that.

SCENE 3. INT. SITCOM SET. DAY.

ANDY IS WITH MAGGIE ON SET.

MAGGIE: (smelling her arm and then ANDY's) Mmm.

ANDY: What are you doing?

MAGGIE: Smell that, nice fabric conditioner. I like smells. Do you know, I once had this bar of soap and it smelt so nice that I bit into it 'cause I wanted to see what it tasted like. It tasted of soap.

A THIRD ASSISTANT DIRECTOR APPEARS.

THIRD A.D.: Andy, Reception say they've got a guy here who says he knows you.

ANDY: Oh, God. Who is it?

THIRD A.D.: He says he went to school with you. Steve Sherwood?

ANDY: Steve Sherwood?

MAGGIE: Who is it?

THIRD A.D.: That's what he said.

ANDY: What, he's here now?

THIRD A.D.: Yeah.

ANDY: Can he come through?

THIRD A.D.: Yeah.
(INTO HER WALKIE-TALKIE)
HIYA, CAN YOU SEND THAT GUY UP?

MAGGIE: Who's that?

ANDY: He was like the coolest kid in the school, everyone wanted to be like him.

MAGGIE: Even you?

ANDY: Well, I suppose so, yeah.

MAGGIE: What does he do now?

ANDY: I think he's something big in the city.

MAGGIE: Well, you could still do that.

ANDY: I don't want to be like him now, do I? I'm doing really well. He probably wants to be like me, if anything.

STEVE SHERWOOD WALKS IN. HE'S TALL AND HANDSOME.

MAGGIE: He definitely doesn't want to be like you.

SHERWOOD: Andy Pandy, you little fat poofter.

ANDY: (batting it away) I'm not a poofter.

SHERWOOD: Hold on, hold on, you're with a pretty girl. There can only be one explanation.
(TO MAGGIE)
Are you a prostitute, darling?

MAGGIE: (laughing girlishly) Pretty girl . . .

SHERWOOD: So, you're doing all right?

ANDY: Yeah, not bad, yeah.

SHERWOOD: Is this the missus?

ANDY: No, no, no.

SHERWOOD: Oh, why do you protest so much? What, you find the idea so repulsive? She's an attractive lady.

MAGGIE: (still girlish) Stop it.

SHERWOOD: You know, we always thought you were gay at school.

ANDY: No, you didn't. Why?

SHERWOOD: Well, you never had a girlfriend.

ANDY: I . . . not in front of you, I didn't.

SHERWOOD: Oh, so you had a girlfriend then, did you?

ANDY: Yes.

MAGGIE: No, not until he was twenty-eight.

SHERWOOD: Twenty-eight?

ANDY: (to MAGGIE) What?

MAGGIE: And she looked like Ronnie Corbett.

ANDY: Oh, not this again, no.

SHERWOOD: Ronnie Corbett?

ANDY: No, it's er, it's er, it's er— why do you think I'm gay? You don't, do you? I'm not . . .

SHERWOOD: Well, you are an actor.

MAGGIE: That is the gayest profession.

ANDY: Yeah, I think rent boy's gayer.

SHERWOOD: Yeah, well, I wouldn't know.

ANDY: Well, of course it is, if we're . . .

SHERWOOD: Well, you tell me, you seem to know all about rent boys.

MAGGIE LAUGHS.

ANDY: Oh . . .
(SUDDENLY CURT)
I'm not gay, I never have been and I never will be.
(HIS OUTBURST KILLS THE MOOD)
Let's nip that in the bud.

SCENE 4. INT. SITCOM SET. DAY.

PASSAGE OF TIME SHOTS, THEN: ANDY IS SAT NEAR THE TEA AND COFFEE AREA. THE AGENT APPROACHES.

AGENT: Andy!

HE WALKS STRAIGHT INTO A CHAIR.

ANDY: Oh for—
(THE AGENT SITS NEXT TO ANDY)
What do you want?

AGENT: The play. I've been talking to one of my contacts . . .

ANDY: You mean Barry from *EastEnders*?

AGENT: Yeah and he's got a friend who's an actor who's just had a meeting with Sir Ian McKellen, who's directing a new play. So I put in some calls and you've got a meeting with McKellen on Wednesday.

ANDY: Really?

AGENT: Yeah, yeah, I don't know . . .

STEVE SHERWOOD WANDERS BACK FROM A STROLL AROUND THE SET.

SHERWOOD: Bloody hell, there's some nice birds round there.

ANDY: (playing it cool) Suppose so.

THE (FEMALE) THIRD A.D. APPROACHES.

THIRD A.D.: Andy, we'll be ready in about five minutes.

ANDY: Cheers.

SHERWOOD: Five minutes is all I need.

THIRD A.D.: What?

SHERWOOD: Steve Sherwood. What's your name?

THIRD A.D.: Suzi.

SHERWOOD: Nice to meet you, Suzi. What time do you finish here?

THIRD A.D.: About ten o'clock.

SHERWOOD: Right. Do you mind if I give you a call?

THIRD A.D.: Sure, okay.

SHERWOOD: What's your number?

(SHE WRITES IT DOWN FOR HIM. ANDY AND THE AGENT LOOK ON, AMAZED. STEVE SHERWOOD COOLLY FLIPS A BOTTLE OF WATER A FEW TIMES, OPENS IT AND TAKES A SWIG)

Speak to you later.

THIRD A.D.: Okay.

SHE WALKS OFF.

AGENT: (laughing) Playa.

ANDY: Oh.

AGENT: Respect, man.

(HE GIVES STEVE A 'STREET' HAND-SLAP)

Darren Lamb, agent to Andy Millman.

ANDY: This is Steve Sherwood, friend of mine.

AGENT: (to ANDY) Are you a friend of his? I don't think so, this guy's an absolute playa. Respect again. Listen, if we're talking about the honeys, there's a chick I've got my eye on actually.

ANDY: Who?

AGENT: Her. Maggie.

ANDY: Maggie? Forget it.

AGENT: Yeah, from what I've heard she's pretty easy.

ANDY: Yeah, she's not that easy. Good luck.

AGENT: (to SHERWOOD) How would you approach it? I mean, what sort of . . . ?

SHERWOOD: Just walk straight up to her and say, 'I've been admiring you from afar for a long time and I haven't said anything but I would love to take you out one night and see if we have as good a time as I think we will. Would you like to have dinner with me sometime?' Bang.

AGENT: Okay.

SHERWOOD: Don't think about it, just do it.

AGENT: Just do it.

ANDY: (laughing) No, don't do it, please.

AGENT: Well, he says do it.

SHERWOOD: Get over there, go on.

ANDY: Oh, look at him.

SCENE 5. INT. SITCOM SET. DAY.

THE AGENT WALKS UP TO MAGGIE, WHO IS READING A MAGAZINE.

AGENT: Maggie . . . hello, sorry to . . .

MAGGIE: Hi.

AGENT: Erm, just wanted to let you know that I've been . . . er . . . watching you secretly without you knowing and, erm, be very keen to spend the night with you and see if you enjoy it as much as I know I will and, erm, happy to pay for it as well if . . . you know, for dinner. If you want to . . . if you eat dinner, obviously you eat dinner . . .

MAGGIE: Are you asking me out?

AGENT: Yeah.

MAGGIE: What, and cook me dinner?

AGENT: I can cook you dinner if you want, yeah.

MAGGIE: Can you cook?

AGENT: Yes.

MAGGIE: (turns back to her magazine) Yeah, okay then.

AGENT: Really?

MAGGIE: Yeah.

AGENT: Okay, cool. I'll give you a call, shall I?

MAGGIE: Yeah.

AGENT: Yeah. See you later.

MAGGIE: Bye.

SCENE 6. INT. SITCOM SET. DAY.

THE AGENT WALKS BACK OVER TO ANDY AND STEVE SHERWOOD.

ANDY: What did she say?

AGENT: She said 'yes'.

ANDY: (incredulous) Really? Oh my God, it's worse than I thought. She's hit rock bottom.

AGENT: Yes she has.

HE RUBS HIS HANDS TOGETHER AND SMILES. ANDY CAN'T BELIEVE IT.

AGENT: (to STEVE, gesturing to ANDY) Do you know what, I've never seen him even try and chat up a woman.

ANDY: No, no, no, 'cause I wouldn't do it in front of you, would I?

AGENT: I'm actually beginning to think he might be a bit gay.

ANDY: No.

SHERWOOD: Join the club.

ANDY: Well, no, don't join any club 'cause I'm not.

SHERWOOD: Sure. You, you could chat up a woman right now, couldn't you?

ANDY: Yes, if I wanted to, yeah.

AGENT: Go on then.

ANDY: I don't want to.

SHERWOOD: We've both done it. Go on. This one coming now, go on.

ANDY: No, no, no, no.

A WOMAN APPROACHES THE TEA TABLE. STEVE SHERWOOD AND THE AGENT BEGIN TO MAKE CHICKEN NOISES AT ANDY WHO TAKES THE BAIT AND LEAPS UP.

ANDY: Hi.

WOMAN: Hello.

ANDY TRIES TO LOOK CASUAL, FLIPPING A BOTTLE OF WATER LIKE STEVE SHERWOOD HAD EARLIER.

ANDY: Hi, do you know what time we finish tonight?

WOMAN: Oh, I don't know, about ten-ish, I think.

ANDY: Ten, hey, I wonder—

(AS HE SPEAKS, ANDY OPENS THE BOTTLE OF WATER HE HAS BEEN FLIPPING OVER. HOWEVER, UNLIKE STEVE SHERWOOD, ANDY HAS PICKED UP A BOTTLE OF SPARKLING WATER AND WHEN HE OPENS IT, THE FIZZY WATER SPRAYS UP AT HIM. IN ORDER TO STOP THE SPRAY, ANDY JAMS HIS OWN MOUTH OVER THE TOP OF THE BOTTLE BUT IT FIZZES UP INTO HIS MOUTH, BLOWING OUT HIS CHEEKS AND FORCING HIM TO SPLUTTER WATER EVERYWHERE. CHOKING:)

Just wanted to know what time we finished. Cheers.

(HE WAVES THE WOMAN AWAY, STILL STRUGGLING TO CATCH HIS
BREATH. THE WOMAN EXITS AS ANDY MOVES BACK TOWARDS STEVE
SHERWOOD AND THE AGENT)

That was unlucky. She answered me and everything. Ten o'clock, she said.

(HE POINTS TO STEVE SHERWOOD'S BOTTLE)

You used still.

(HE POINTS TO HIS OWN BOTTLE)

Sparkling . . . She definitely noticed.

SCENE 7. INT. THEATRE
REHEARSAL ROOM. DAY.

SIR IAN MCKELLEN IS DISCUSSING CASTING OPTIONS WITH HIS
PRODUCTION TEAM. ANDY ENTERS NERVOUSLY. MCKELLEN NOTICES HIM.

IAN MCKELLEN: Hello.

ANDY: Hello, Andy Millman.

IAN MCKELLEN: Andy, do sit down.

THEY SHAKE HANDS.

ANDY: Hi. It's a pleasure to meet you, Sir Ian.

IAN MCKELLEN: Please, no titles in the workplace. Thank you.
(LOOKING AT ANDY'S DETAILS IN FRONT OF HIM)
Andy Millman. Good, good . . . Not much theatre work of late?

ANDY: No, no.

IAN McKELLEN: (light-hearted) Oh, that's fine. You're in good hands here.

(ANDY CHUCKLES. FROM NOWHERE, GRANDLY:)

How do I act so well?

(ANDY REACTS)

What I do is, I pretend to be the person I'm portraying in the film or play.

ANDY: Yeah.

IAN McKELLEN: You're confused.

ANDY: No.

IAN McKELLEN: It's perfectly simple. A case in point: *Lord of the Rings*. Peter Jackson comes from New Zealand, says to me, 'Sir Ian, I want you to be Gandalf The Wizard.' And I say to him, 'You are aware that I am not really a wizard?' And he said, 'Yes, I am aware of that, what I want you to do is to use your acting skills to portray the wizard, for the duration of the film.' So I said, 'Okay.' And then I said to myself, 'Hmm, how would I do that?' And this is what I did. I imagined what it would be like to be a wizard and then I pretended and acted in that way, on the day . . .

ANDY: Yeah.

IAN McKELLEN: And how did I know what to say?

(WHISPERING LIKE IT'S A BIG SECRET)

The words were written down for me in a script. How did I know where to stand? People told me. If we were to draw a graph of my process, of my method, it would be something like this:

(MIMES WALKING, WITH HIS FINGERS)

Sir Ian, Sir Ian, Sir Ian. 'Action!'

(ADOPTS A 'GANDALF' VOICE)

'Wizard, you shall not pass!' 'Cut.'

(MIMES WALKING AGAIN)

Sir Ian, Sir Ian, Sir Ian.

ANDY: Okay.

IAN MCKELLEN: Do you see?

ANDY: Yeah.

IAN MCKELLEN: So, now, you would be pretending to be John in this play, and how would you know what to say? Well, the words will be in the script.

ANDY: Yeah.

IAN MCKELLEN: And you would learn the words, they – you would not have the script on the night. That goes for everybody, there will be no scripts on the night! You'll learn the words!

ANDY: Yeah – no, I . . .

IAN MCKELLEN: And you will speak them as if you were saying them for the first time.

ANDY: I didn't think we would have the script on the night.

IAN MCKELLEN: No, well, you won't.

ANDY: No, I . . .

IAN MCKELLEN: Because if you did have the script it would break the illusion and the whole thing is illusion. Do you see?

ANDY: Of course.

IAN MCKELLEN: You are not really John.

ANDY: No, I know.

IAN MCKELLEN: You are pretending, and that is acting.

MCKELLEN BECOMES INEXPLICABLY EMOTIONAL AT THIS AND WIPES AWAY A TEAR. ANDY LOOKS ON, PERPLEXED.

ANDY: What's the play about?

IAN MCKELLEN: It's a new play by Charley, Charley Heyward.

ANDY: Mmm.

IAN MCKELLEN: And, as I say, you would be the part of John and you're in love with Fran, and the whole centrepiece of the play is the emotional confrontation when the two of you address those unspoken feelings that you've been bottling up.

ANDY: (thrilled) That sounds challenging.

IAN MCKELLEN: Oh, I hope so and, I don't know, is it anything that you'd be interested in?

ANDY: (excited) Oh, definitely, yeah, yeah, yeah, yeah, yeah.

IAN MCKELLEN: Great. So let me introduce you to the team. There's Fran – who's your lover . . .

ANDY: Yeah.

IAN MCKELLEN: Played by Leslie. Leslie, this is Andy.

A MALE ACTOR GETS UP AND SHAKES ANDY'S HAND. ANDY REACTS.

LESLIE: Good to meet you.

ANDY: F— You're Fran. Fran's a man?

IAN MCKELLEN: Yes.

ANDY: Can be, 'cause Fran Healey out of Travis . . .

IAN MCKELLEN: What?

ANDY: Yep.

IAN MCKELLEN: And our clever little writer, Charley.

A WOMAN WAVES.

ANDY: Who's a woman! I didn't . . .
(SUDDENLY PANICKED)
I'm Fran's lover in this?

IAN MCKELLEN: Yes.

ANDY: Could I . . . could I have a quick look at the script? Just before . . .

IAN MCKELLEN: Yeah, sure.

ANDY GRABS THE SCRIPT AND THUMBS THROUGH THE PAGES IN A PANIC.

ANDY: No one said anything about the . . .

IAN MCKELLEN: And I don't know if you'd be happy to do this . . .

ANDY: Yeah, I just want to . . .

IAN MCKELLEN: But we thought we might do a little workshop of some of the lines, you know, and get it up on its feet.

ANDY: Yeah.

IAN MCKELLEN: Kick it around a bit, I don't know, do you have time for that?

ANDY: Yeah.

IAN MCKELLEN: Andy?

ANDY: (lost in thought desperately scanning the script) Yeah.

IAN MCKELLEN: Good. Can I get you something? Some water, cup of tea?

ANDY: Yeah, yeah. Tea.

IAN MCKELLEN: George, will you get Andy a cup of tea?

GEORGE: Ah, yeah, no problem.

ANDY SEES THAT GEORGE IS A WOMAN.

ANDY: George. 'Course.

SCENE 8. INT. AGENT'S OFFICE. DAY.

ANDY ENTERS.

AGENT: All right?

ANDY: (staring at the AGENT). Moron.

AGENT: (looking around) What? Are you talking to me?

ANDY: Yeah, I'm talking to you. Why didn't you tell me it was a gay play?

AGENT: What, what gay play?

ANDY: The play I'm in that you got me: *A Month of Summers*. It's a gay play. I've got to play a gay, with another gay, acting all gay, all through the play. It's so gay.

AGENT: Do not worry, do you know why? Gay, my friend, is all the rage.

ANDY: What does that mean?

AGENT: Let me tell you what it means. It will show you are sensitive, it will show that you are versatile, all right? Case in point: Mr Thomas Hanks, okay? Now, people weren't interested in Tom Hanks, suddenly there's that film *Philadelphia*, yeah? Now remember, in that film he played a skinny little bent fella, remember?

ANDY: Yeah.

AGENT: Right, after that everyone loved him, do you know what I mean? Or those two guys from *Brokeback Mountain*, now, they're not even gay and I was watching that, right, and they were getting off with each other. Oh, I was sick to the stomach, they were so convincing that even though I was going, 'They're not really queer, they're not really queer,' I was still repulsed . . . because of how good they were.

ANDY: When did you go and see *Brokeback Mountain*?

AGENT: I watched it on DVD with Bar.

ANDY MUSES ON THE AGENT'S INCREDIBLY PERSUASIVE ARGUMENT.

ANDY: I don't know.

SCENE 9. INT. THEATRE REHEARSAL ROOM. DAY.

MUSIC MONTAGE OF ANDY REHEARSING THE PLAY WITH HIS CO-STAR LESLIE AND IAN MCKELLEN. AT ONE POINT, WE SEE LESLIE AS FRAN KNEELING ON THE FLOOR. ANDY IS SAT ON A CHAIR. LESLIE CRAWLS OVER AND PUTS HIS HEAD ON ANDY'S LAP.

LESLIE: John, I love you.

ANDY: I know.

IAN MCKELLEN: Yes, that's lovely.

LESLIE: Thanks.

MONTAGE ENDS.

SCENE 10. INT. THEATRE LOBBY. NIGHT.

A FEW AUDIENCE MEMBERS ARE MILLING ABOUT. ANDY APPEARS AND APPROACHES THE BOX OFFICE.

ANDY: Hi, can I just check there are some tickets for my colleagues from the BBC who should be coming down: Damon Beesley, plus one, and Iain Morris, plus one.

THE BOX OFFICE ATTENDANT CHECKS HER TICKETS.

BOX OFFICE ATTENDANT: Yeah, we've got them.

ANDY: Oh, great, okay, well . . .

SHERWOOD: (off-screen) Oi! Andy Pandy!

ANDY LOOKS ROUND. STEVE SHERWOOD AND A BUNCH OF BLOKES ARE CALLING HIM OVER. ANDY'S FACE DROPS.

ANDY: Oh – what?

SHERWOOD: You remember these boys from school, don't you? Nobby, Boss Hogg, Gut Rot.

THE LADS ARE REAL 'BLOKES', THE SORT WHO DRINK TEN PINTS AND GO LOOKING FOR A FIGHT.

ANDY: Oh, right, w-w-what are you doing here? You're not here for the play, are you?

SHERWOOD: Yeah. We've got tickets.

ANDY: Oh, not your type of thing.

SHERWOOD: No, no, no, we're looking forward to it. What's it about?

ANDY: It's all feelings and emotions, I'm just here for the . . .

ANDY RUBS HIS FINGERS TOGETHER TO INDICATE MONEY.

SHERWOOD: Oh, no, oh God, look at that – poofters at twelve o'clock.

ANDY: What can you do?

DAMON AND IAIN FROM THE BBC ARE ARRIVING AT THE BOX OFFICE, HOLDING HANDS WITH THEIR MALE PARTNERS.

SHERWOOD: That your audience, is it?

ANDY: No way.

DAMON: (calling out) Andy? Hiya!

ANDY: (to the LADS) Fans.

DAMON: (calling) Thanks for sorting out tickets, love.

ANDY: No worries.

SHERWOOD: Why are you sorting the Village People out with tickets?

ANDY: (laughing) Village People.

AS IF FROM NOWHERE BUNNY (FROM EPISODE 4, SERIES 1) APPEARS AND PUTS HIS HANDS OVER ANDY'S EYES.

BUNNY: Guess who!

ANDY: Bunny, Christ.

BUNNY: (grabbing ANDY's arm) I couldn't miss my little genie in his first 'gwown up pway'.
(HE NODS AT THE LADS)
Oh, you do hang around with all the butch boys, don't you?
Hello, I'm Bunny.

THE LADS JUST STARE AT BUNNY LIKE HE HAS LANDED FROM ANOTHER PLANET.

ANDY: (trying to disguise BUNNY's campness) How's the wife?

BUNNY: Oh, gone. I was living a lie and she knew it. But now I'm able to go out and enjoy some serious cock, guilt free. Yuma, yuma, yuma, yuma. Break a leg.

HE SMACKS ANDY'S ARSE AND TROTS OFF. THE LADS LOOK AT ANDY, APPALLED.

ANDY: (trying to act cool and blokeish) I'm going to . . . er . . . get down, get changed. Come down for a few beers if you want, but don't hang around for this shit.

HE WALKS OFF. THE LADS NOD NOD, STILL IN SHOCK.

SCENE 11. INT. ANDY'S DRESSING ROOM. THEATRE. NIGHT.

ANDY IS GETTING CHANGED. THERE IS A KNOCK AT THE DOOR AND IAN MCKELLEN ENTERS.

IAN MCKELLEN: Hello.

ANDY: Hi.

ANDY IS IN HIS SHIRT AND BOXER SHORTS. HE FEELS SELF-CONSCIOUS.

IAN MCKELLEN: How you doing?

ANDY: Good . . .

IAN MCKELLEN: Good, now look, I've just been talking to Leslie and we think it would be better if at the end of act two, you were to kiss each other.

ANDY LAUGHS NERVOUSLY AND SHAKES HIS HEAD.

ANDY: No.

IAN MCKELLEN: No? Leslie and you kiss each other at the end of act two?

ANDY: Ah. No, no.

IAN MCKELLEN: No?

ANDY: No.

IAN MCKELLEN: No, why?

ANDY: 'Cause it's too obvious.

IAN MCKELLEN: Oh, now dear, don't forget that you've finally been able to express your feelings toward each other for the first time in twenty years, and I think a kiss would be a sort of physicalisation of this emotional liberation, you know, your freedom to show the world what you are.

ANDY: Not the whole world, though. Let's . . . let's give 'em a clue, but let's keep it subtle.

IAN MCKELLEN: Oh, no.

ANDY: Yeah.

IAN MCKELLEN: But imagine if he just leans over you and then kisses—

ANDY: Kisses me on the cheek, shake hands, curtain comes down. 'Bravo, encore, what a brilliantly directed play. Well done.'

IAN MCKELLEN: Well, well, thank you, dear. But no, no dear, he must kiss you on the lips.

ANDY: No, he can't kiss me on the lips.

IAN MCKELLEN: Why is that?

ANDY: Cold sores.

IAN MCKELLEN: Where?

ANDY: Yeah, opening night. Sod's Law.

IAN MCKELLEN: What, let me see.

ANDY: (covering his lip) Well, you can't really – it's underneath . . .

IAN MCKELLEN: No.

ANDY: No – yes.

IAN MCKELLEN: Don't you worry about that.

ANDY: I do worry about that.

HE TAKES ANDY'S HAND.

IAN MCKELLEN: No, we'll soon sort that out, old theatre trick.
(MCKELLEN OPENS THE DOOR AND CALLS TO HIS PERSONAL ASSISTANT. STEVE SHERWOOD AND THE LADS ARE APPROACHING DOWN THE CORRIDOR. THEY SEE THE TABLEAUX: ANDY WITH NO TROUSERS ON AND SIR IAN SHOUTING:)
George, can you get us some Vaseline?

ANDY OPENS HIS MOUTH TO EXPLAIN BUT MCKELLEN CLOSES THE DOOR.

SCENE 12. INT. AGENT'S FLAT. NIGHT.

THE AGENT OPENS THE DOOR. IT'S MAGGIE. HE WELCOMES HER INTO HIS KITCHEN/DINING AREA.

AGENT: Hello, all right?

MAGGIE: Hello, yes.

AGENT: Come in, come through, this is the crib.

MAGGIE: God, it's big!

AGENT: No . . . well, er, yes. Yeah, it's all right.

MAGGIE: I've bought you . . .

MAGGIE HANDS OVER A BOTTLE OF WINE.

AGENT: Oh, thank you very much, is that red or . . .

MAGGIE: It's red, but I'll drink anything.

AGENT: No, I got red myself.

MAGGIE: Oh, right, okay.

AGENT: So, obviously we're both fans of red.

MAGGIE: Fine.

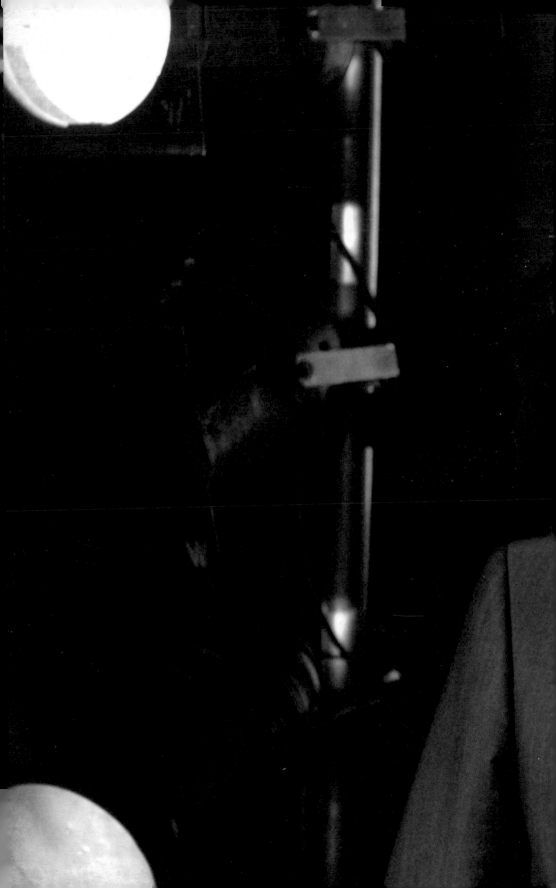

AGENT: I quite like wine.

MAGGIE: I like anything, me.

AGENT: Do you want to, sorry, do you want to take your coat off? 'Cause it's quite hot in here, 'cause of the cooking.

MAGGIE: It's a nice smell.

AGENT: Yeah, no, it's . . . well, we're going sort of oriental.

MAGGIE: (taking her coat off) Will I just hang it up?

AGENT: Well, no, yeah, just hang it up, yeah.

MAGGIE: Okay.

SCENE 13. INT. THEATRE. NIGHT.

THE AUDIENCE IS SETTLING DOWN AS THE LIGHTS DIM. SOUND FX OF THE SEA, WAVES LAPPING ON A BEACH, SEAGULLS, ETC. BLUE WASH ON BACKDROP. AN EMPTY STAGE. ANDY, AS JOHN, RUNS ON, IN T-SHIRT AND SHORTS, CALLING BEHIND HIM.

ANDY: C'mon Fran! You're like an old lady.

HE SITS CROSS-LEGGED, STARING OUT AT THE AUDIENCE. LESLIE (PLAYING FRAN) ENTERS, CARRYING A LARGE SEASHELL.

LESLIE: I stopped to pick up this shell. Look, it's beautiful.

HE SITS CROSS-LEGGED NEXT TO ANDY.

ANDY: It is. Do you remember the first time we came here?

LESLIE: (sad) Yeah, with Paul.

ANDY: Yeah.
(THEY PAUSE, MUSING ON THE MEMORY OF PAUL. ANDY JOLTS BACKWARDS, AS THOUGH THE SEA HAS JUST SWEPT UP THE BEACH)
Ah. Bloody sea.

LESLIE: Why are you so scared of the sea?

ANDY: I'm not scared of the sea. It's just, when it gets in your shoes, the salt water just rots away the stitches and they fall apart . . . and you have to throw them away.

LESLIE: (serious) Are you still talking about the sea?

ANDY: 'Course. What else?

PAUSE.

LESLIE: You're mad.

LESLIE RUFFLES ANDY'S HAIR AND RUNS HIS HAND SUGGESTIVELY DOWN ANDY'S ARM. STEVE SHERWOOD AND THE LADS ARE IN THE AUDIENCE WATCHING THIS. ANDY NOTICES THEM, FEELING SELF-CONSCIOUS.

LESLIE: I'm going back to the beach house.

HE GETS UP AND RUNS OFF. ANDY STARES AT 'THE SEA' A MOMENT LONGER, THEN JUMPS UP.

ANDY: (calling) Fran! Wait for me!

HE RUNS AFTER HIM.

ANOTHER REACTION SHOT OF SHERWOOD ET AL. PUZZLED AND A LITTLE CONCERNED BY DEVELOPMENTS.

SCENE 14. INT. AGENT'S FLAT. NIGHT.

A BRIEF MONTAGE OF THE AGENT COOKING IN HIS SURPRISINGLY
SLEEK, DESIGNER KITCHEN, THROWING THINGS CONFIDENTLY INTO
A LARGE WOK AS HE CHATS WITH MAGGIE, WHO IS STOOD NEARBY,
SIPPING WINE, ADMIRING HIS FLAIR. THEY CHAT, LAUGHING WITH
EACH OTHER, ENJOYING DINNER AND EACH OTHER'S COMPANY.
THEY APPEAR TO BE HITTING IT OFF.

CUT TO: MAGGIE IS SAT ALONE EATING HER DESSERT. WE HEAR THE
SOUND OF THE TOILET FLUSHING. THE AGENT APPEARS FROM THE
BATHROOM. HE WANDERS OVER TO THE DINING TABLE BUT INSTEAD OF
SITTING BACK DOWN HE HOVERS. MAGGIE LOOKS AT HIM AND SMILES.
HE SMILES BACK.

MAGGIE: You okay?

AGENT: Yeah, just waiting for the cistern to refill. There's . . . just left a
bit of, erm . . . Didn't, you know, flush away completely so . . . annoying.

HE STANDS AND WAITS. MAGGIE FEELS AWKWARD AND CONTINUES
EATING TO COVER THE SILENCE.

MAGGIE: Are you going to sit down?

AGENT: No, 'cause it's, it's on my mind, to be honest so . . .

MAGGIE: Okay, right, right.

AGENT: I'd rather – I want to get it sorted.
(MAGGIE ROLLS HER EYES. THE AGENT POINTS TO HER DESSERT)
Is that all right?

MAGGIE: Yes.

AGENT: Yeah?

MAGGIE: Fine, just ...

WE HEAR THE CISTERN FINISH REFILLING.

AGENT: Let's have another go.

MAGGIE: Mmm.

THE AGENT WALKS BACK INTO THE BATHROOM. WE HOLD ON MAGGIE.

WE HEAR THE TOILET FLUSH AGAIN. PAUSE.

AGENT: (off-screen) Oh, for fuck's sake.

HOLD ON MAGGIE'S REACTION. THE AGENT REAPPEARS FROM THE
BATHROOM AND GOES TO A KITCHEN DRAWER.

MAGGIE: Don't worry about it.

AGENT: Do you know, I don't want you to have to see it. To be honest,
I don't want you to have to worry about it.
(THE AGENT WRAPS A POLYTHENE BAG AROUND HIS HAND AND PICKS
UP A WHISK)
That'll sort it.

(HE MARCHES BACK INTO THE BATHROOM. MAGGIE TAKES THE
OPPORTUNITY TO GRAB HER COAT AND LEAVE)
That's just mashing it up.
(THE AGENT REAPPEARS FROM THE BATHROOM AND NOTICES
THAT MAGGIE HAS GONE)

SCENE 15. INT. THEATRE. NIGHT.

THE PLAY IS STILL GOING. LESLIE IS SAT ON THE FLOOR. ANDY IS SAT ON A ROCK, LOOKING AT THE SEASHELL FROM THE PREVIOUS SCENE. THEY ARE BOTH WEARING TUXEDOS, TIES UNDONE.

LESLIE: You kept the shell?

ANDY: 'Course I did. You gave it to me.

LESLIE: It wasn't mine to give.

ANDY: I kept it anyway.

LESLIE CRAWLS OVER AND PUTS HIS HEAD ON ANDY'S THIGH. ANDY NOTICES STEVE SHERWOOD AND THE BOYS REACT. ANDY PUSHES FRAN'S HEAD AWAY FROM HIS GROIN.

ANDY: Nearer the knee.

LESLIE: John, I love you.

ANDY: (to audience) In the play.
(TO JOHN)
I know.

LESLIE LOOKS ANDY IN THE EYE.

LESLIE: I'm going to kiss you.

ANDY: No point.

LESLIE: (thrown, ad libbing) Silly. Sometimes I don't know what you're talking about.

ANDY: You do, we agreed. If any nonsense happens, I'm going home!
(LESLIE LEANS FORWARD TO KISS ANDY AGAIN. ANDY JUMPS UP TO AVOID THE KISS)
Let's just have a lovely evening and appreciate the stars and the moon, as agreed, okay? So, just run to the next bit.
(LESLIE, TRYING TO STICK TO THE SCRIPT, LUNGES INTO KISS ANDY WHO HOLD HIM OFF. HE BACKS TOWARDS THE EDGE OF THE STAGE)
It's not going to happen.
(A HAND APPEARS FROM THE WINGS AND TRIES TO FORCE THE BACK OF HIS HEAD TOWARDS LESLIE)
Who the fuck's that?
(WE REVEAL THAT IT IS SIR IAN MCKELLEN'S HAND PUSHING THE BACK OF ANDY'S HEAD)
What are you doing? It's like *Deliverance* in here.
(HE BREAKS AWAY)
What are you playing at? I said I wouldn't do the kiss.

(HE STARES AT THE AUDIENCE)

McKellen comes to me, five minutes before, and drops that bombshell on me. 'Oh, we'd like you to do the kiss.' Not my cup of tea, mate. And then all that – no. And him a Knight of the Realm.

(TO IAN MCKELLEN)

Do you want to do the end bit without that? Oh, he's got the hump. No understudy, so I'm afraid that's the end of the run, sorry about that. We'd nearly finished anyway, to be fair. Only about five minutes to go, wasn't there? All you missed was, er, we find out me and Fran were both having it off with Paul, do you remember Paul we mentioned earlier? Erm, Paul killed himself 'cause he was wracked with guilt about doing both of us behind the other one's back. So . . .

(HE NOTICES GERMAINE GREER MAKING SOME NOTES)

Oh look, she's writing all this down. That's not going to be good, is it?

(GERMAINE GREER SHAKES HER HEAD. ANDY SPOTS GREG IN THE AUDIENCE, SHAKING HIS HEAD AND SMILING. ANDY LOOKS AT THE AUDIENCE. THEY STARE BACK AT HIM IN SILENCE.

'Are you having a laugh? Is he having a laugh?'

(THE AUDIENCE DO NOT REACT)

Not my audience, so what.

HE TAKES AN UNEARNED BOW, WAVES AND WALKS OFF-STAGE, PAST AN UNDERSTANDABLY FURIOUS SIR IAN MCKELLEN.

EXTRAS
Episode 6

CAST LIST
Andy Millman RICKY GERVAIS
Maggie Jacobs ASHLEY JENSEN
Agent STEPHEN MERCHANT
Shaun SHAUN WILLIAMSON

Guest Starring ROBERT LINDSAY
JONATHAN ROSS

Special Guest Star ROBERT DE NIRO

Joe COREY J SMITH
Mother of Joe REGINA FREEDMAN
Maggie's Date PAUL ALBERTSON
Date's Mother JENNIE GOOSSENS
Date's Father DAVID MCKAIL
Parents' Friend PENNY RYDER
Make-up Woman SARAH PRESTON
Researcher LAWRY LEWIN
Nurse CATHY MURPHY

Written & Directed by
RICKY GERVAIS &
STEPHEN MERCHANT

Extras   series two

501

TV CLIP: 'FRIDAY NIGHT WITH JONATHAN ROSS'

ANDY IS BEING INTERVIEWED BY THE CHAT-SHOW HOST.

JONATHAN ROSS: A lot of people when they get famous they find a lot of temptations in their way, they maybe drink too much, they eat too much, they get invited to parties and so forth, and, you know, weight can be a problem. You look like you have always struggled a little bit with your weight . . .

(THE AUDIENCE AND ANDY LAUGH)

Would I be right in that? Is it a struggle?

ANDY: It's not a struggle, the more I eat, the fatter I get . . .

MORE AUDIENCE LAUGHTER.

JONATHAN ROSS: But you're comfortable?

ANDY: It's easy, it's easy.

JONATHAN ROSS: What are your ambitions? I mean, obviously this has been a big hit for you, a surprise hit some would say, but what are your ambitions over and above this? You going to do more of the same or do you want to branch out?

ANDY: I suppose I would like to do, you know, serious acting and I would like to do films.

JONATHAN ROSS: Who would you like to meet? Who would you like to work with?

ANDY: You don't know anyone.

JONATHAN ROSS: I know most people in Hollywood, I've interviewed most of them, I've interviewed Tom Cruise many times, I've interviewed Robert De Niro. I interviewed . . .

ANDY: Well . . .

JONATHAN ROSS: I've interviewed all the greats.

ANDY: Yeah, obviously Robert De Niro's the greatest actor in the world so I'd obviously like to work with him . . .

JONATHAN ROSS: All right, that's . . . challenge accepted. Challenge accepted.

(ANDY LAUGHS)

No, challenge accepted. De Niro. I will hook you up with De Niro.

ANDY: You can get me De Niro?

JONATHAN ROSS: Yeah, but lose some weight first.

SCENE 1. INT.
BBC BACKSTAGE AREA. NIGHT.

ANDY IS SORTING HIS STUFF OUT IN HIS DRESSING ROOM.
JONATHAN ROSS APPEARS AT THE DOOR.

JONATHAN ROSS: Andy?

ANDY: Hi.

JONATHAN ROSS: Well done, that was great.

ANDY: Really?

JONATHAN ROSS: Yeah, it was fantastic, you were fantastic.

ANDY: Cheers.

JONATHAN ROSS: Are you going to stay for a drink?

ANDY: Yeah.

JONATHAN ROSS: All right, well, look, wait for me in there. I've got to pop downstairs but don't go without seeing me. I'd really love to chat.

ANDY: Okay.

JONATHAN ROSS: Wait for me.

ANDY: All right.

JONATHAN ROSS: Okay, I'll be a minute.

ANDY SMILES, PLEASED TO HAVE WON OVER ROSS.

SCENE 2. INT. BBC GREEN ROOM. NIGHT.

ANDY IS HAVING A CHAT WITH FELLOW GUEST ROBERT LINDSAY.

ROBERT: Was that your first chat show?

ANDY: Yeah.

ROBERT: You're not serious?

ANDY: Yeah, I was nervous as well.

ROBERT: Yeah, well it didn't show.

ANDY: Oh, really?

ROBERT: No, I didn't notice.

ANDY: You were great.

ROBERT: Well, I mean, I'm used to it. I've done loads, you'll get used to it.

A BBC RESEARCHER APPROACHES ANDY.

RESEARCHER: Sorry, sorry, you got a minute to talk to a big fan of yours from the audience?

ANDY: Er, yeah. What, now?

RESEARCHER: Yeah, is that all right, yeah? Sure?

ANDY: Yeah, yeah.

THE RESEARCHER CALLS IN A MOTHER AND HER YOUNG SON WHO
IS IN A WHEELCHAIR AND CLEARLY UNWELL.

RESEARCHER: Joe, this is Andy. Andy, Joe.

ANDY: (to the boy) Hi. You all right?

MOTHER: Can I ask – Joe's going into hospital next week, St Matthews.
He may be in for quite a long time and would you pop in and say hello?

ANDY: Would I . . . ?

MOTHER: Can you pop in and visit him whilst he's in hospital?

ANDY: I, I, I, I'm not sure what I'm doing.

MOTHER: All right, well give me your number and we can arrange
something.

ANDY: Er, yeah, if you call my agent on 02—

MOTHER: Not your agent.

ANDY: Not my agent?

MOTHER: No. They fob you off, agents. What's your mobile?

ANDY: Erm, I lost my mobile. I don't know where it is at the moment.

THE SICK BOY PIPES UP.

JOE: It's in your pocket.

ANDY: It's in my what?

JOE: It's in your pocket.

ANDY: (pretending to discover his 'missing' phone) Oh, I thought I looked there. Why didn't I look in there? I usually look in my pocket. Well done, kid.

MOTHER: (typing into her phone) What's your number?

ANDY: Mine?

MOTHER: Yeah.

ANDY: (lying) Can I remember it? 07700 . . . 900 . . . 15 . . . 8.

MOTHER: Oh, I'll just ring it so I've got it in there.

ANDY: Well, don't, no! That's my old one. That's the one I lost. That's the one I lost, no. If you're going to test it, it's 07700 900 168.

MOTHER: Okay, all right, well, I'll ring to confirm Monday.

ANDY: Well, I don't know if I can . . .

MOTHER: You can make it Monday, it's just, it's half an hour.

ANDY: Yeah.

MOTHER: Get a cab, you can afford it.

ANDY: Yeah, I know, but . . .

MOTHER: Six o'clock, St Matthews. He's going to be on the Parrot Ward, neurology block.

ANDY: Okay.

MOTHER: And six o'clock.

ANDY: Okay.

MOTHER: See you at six.

ANDY: Yeah.

MOTHER: Great, thank you very, very much.

ANDY: Oh.

MOTHER: Say goodbye.

JOE: Bye.

ANDY: Cheers.

MOTHER: Bye, bye, thanks.

ANDY: Bye.

MOTHER: This way.

THEY LEAVE. ANDY IS LEFT WITH ROBERT LINDSAY.

ROBERT: Bit weird, isn't it?

ANDY: Bit presumptuous.

ROBERT: No, I mean it's weird she didn't ask me. I mean, knowing what I can do and how much joy I bring to people. Well, maybe she didn't notice me.

ANDY: Maybe.

ROBERT: (curt) Unlikely. I think you're going to notice Robert Lindsay in a room. No, she probably saw me and thought, 'I'd love to ask him first, being one of Britain's best-loved actors and let's not forget, you know, he can sing, he can dance and he has won awards on Broadway for Christ's sake.' No, I know what it was, she was intimidated and she thought, 'Bird in the hand, I'll definitely get a "yes" from the nobody.'
(HE POINTS AT ANDY)
Worried about this kid though, aren't you?

ANDY: Yeah, well that's . . .

ROBERT: No, I'm worried. I'm worried about the kid because if this so-called mother is making stupid mistakes like that, you know, choosing you over me, then what other mistakes is she making? Is she screwing up his medication? Is she? Is she? I don't know . . .

ANDY: I don't know, I don't know.

ROBERT: No, no.
(ROBERT BEGINS TO WANDER OFF)
Good luck. Keep 'em laughing.

ANDY: Cheers.

ROBERT EXITS. ANDY IS TAKEN ABACK BY ROBERT'S MANNER.

SCENE 3. INT. BAR. NIGHT.

MAGGIE ON A DATE WITH A DISHY GUY WHO LOOKS LIKE HE'S PROBABLY A DOCTOR OR A LAWYER. THEY'RE LAUGHING AND DRINKING.

DISSOLVE TO MAGGIE AND HER DATE AS THEY PREPARE TO LEAVE THE BAR.

DISHY GUY: Would you like to come back for a nightcap?

MAGGIE: Yeah, I'd love to.

SCENE 6. INT.
BBC GREEN ROOM. NIGHT.

ANDY IS HAVING A GREAT TIME CHATTING WITH JONATHAN ROSS.

JONATHAN ROSS: Do you play at all?

ANDY: Mmm.

JONATHAN ROSS: Well, we should definitely have a game.

ANDY: I used to play all the time at school. I haven't played for a while.

JONATHAN ROSS: Well, I can see that, but I've got a court in my
back garden.

ANDY: Right, money on it.

JONATHAN ROSS: I will knock you all over the place. Actually, I've got
two courts.

ASSISTANT: (handing JONATHAN ROSS a box) Jonathan?

JONATHAN ROSS: Oh, brilliant, thank you. Right, I'm going to show
you this.

ANDY: Is that your wages?

JONATHAN ROSS: No, I got two of these. I got one in Japan, one in New York, right.

ANDY'S MOBILE RINGS.

ANDY: Oh, oh, sorry.

JONATHAN ROSS: I'll set it up.

HE ANSWERS THE CALL. IT'S MAGGIE. WE CROSSCUT BETWEEN ANDY AND MAGGIE DURING THE CONVERSATION.

ANDY: Hello?

MAGGIE: Hello, it's me.

ANDY: Hi, yeah, what can I do for you?

MAGGIE: Nothing, I'm just phoning for a chat. Oh God, I've got to tell you about this date that I've just been on.

ANDY: Do you have to tell me right now?

MAGGIE: What, are you busy?

ANDY: Yeah, I'm, er, I'm right in the middle of something at the moment.

ANDY LOOKS DOWN AT JONATHAN ROSS WHO IS NOW PLAYING WITH TWO ROBOT DOGS ON THE FLOOR.

MAGGIE: All right, well, I'll call you later then?

ANDY: (distracted by JONATHAN ROSS and the robot dogs) Yeah, I . . . don't know when I'll be finished though.

JONATHAN ROSS: He's stretching, look at this.

ANDY: Sort of really snowed under. I've got to go, I'll speak to you soon, yeah?

MAGGIE: All right, well, I'll speak to you tom—

ANDY HANGS UP THE PHONE AND EAGERLY JOINS JONATHAN ROSS AND THE TOYS.

JONATHAN ROSS: That's my toy right, but this is his toy. I had to buy this separately, check this out.

ANDY: I love the fact that your toys have got toys.

JONATHAN ROSS: Well, of course.

SCENE 7. INT. MAGGIE'S FLAT. NIGHT.

MAGGIE WATCHES TV IN HER EMPTY, LONELY FLAT.

SCENE 8. INT. AGENT'S OFFICE. DAY.

ANDY IS ANNOYED.

ANDY: Okay, so, how are you getting on with the De Niro thing?

AGENT: What's that?

ANDY: Oh for f— I told you, it . . . Jonathan Ross told me he's over here doing a film. You said you'd get me an audition, you said you'd make a few phone calls.

AGENT: Well, no, no, I've been looking into that.

ANDY: Have you?

AGENT: But it's tricky because all his people are in Los Angeles and . . .

ANDY: So? You've got a phone!

AGENT: Yeah, it's complicated though 'cause it's like . . . it took me two days to realise they're eight hours ahead.

ANDY: They're behind.

AGENT: Are they?

ANDY: Yes.

AGENT: That explains quite a lot. So, what time would it be over there now?

ANDY: Right, it's four o'clock here, so eight hours.

AGENT: (counting on fingers, left to right) Five, six, seven . . .

ANDY: No, you're going up.

AGENT: (counting on fingers, right to left) Five, six, seven . . .

ANDY: You're still going up.

AGENT: No, that's 'down', look.

ANDY: No, it's four o'clock here, so eight hours . . . eight o'clock.

AGENT: That's four hours ahead.

ANDY: (very annoyed) In the morning!

AGENT: Oh, okay, yes.

ANDY: Supposing they get in at nine . . .

AGENT: Ten, yeah, have a cup of coffee, say hello to people and . . . yeah.

ANDY: Right, add eight.

AGENT: To what?

ANDY: Ten!

AGENT: Ten – eighteen?

ANDY: What do you mean, eighteen?

AGENT: Oh, no, add eight hours, you mean.

ANDY: Well, of course.

AGENT: Yeah. Sorry.

ANDY: So call them at six o'clock.

AGENT: Right. Their time?

ANDY: Our time!

AGENT: Our time. Yeah. And what time will it be over there?

ANDY: Ten.

AGENT: Ten. At night?

ANDY: (exhausted) In the morning! Forget it. If I can get hold of Robert De Niro before you, you're fired. Okay? I've outgrown you, I don't know what you're for. Have another go but if I beat you to him . . . you're fired.

ANDY IS DEADLY SERIOUS AND FOR ONCE THE AGENT IS SHOCKED INTO SILENCE.

SCENE 9. INT. SITCOM SET. DAY.

ANDY IS HAVING HIS WIG ADJUSTED BY A MAKE-UP WOMAN.
MAGGIE APPEARS.

MAGGIE: Hey, hello.

ANDY: All right? What you doing here?

MAGGIE: Some more extra work, obviously.

ANDY: (distracted, to MAKE-UP WOMAN) That's where it's tight, there.

MAKE-UP WOMAN: Well, it's the same as it was before.

MAGGIE: Listen, Andy, I've got to tell you about this date that I went on. This guy, right, to look at him you would think that he was Mr Perfect.

ANDY: Your dad?

MAGGIE: What?

ANDY: What did you say, 'your dad' what?

MAGGIE: No, a date, I said. I went on a date.

ANDY: Oh, right.

MAKE-UP WOMAN: Try it now.

ANDY: Cheers.

MAGGIE: Is this a really bad time 'cause I can easily come back and catch you at a . . .

ANDY: (still not paying attention to MAGGIE) That's better . . .

MAGGIE: . . . At a later date.

ANDY: . . . Whatever you did.

MAGGIE: Listen, we should hook up 'cause I've hardly seen you. Well, not in the flesh. I've seen you in the paper, in fact, a photograph of you here with your new best friend.

SHE OPENS A TABLOID PAPER AND HANDS IT TO ANDY. IT'S A PICTURE OF JONATHAN ROSS RIDING A PUSHBIKE WITH ANDY BALANCED ON THE HANDLEBARS, A LA *BUTCH CASSIDY & THE SUNDANCE KID*. BOTH ARE LAUGHING HYSTERICALLY, HAVING A WILD OLD TIME. ANDY READS THE HEADLINE.

ANDY: Oh, wow, 'Wossy takes fwiend for a wide.'
(CHUCKLING AT THE MEMORY)
That's at his house in Swanage. That was a brilliant day.

MAGGIE: Yeah. Well, we should go and get a cup of tea or something, sometime.

ANDY: Yeah, don't you get it, get a runner to get it.

MAGGIE: No, not, not now, I'm saying we should get together and have a cup of tea.

ANDY: Tell you what, if you do want to hook up and do me a favour at the same time, I've got to go and see this sick kid in hospital Monday and I'm dreading it. I don't know what to say to him. At least if you're there I'll have someone to talk to.

MAGGIE: (sarcastic) Are you sure you want me to come? Sounds like you should be asking some hot date.

ANDY: No, it'll be awful, no, you're great.

MAGGIE: Buy myself a new dress then.

ANDY: Uh?

MAGGIE: Nothing. Right, well, I'll, I'll leave you to it then.

ANDY: (still reading the paper, not noticing MAGGIE leaving) Look at his face.

MAGGIE: Bye.

ANDY: Why's he on a bike when he's got about five cars?

SCENE 10. EXT.
OPEN ROAD. DAY.

MUSIC MONTAGE: ANDY AND JONATHAN ARE DRIVING ALONG IN AN
OPEN-TOP SPORTS CAR, WEARING TENNIS WHITES, SMOKING CIGARS,
LAUGHING AND JOKING TOGETHER.

CUT TO: ANDY AND JONATHAN HAVING A PICNIC IN THE GARDENS
OF ROSS'S PALATIAL COUNTRY HOME.

CUT TO: MAGGIE DRESSED IN MEDIEVAL GARB, STRUGGLING ACROSS
A MUDDY FIELD, CARRYING TWO HEAVY-LOOKING PAILS OF WATER
TOWARDS THE CAMERA. SHE TOPPLES BACKWARDS INTO THE MUD
AND AN ANGRY ASSISTANT DIRECTOR MARCHES TOWARDS HER.

CUT TO: ANDY AND JONATHAN ROSS PLAY-FIGHTING. THEN, WHILE
ANDY SUNBATHES TOPLESS, AN EQUALLY TOPLESS ROSS SNEAKS UP
ON HIM AND SQUIRTS HIM WITH A 'SUPER SOAKER' WATER PISTOL.
ANDY LEAPS UP AND CHASES ROSS ROUND THE GARDEN.

CUT TO: MAGGIE STILL STRUGGLING IN THE MUD. SHE TRIPS AND FALLS
AND THE A.D. APPEARS AGAIN, FURIOUS THAT SHE'S RUINED THE SHOT.

A.D.: Cut, cut, cut.

MAGGIE: Sorry, the bucket fell off the thing.

A.D.: Yes, erm, I'm sure it did.

SCENE 11. INT. HOSPITAL ROOM. DAY.

JOE, THE SICK CHILD, IS SAT IN BED. HIS MOTHER IS FUSSING.

JOE: Can you just tuck that in?

ANDY AND MAGGIE ARRIVE.

MOTHER: Look who's here.

ANDY: Hello.

JOE: Hello.

ANDY: Hi!

JOE: Do the catchphrase.

MOTHER: Let him sit down. Sit down.
(ANDY AND MAGGIE SIT)
Now do the catchphrase.

ANDY: 'Are you having a laugh? Is she having a laugh?'

MOTHER: Oh, it's good that, it's very clever.

ANDY: This is my friend, Maggie.

MAGGIE: Hi, hi.

AN AWKWARD SILENCE DESCENDS.

ANDY: What you been doing?

JOE: Just lying here.

ANDY: Yeah.

PAUSE.

MAGGIE: Comfy?

JOE: Erm, it's pretty comfy, yeah. And I'm on morphine so I can't really feel anything.

ANDY SEARCHES FOR SOMETHING TO SAY.

ANDY: Rather that than terrible pain. Erm . . .

ANOTHER AWKWARD SILENCE.

JOE: (to MAGGIE) Are you his girlfriend?

MAGGIE: No.

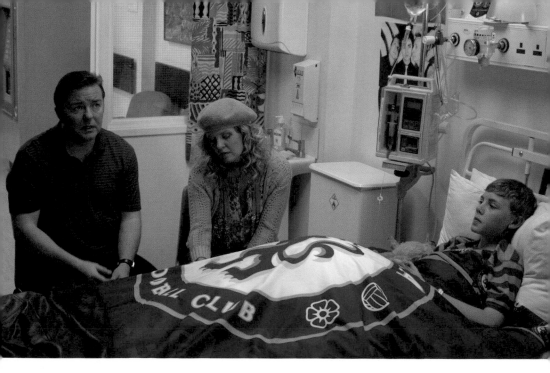

ANDY: No, just a friend.

JOE: Why'd you have a friend who's a girl? Boring.

ANDY: They're usually boring, but because she's so stupid that amuses me.

MAGGIE: I'm not stupid.

ANDY: She's very dim.

MAGGIE NOTICES JOE'S IV DRIP.

MAGGIE: Oh, that looks like one of those things that you get a goldfish in at the fair. Could you keep a goldfish in that?

ANDY: See.

JOE LAUGHS.

MOTHER: Andy, can I have a word?

ANDY: Yeah, sure.

MOTHER: Out—

ANDY: Outside?

MOTHER: Mmm, please.

ANDY: (to MAGGIE) Don't touch anything, they're not toys.

MAGGIE: Are you a Chelsea fan?

SCENE 12. INT.
HOSPITAL CORRIDOR. DAY.

ANDY AND THE MOTHER WALK OUT TO THE CORRIDOR.

MOTHER: Can I just ask, and it's a very sensitive issue, but if, heaven forbid, Joe did pass away . . .

ANDY: Who's Joe?

MOTHER: Joe, my son.

ANDY: Oh, no, no, sorry, yeah, I know.

MOTHER: Yeah.

ANDY: Yeah, I knew.

MOTHER: If he did pass away, would you say a few words at his funeral?

ANDY GOES QUIET, STUCK FOR AN EXCUSE.

ANDY: Oh, I don't even want to think about that.

MOTHER: Well, we have to think about it now.

ANDY: I know but . . .

MOTHER: Yeah, but it's something the whole family would really very much appreciate, you know, knowing how much you mean to Joe and how much he means to you. So, if you could tell me yes, you'd be happy to, to say a few words.

ANDY: But, I think he's going to live a very long time.

MOTHER: He may not.

ANDY: He will.

MOTHER: He may not.

ANDY: Oh, but, yeah, I know, but it's mad to hold someone to plans that far ahead.

MOTHER: We may even lose him in the next six months.

ANDY: Yeah, six months is a long time with my schedule 'cause things change and I don't want to . . .

MOTHER: Can I just say that you've promised you'll be there unless it's something like literally impossible for you to get out of?

ANDY: Like filming or . . . ?

MOTHER: Not filming.

ANDY: Not filming. That's not important enough?

MOTHER: No.

ANDY: Well, what do you consider a good enough excuse to get me out of this? Just so . . . so I don't bother you with, like, I'm phoning you up going, 'Oh, I can't make it 'cause of this' and you're going, 'That's not an excuse.'

MOTHER: Right.

ANDY: What we talking? What sort of, er . . .

MOTHER: Can we just talk about it later?

ANDY: Yeah.

MOTHER: Let's go back in.

ANDY: Yeah.

SCENE 13. INT.
HOSPITAL ROOM. DAY.

AS ANDY AND THE MOTHER SIT BACK DOWN, ROBERT LINDSAY APPEARS
UNINVITED.

ROBERT: Where is he? Ah, there he is, there he is, there is the boy!
Look at his face. Dumbstruck! I know, I understand, it's okay, it's okay,
you were expecting a one-hit-wonder.

HE POINTS TO ANDY.

ANDY: You all right?

ROBERT: . . . And what d'you get? Bloody British legend. I know you know me from *My Family*, the biggest and most popular sitcom in England, but did you know I'm a serious actor? Oh, yeah, and I can sing and dance.

(SINGING)

'Make 'em laugh, make 'em laugh, don't you know that the world wants to laugh . . .'

ROBERT BEGINS AN OVER-ENTHUSIASTIC SONG AND DANCE NUMBER. ANDY FINDS THE WHOLE THING EXCRUCIATING. ROBERT FINISHES WITH A FLOURISH AND WAITS FOR HIS APPLAUSE. IT DOESN'T COME.

HE NOTICES JOE HAS DOZED OFF AND THROWS A TEDDY AT HIM VICIOUSLY.

ROBERT: Oy!

JOE: Sorry. It's the morphine. I'm tired. I wasn't really enjoying it, to be honest.

ROBERT: Rude.

JOE: Well, I'm not really into musicals.

ROBERT: So, what are you into?

JOE: Well . . . comedies, with catchphrases, like Andy's . . .

ROBERT: 'Freedom for Tooting!' 'Power to the people!'

JOE GIVES A BLANK LOOK.

JOE: What's that?

ROBERT: (annoyed, to MOTHER) Your kid does not know comedy, sort it out, now. *Citizen Smith*, biggest sitcom of the seventies. Come on!

JOE: I wasn't born till 1993.

ROBERT: I wasn't born until 1949 but I know who Queen Victoria is, for God's sake. Something wrong with your brain?

MAGGIE AND ANDY EXCHANGE A LOOK.

ROBERT: Right, you'll love this. This anecdote has people on the floor at any function, any dinner party, and if you think that's because they're drunk, think again because Richard E. Grant loves this story and he doesn't even drink. So, I'm on the set of *GBH*, I'm in my trailer, knock on the door, guess who it is? Go on, guess.

JOE: Erm . . .

ROBERT: Alan Bleasdale—

JOE: I don't know who that is.

ROBERT: Oh, fuck off!

HE TURNS TO LEAVE.

ROBERT: (to MOTHER) Kid's a waste of space.

HE STORMS OUT. THE ROOM GOES QUIET.

ANDY: Oh, that was a nice surprise, wasn't it?

SCENE 14. INT. HOSPITAL CORRIDOR. DAY.

ANDY AND MAGGIE ARE WALKING OUT.

MAGGIE: Well, that was interesting.

ANDY: Yeah.

MAGGIE: Do you want to go for a quick pint?

ANDY: I can't tonight.

MAGGIE: Why? What you doing?

ANDY: I am going to The Ivy restaurant. You know Vernon Kaye and Tess Daly? They have invited me out for a meal.

MAGGIE: Why?

ANDY: Just want to hang out with me.

MAGGIE: Is there room for one more?

ANDY: No, I think the four's made up.

MAGGIE: Who's the fourth?

ANDY: Jamie Theakston, nutter! But I promised I'd come and visit the kid again next week, if you want to come along again?

MAGGIE: Yeah, all right, okay.

ANDY: Yeah? Brilliant.

MAGGIE: It's a date.

ANDY: (laughing) What's Theako going to be like after a few beers? He's mental enough sober!

SCENE 15. INT. AGENT'S OUTER OFFICE. DAY.

SHAUN WILLIAMSON IS SAT BEHIND HIS LITTLE DESK, STARING INTO SPACE.

FOR AGES. FINALLY, ANDY ENTERS THE AGENT'S OUTER-OFFICE.

SHAUN: Yes?

ANDY: Oh! You all right? Is he in?

SHAUN: Yes.

SCENE 16. INT.
AGENT'S OFFICE. DAY.

ANDY BURSTS INTO THE AGENT'S OFFICE. AS ANDY ENTERS WE SEE THE AGENT DROP TO HIS KNEES BEHIND HIS DESK AND LOOK UP AT ANDY SHEEPISHLY.

AGENT: Hiya.

ANDY: I haven't got long, just want to find out what's going on with this De Niro thing.

AGENT: Er, what, did we have a meeting or . . . I don't remember planning anything.

ANDY SITS DOWN, A LITTLE CONFUSED BY THE AGENT'S CURIOUS DEMEANOUR AND THE FACT THAT HE IS STILL KNEELING ON THE FLOOR. ANDY PEERS OVER THE DESK AND WHATEVER HE SEES SHOCKS HIM INTO SILENCE. PAUSE.

ANDY: Were you masturbating?

AGENT: Was I what . . . ?

ANDY: Were you masturbating? When I came in?

PAUSE. THE AGENT LOOKS AWAY.

AGENT: Sort of, yeah. Don't tell anyone, though.

ANDY: I'm not going to tell anyone.

AGENT: No.

ANDY: Why didn't you lock the door?

AGENT: Well, I should have locked the door, but I didn't think ahead, I just . . . the moment took me and . . . I just went, you know, crazy. It wasn't anything weird . . . Well, if you must know what it was, it was the lady on this pen.

THE AGENT PRODUCES A NOVELTY PEN WITH A PICTURE OF A WOMAN ON IT WHOSE CLOTHES FALL OFF IF YOU TURN THE PEN UPSIDE DOWN.

ANDY: I don't need to – oh.

AGENT: It just looks like a regular lady, nice attractive lady wearing a bathing costume, but when you turn it up the other way, it comes off and then she's nude.

ANDY JUST STARES AT HIM. SHAUN ENTERS.

SHAUN: Have you got my pen?

AGENT: Yes. Take your pen please for . . .

SHAUN SURVEYS THE SCENE.

SHAUN: Were you having a wank?

AGENT: I was trying to have a quick one, yes, but it's like bloody Piccadilly Circus in here.

ANDY: I didn't know, I just walked in and he was . . .

AGENT: (to SHAUN) If it's anyone's fault it's yours, for leaving your erotic material lying around. If you leave that stuff about I'm only going to do one thing, aren't I? So . . .

SHAUN: Well, why didn't you have one before you came out?

AGENT: I did have one before I came out, Barry, thanks for asking, but I'm a very sexual being if you must know, and I produce an ungodly amount of—

ANDY: Fine.

SHAUN EXITS.

AGENT: Tha— thank you.

ANDY: This is what I'm talking about.

AGENT: We haven't talked about this.

ANDY: I didn't think I had to. I didn't think I had to make a list of things that you shouldn't do at work, one of them: tossing off over a pen.

AGENT: No.

ANDY: Do you really think you're earning your twelve and a half per cent by doing that sort of thing under the table?

AGENT: No.

ANDY: No, nor do I. So why am I paying you? That's it, this is pathetic really. I gave you a chance to sort something out and you'd rather be doing that so . . . let's call it quits.

AGENT: No, no don't start . . .
(ANDY STARTS TO LEAVE SO THE AGENT STANDS UP. WE SEE THAT HE STILL HAS HIS TROUSERS ROUND HIS ANKLES.)
Look at that. Ah! God Almighty.
(THE AGENT PULLS HIS TROUSERS UP)

As far as I'm concerned. you're fired. That's it.

AGENT: Well, if you fire me then you won't know anything about the Robert De Niro meeting that I've set up.

ANDY: You got a meeting with Robert De Niro?

AGENT: Yeah, next week. What you doing next Monday?

ANDY: What time?

AGENT: Six o'clock.

ANDY: Where?

AGENT: At his hotel.

ANDY: What hotel?

AGENT: Dorchester Hotel.

ANDY: So, next Monday at six o'clock at the Dorchester Hotel, I'm meeting Robert De Niro?

AGENT: Yeah.

ANDY: Brilliant, and if he doesn't turn up you're fired then.

AGENT: Well, if he doesn't turn up that's not my fault.

ANDY: Well, no, no, no, you've arranged it so it's win–win for me. Either I turn up and he's there, I meet De Niro, or I turn up and he's not there and you're fired and I get a proper agent.

ANDY PAUSES TO LET THE AGENT TAKE IN THE ULTIMATUM, THEN TURNS TO LEAVE.

AS HE ENTERS THE OUTER OFFICE, SHAUN DROPS TO THE FLOOR BEHIND HIS DESK JUST AS THE AGENT HAD EARLIER. ANDY ROLLS HIS EYES AND LEAVES.

ANDY: Ah, for fuck's sake.

HE EXITS.

MAGGIE HAS HER COAT ON. SHE IS ABOUT TO LEAVE WHEN HER
PHONE GOES.

MAGGIE: (answering phone) Hello.

CROSS-CUT WITH ANDY, TALKING ON HIS MOBILE IN THE BACK OF
A BLACK CAB.

ANDY: Hi, you all right?

MAGGIE: Oh, hi, yeah, I'm just on my way to the hospital. I'm taking
'Operation'. I thought it seemed appropriate.

ANDY: Yeah. Erm, look, I'm not going to make it later.

MAGGIE: Oh, what do you mean?

ANDY: I've got a really important meeting.

MAGGIE: What, at that exact time?

ANDY: Yeah, I couldn't . . .

MAGGIE: And no other time was available?

ANDY: No, he couldn't do any other time.

MAGGIE: Who?

ANDY: Robert De Niro.

MAGGIE: He couldn't do any other time?

ANDY: Sorry, did you hear what I said? Robert De Niro wants a meeting.

MAGGIE: It's just . . . it's the only time that I ever see you.

ANDY: I'll move it, shall I? 'Sorry, Mr De Niro, I know you wanted to
meet me and you've been my hero all my life, but I meet up with Maggie
at a very specific time every week. It can't be moved.'

MAGGIE: All right, I'm not having a go. I'm just disappointed, that's all.

ANDY: Well, I can't move it, obviously not, it's really important. Sorry, I'll see you next week.

MAGGIE: Okay.

ANDY: Okay.

MAGGIE: Bye.

HE HANGS UP, ANNOYED BUT FEELING GUILTY. DEFLATED, MAGGIE GETS HER BAG AND HEADS OUT OF THE DOOR.

SCENE 18. INT. HOSPITAL CORRIDOR. DAY.

MAGGIE WALKS DOWN THE CORRIDOR.

SCENE 19. INT. HOSPITAL ROOM. DAY.

JOE IS SAT UP IN BED, READING. MAGGIE KNOCKS AND ENTERS.

MAGGIE: Knock, knock.

JOE: Hello.

MAGGIE: Hello. How are you?

JOE: Good.

MAGGIE: Bit of bad news, I'm afraid. Andy can't make it. He's got a really important meeting. So, you're stuck with me. But I've brought you this – look.
(SHOWING JOE THE GAME)
Ta da! All right?

JOE: Yeah, all right.

MAGGIE: Even though I'm a girl?

JOE: No, it's okay.

MAGGIE: Come on then, you set it up.

JOE: Okay.

SCENE 20. INT. BLACK CAB. DAY.

ANDY IS TRAVELLING ALONG. HIS MOBILE PHONE BLEEPS. IT'S A TEXT MESSAGE. IT READS: 'SORRY FOR NOT BEING SUPPORTIVE. GOOD LUCK WITH THE MEETING. MAGGIE X.'

SCENE 21. INT. HOSPITAL ROOM. DAY.

MAGGIE AND JOE ARE PLAYING 'OPERATION'. MAGGIE IS REMOVING AN ITEM BUT MAKES THE BOARD BUZZ.

MAGGIE: Oh.

JOE: You're so rubbish. I hope the surgeon working on me's better than you.

MAGGIE: Well, this is just a tiny wee thing I'm trying to get out here. From what I've overheard, your tumour is massive ...

(SHE REALISES WHAT'S SHE'S SAID AND STARTS TO BACKTRACK)

So, it'll be easy ... to get it out, you know ...

JOE LAUGHS, LETTING HER OFF THE HOOK. MAGGIE LAUGHS WITH RELIEF.

SCENE 22. INT. HOTEL ROOM. DAY.

THE AGENT IS SAT, LOOKING NERVOUSLY AT THE DOOR. WE REVEAL THAT ROBERT DE NIRO IS SAT OPPOSITE HIM, GROWING IMPATIENT. THEY SIT IN AGONISING SILENCE. ROBERT DE NIRO LOOKS AT HIS WATCH.

AGENT: Very strange, I'm sure he'll be here in a second. It's very unusual for him to, to be late.

(SILENCE. THE AGENT SEARCHES FOR SOMETHING TO SAY. A LONG, LONG. LONG PAUSE. THEN:)

Have you ever driven a taxi for real?

ROBERT DE NIRO JUST STARES AT HIM.

ROBERT DE NIRO: No.

SCENE 23. INT. HOSPITAL ROOM. DAY.

MAGGIE AND JOE ARE STILL PLAYING THE GAME. AS IF FROM NOWHERE, ANDY APPEARS. HE TAKES OFF HIS COAT AND SITS DOWN.

ANDY: I used to have that.

MAGGIE: What are you doing here? Has the meeting happened already?

ANDY: I didn't go, I came here instead.

MAGGIE: Why?

ANDY: Well, you know, don't want to let people down.

MAGGIE: But that's madness. It's Robert De Niro.

ANDY: I know but—

MAGGIE: No, but that's madness!

ANDY: What do you mean, it's madness?

MAGGIE: Because it's Robert De Niro.

ANDY: I know it is.

MAGGIE: Yeah, well, this is, this is a, a once in a lifetime opportunity.

ANDY: Yes, I know, but I thought you were upset about being put second best so that's why I came here.

MAGGIE: Oh, no, don't you turn it round on me, no, I wasn't trying to make you feel bad.

ANDY: I got a text from you going, 'Oh, have a . . .'

MAGGIE: Don't make me feel guilty.

ANDY: It made me feel guilty, that's why . . .

MAGGIE: Yes, I know but that was supposed to be nice; it was supposed to be encouraging . . .

ANDY: I know, I know what it was, I know and it worked so . . .

MAGGIE: Look if you go now . . .

ANDY: Don't be stupid!

MAGGIE: Just get a taxi.

ANDY: I don't believe this. I do not believe this.

MAGGIE: It might not be too late, it's Robert De Niro!

ANDY: I know who it is!

MAGGIE: All right, well now I'm going to feel guilty for the rest of my life . . .

ANDY: Well, don't make me feel bad about you feeling guilty.

MAGGIE: I know but what if your career goes down the pan?

ANDY: I wouldn't worry about it. My career is already down the pan.
(DRAGGING THE GAME TOWARDS HIM)
Now it's my turn to operate.
(BUZZING THE BOARD AGGRESSIVELY)
He's dead.

SCENE 24. INT. HOTEL ROOM. DAY.

THE AGENT AND ROBERT DE NIRO ARE STILL SAT IN SILENCE, WAITING
FOR ANDY. THE AGENT COMES UP WITH SOMETHING TO BREAK THE
SILENCE.

AGENT: (producing the novelty pen from his pocket) You're a man
of the world, you'll like this. Right, it's just an ordinary pen, so it seems,
with a picture of a lady on it, just in a bathing costume, just normal.
Turn it upside down, oh, what's happened there? Nudey lady! 'You
looking at me?' I am now.

ROBERT DE NIRO: Oh.

AGENT: It's good, isn't it?

ROBERT DE NIRO: (intrigued) Yeah, where d'you get this?

AGENT: My friend, Barry gave it to me. Look at that, back on, nothing suspicious, turn it up the other way, oh, hang on, hello . . .

ROBERT DE NIRO: Can I have this?

AGENT: Do you want it? Take it.

(DE NIRO, INEXPLICABLY CHARMED BY THE PEN, PUTS IT IN HIS POCKET)

Do you want to go for a pint?

SCENE 25. INT. HOSPITAL ROOM. EVENING.

ANDY, MAGGIE AND JOE ARE PLAYING 'OPERATION' BUT THERE IS A HEAVY ATMOSPHERE. MAGGIE IS TAKING AGES TO LIFT A PIECE OUT.

ANDY: Hurry up.

MAGGIE: You're in a bad mood.

ANDY: I'm not in a bad mood but hurry up.

(SHE BUZZES)

Dead.

(SHE BUZZES AGAIN)

Dead.

(BUZZ)

Dead.

MAGGIE: Stop putting me off.

ANDY: If you were hacking at him like that he'd be dead.

(ANDY'S MOBILE PHONE RINGS)

Oh. Oh, it's Darren.

(HE ANSWERS)

What?

WE HEAR THE AGENT'S VOICE.

AGENT: Hello, mate, what happened to you? I'm still here with
Mr Robert De Niro.

ANDY: You're with him now?

AGENT: Yeah. We're just cruising down to a club, come down, mate.

ANDY: Erm, can I bring Maggie?

AGENT: (to ROBERT DE NIRO, in the background) He wants to bring
his friend, is that all right?

ROBERT DE NIRO: (on the phone) Who's that?

AGENT: Friend of his . . . Lady!

ROBERT DE NIRO: The lady on the pen?

AGENT: I wish.

THEY GIGGLE.

ROBERT DE NIRO: Yeah, sure.

AGENT: All systems go, mate.

ANDY: (to MAGGIE) What you doing after this?

MAGGIE: Me? Nothing.

ANDY: Do you want to meet Robert De Niro?

MAGGIE: Nah.

ANDY: Really?

MAGGIE: I'm only joking, yeah.

ANDY: (to AGENT) Okay, all right then.

AGENT: We'll find somewhere, I'll text you the 'detes'.

ANDY: Okay.

AGENT: See you later, mate.

ANDY: See you there.

ANDY HANGS UP.

MAGGIE: Really?

ANDY: Amazing, let's go.

MAGGIE: Now?

ANDY: Yeah.

JOE: What about the game?

MAGGIE: We can't just leave him.

ANDY: We can, just give him an extra couple of drops of morphine, he'll be out cold. No, I'm joking. Right, whose go is it?

MAGGIE: You have a go.

ANDY: Okay, okay.

THEY SETTLE BACK INTO THE GAME IN A BRIGHTER MOOD.

SCENE 26. INT.
HOSPITAL CORRIDOR. EVENING

ANDY AND MAGGIE ARE WALKING OUT OF THE HOSPITAL.

MAGGIE: What would you rather do, right . . .

ANDY: Oh.

MAGGIE: No, listen, would you rather die a sad, lonely, bitter old man in a cold and empty flat or, if we're not with anyone in about five years' time, just move in together?

ANDY: I know what you've tried to do there, you've tried to make the first option sound the worst. Why is it a cold flat?

MAGGIE: Because you're too fat to get up and put the heating on.

ANDY: What, I've got five years to decide, have I?

MAGGIE: Why's it taking you so long to actually think of the answer?

ANDY: I want to keep my options open. I don't want to commit . . .

WE HOLD ON ANDY AND MAGGIE AS THEY AMBLE SLOWLY OUT OF THE HOSPITAL, CHATTING HAPPILY TO ONE ANOTHER. AS THEY DISAPPEAR INTO THE DISTANCE, ROBERT LINDSAY APPEARS AT THE RECEPTION DESK.

ROBERT: Hi.

NURSE: He doesn't want to see you, Robert.

ROBERT: Yes, he does, he does because I've brought DVDs of *My Family*. Come on, everyone likes these.

NURSE: No, I don't. I prefer that edgier stuff on BBC2.

ROBERT: What are you, a critic?